MINING IDEAS FOR
DIAMONDS

**Comparing China and US IP Practices from
Invention Selection to Patent Monetization**

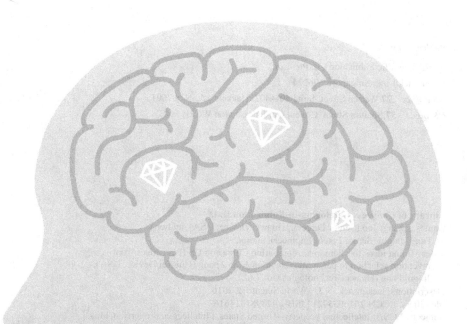

MINING IDEAS FOR
DIAMONDS

Comparing China and US IP Practices from Invention Selection to Patent Monetization

TAO ZHANG ❖ JINGUI FANG

World Scientific

NEW JERSEY · LONDON · SINGAPORE · BEIJING · SHANGHAI · HONG KONG · TAIPEI · CHENNAI · TOKYO

Published by

World Scientific Publishing Co. Pte. Ltd.
5 Toh Tuck Link, Singapore 596224
USA office: 27 Warren Street, Suite 401-402, Hackensack, NJ 07601
UK office: 57 Shelton Street, Covent Garden, London WC2H 9HE

Library of Congress Cataloging-in-Publication Data
Names: Zhang, Tao (Senior Director, Huawei Device, USA), author. |
    Fang, Jingui (Senior Patent Engineer), author.
Title: Mining ideas for diamonds : comparing China and US IP practices from
    invention selection to patent monetization / Tao Zhang (Huawei Device, USA),
    Jingui Fang (Huawei Technologies Co., Ltd.).
Description: Hackensack, N.J. : World Scientific, 2016.
Identifiers: LCCN 2016035721 | ISBN 9789813146167
Subjects: LCSH: Intellectual property--United States. | Intellectual property--China. |
    Patent laws and legislation--United States. | Patent laws and legislation--China.
Classification: LCC K1401 .Z4519 2016 | DDC 346.5104/86--dc23
LC record available at https://lccn.loc.gov/2016035721

British Library Cataloguing-in-Publication Data
A catalogue record for this book is available from the British Library.

Desk Editor: Shreya Gopi

Typeset by Stallion Press
Email: enquiries@stallionpress.com

Printed in Singapore

Disclaimer

The views expressed herein are opinions of the authors and do not represent those of the authors' past or current employers. The discussions in this book are general recommendations based on personal observations and do not constitute specific legal advice. Please consult with your own counsel for legal analysis and advice.

About the Authors

Tao Zhang is senior director of IP strategy at Huawei Device USA. Jingui Fang is senior patent engineer at Huawei Technologies.

Graphic Designer for book cover: Zara T. Dickinson

Contents

List of Figures

List of Tables

Preface

This book is targeted at EVERYONE. It offers ample first-hand tips for the reader, regardless whether you are an individual wanting to improve a product or process, a patent drafter needing to provide client satisfactory results, a patent asset manager desiring to create a bullet proof portfolio, or an IP business executive wishing to deliver much needed financial results to your company's bottom line. The objective is to help you truly understand how patents are used eventually so that you spend time on generating high quality patents from the very beginning.

More importantly, with the increasing interest for US IP practitioners to test out China market and Chinese companies planning to enter US commerce, this book compares the differences in the IP policies for these two exemplary countries. By highlighting potential issues in these two systems, the authors hope to assist readers more quickly reach their goals.

Preface

Chapter 1

The Objective of This Book

1.1. Target Audience

This book is targeted at EVERYONE, covering intellectual property (IP) practices from invention selection to patent monetization. It intends to help anybody who has had, even if momentarily, an idea to improve something around them. It offers ample first-hand tips for the reader, regardless of whether you are an individual wanting to improve a product or process, a patent drafter needing to provide client satisfactory results, a patent asset manager desiring to create a bullet proof portfolio, or an IP business executive wishing to deliver much needed financial results to your company's bottom line.

The objective is to guide and channel your creative energy towards a realistic result, something which is likely to provide you with actual return on your investment (ROI), regardless of whether the investment is your time, money, or both. We want to help you truly understand how patents are used eventually so that you spend your valuable time on generating high quality patents from the very beginning. The book is not merely useful for working professionals, some of the chapters should be equally helpful to retirees or even teenagers.

More importantly, with the increasing interest from US IP practitioners to test out China market as well as Chinese companies planning to enter US commerce, this book compares the differences in the IP policies for the two exemplary countries, China and US. By highlighting potential issues

1

you may face in these two systems, the authors hope to assist readers to more quickly reach your IP goals.

1.1.1. *Everyone has sparks of ideas*

We write this book truly with a broad audience in mind because each of us once and awhile has sparks of ideas. At times you probably witness an approach being used by another person and feel that there is an alternative, more advantageous, way to do it. For example, one day you see your neighbor handling his fruit trees awkwardly. You might, on the spot, come up with an idea on how to graft your fruit tree so that it produces better tasting fruits.

Similarly, you might use a particular product frequently and have discovered that the feature or shape could be improved to better meet your needs. For example, your idea might be improving a can-opener's structure so that it opens more easily and quickly.

Another scenario is that you may have encountered a problem that irritated you so much that you wanted to solve it yourself. For example, your alarm clock kept beeping without stopping regardless of whether you are there to turn it off or not, and you came up with a clever solution such that it only goes off when you are in its vicinity.

Indirectly you may have overheard complaints from other people and figured out a good solution. If you are a retired person, you likely have had a lot of real life hands-on experiences and now you have much more quality time to think quietly. Therefore, you should have abundant opportunities to come up with good ideas. Even if you are a teenager, you probably have been exposed to more high tech gadgets than any previous young generations and thus have many innovative ideas. An illustrating example is that the first author's daughter, when at age 14, came up with an interesting idea on customizable shoes and spent weeks trying to make them work. After coming up with various embodiments and producing corresponding proto-types, her idea was eventually turned into a patent application.

Please be aware that many of your ideas may have been previously thought of by others already. However, sometimes your idea is *new, useful, and non-obvious* which might become patentable. Then, you should explore this idea further and determine whether you want to file a patent. The fact that your idea being patentable alone is not sufficient to justify your spending time and money on patenting it. You need to have a clear understanding about what benefits a patent affords you.

Seeking a patent means that you can obtain government protected legal exclusion right preventing others from practicing your idea for a period of time (it is typically 20 years from the filing date for utility patents in the US as well as invention patents in China). Others can only incorporate your idea into their products after they obtain your prior permission or a license from you. Patent exclusion is a powerful and legitimate legal right that you can proudly exercise. However, obtaining a patent takes a lot of time, effort, and money. You should be clear in your mind about why you are patenting and only pursue it when there is a reasonable ROI so you don't waste time.

1.1.2. *Our emphasis on quality — symbolized by "diamond"*

We name this book "Mining Ideas for Diamonds" because *Diamond* symbolizes quality with long-lasting high intrinsic value. We initially thought about naming the book "Mining Ideas for Gold" because Gold also represents universally recognized high value. However, we decided against "Gold" in the end, and instead, chose "Diamond" based on our following strong beliefs and rationale:

(i)　First of all, we favored the "Diamond" symbol because diamond can be used to cut, drill, grind, polish, and shield objects and makes a valuable tool. Depending on the task at hand, you don't need the biggest diamond. The one with the right shape, size, and physical property should suffice. Similarly, as will be discussed in detail in Chapter 6, a high quality patent doesn't necessarily mean the most innovative invention or the biggest technology breakthrough in history. Instead, a patent is considered to have high quality when it is an effective tool enabling you to accomplish your objectives, whether the goal is patent licensing, litigation, patent sales, or IP defense. In fact, many highly effective patents for patent litigations are narrow scoped minor improvement inventions and yet have been proven to be of high value to the patent holder during court "battles".

Most people tend to agree that a patent which has been successfully used to sue another party and survived the litigation ordeal is a high quality patent. On the other hand, if an IP practitioner skillfully uses a patent to persuade a licensee to pay royalty fees to the patent owner, this patent should be considered a high quality patent as well, even if the parties never litigate in court. In fact, if a party is able to use a patent to deter third parties from a potential patent suit, such a patent should also be viewed as a high quality patent. Similarly, if a patent seller is able to develop good claim-chart and convince the patent purchaser to pay reasonably high amount of money for the patent, it is a high quality patent. Therefore, quality means high success rate in IP transactions (or can be referred to as IP motions, since some are preparatory work without consummating any IP transactions), regardless of whether the IP motion is offensive or defensive in nature.

(ii) In addition, many high quality patents do not necessarily come from initially apparent "star" inventions. Often an idea at the time of the patent filing was not a breakthrough idea, but only presented a small improvement in feature, or was simply an alternative approach that was not necessarily considered the most brilliant solution. However, as the market evolves, due to various expected and unexpected reasons (such as advancement in technology development, availability of previously-expensive material at low cost, or finalization of a Standard specification), the feature covered by the idea becomes widely adopted by the mass market. Then, the invention suddenly could become highly valuable. It takes a skilled patent practitioner to recognize early the potential of such inventions and pluck them out from the crowded patent applications or patent portfolios and develop them into high quality patents. The previously casually drafted patent claims often need to be improved according to target evidence of use (EoU) data to gradually "tweak" the application into a high quality patent. This process is vividly described as recognizing a *diamond in the rough*, or in an analogous Chinese phrase "伯乐识马".

Again, as stated in (i), an effective diamond doesn't have to be shiny and gigantic, but only needs to be just the right size for the intended purpose. Similarly, an idea doesn't have to be the best idea, but as long as it is a useful one for the targeted IP motion, then that idea is a potential "diamond".

(iii) Last but not the least, even after finding a "diamond in the rough", it takes a skilled alchemist to cut and polish the surrounding roughness away to produce a shining diamond. If the alchemists are not skilled or not paying enough attention, they could miss a small diamond altogether. Similarly, patent drafters are like the alchemists for diamonds. They need to carefully contemplate the specifications, embodiments, drawings, claim language and structure to bypass prior arts, minimize potential defects so to make the patent most effective in litigation and negotiation. In addition, often the initially drafted parent patent claims may not be exactly on target and you need several continuation cases to get the final claim perfect. Again, this requires the skilled IP practitioners to understand thoroughly patent technology and corresponding competitive landscape. This way, the IP practitioner can better shape the patent application in multiple iterations, and eventually turn it into a high quality patent that is "as sharp as a diamond".

In summary, *a high quality patent means that it is useful and effective.* To generate such high quality patents, you need to recognize the right idea (not necessary the most innovative one), and motivate skilled patent drafters to work on the case while constantly keeping your ultimate objective in mind. We sincerely want this book to help inventors, lawyers, IP professionals, business managers to focus on high quality ideas (i.e. ideas that will lead to high quality patents) that enable them to better accomplish their ultimate goals. Such approach of focusing on quality to increase ROI should be universally applicable, regardless of for which technology area, in which legal jurisdiction, or during what time period that you came up with your idea. In other words, high quality idea is a "Diamond standard" that is recognized worldwide. Only those ideas are worth your time, effort, and money to pursue, protect, and leverage via patenting.

1.1.3. *Driving force behind this book — from invention selection to patent monetization*

Another objective of this book is to share our experiences and knowledge about the differences between China and US IP law/procedure. We use a checklist format to clearly point out optimized processes, best practices, and lessons learned. This will help inventors or IP professionals, both in China and US, avoid unnecessary mistakes so that they are more efficient and effective when pursuing their IP missions or carrying out their IP roles.

When the first author joined a large US enterprise company's licensing team more than 10 years ago and began patent licensing activities, it was difficult because IP licensing business being carried out by an operating company was a relatively new phenomenon and we were truly early pioneers in the field. There were not too many rules written down for us and little relevant guidance. Therefore, most people were just conducting IP licensing deals via trial and error. Considering that now China is trying to reap the benefit of IP as it joins the advanced elite economy, IP is attracting much more attention than before. Companies in China and western companies, who want to operate in China in the future, will need to figure out how to manage IP in China. Due to the fact that IP industry is new to Chinese market, IP professionals as well as inventors will face similar situations as the United States did 10+ years ago. Therefore, we believe that comprehensive IP checklists comparing China and US IP practices, from idea generation to patent monetization, perhaps even including some strategies for litigation defense, would be a good book to write about.

When exchanging opinions with those in the IP industry in US and China who manage patent portfolios, we often detect a disturbing phenomenon. Most of the patent prosecution teams file patents with a "passive activity" mentality, i.e. treating patent filing as a mere byproduct of R&D programs rather than part of strategic planning. We initially had similar lack of appreciation for the role patents play. As a result, we were conducting IP transactions, such as patent sales, without fully understanding patent purchaser's needs.

A few years ago, the first author moved into a patent acquisition role and began to see first-hand the stringent criteria associated with high quality standard required for acquisition patents. Such in-depth insight into the rationales behind patent demand side was indeed awakening. It becomes evidently clear to the authors that there is an urgent need for inventors and patent prosecution teams to understand the ultimate goal of patenting so that their time and effort are spent on the most critical portion of the process. This is part of the motivations behind writing this book.

People always say you should play on your strength. Since English is our second language and not our mother tongue, we never thought about writing a book in English. However, when a few of us felt strongly about certain IP issues and published two patent related articles (discussions from which are included in various chapters in this book) on *IAM Magazine*, we received good feedback. When we presented our proposal or analysis at conferences, people would come up to us and tell us that our methodology is very insightful and helpful. As a result, we decided that we should put our good practices down on paper and write an IP book so that more people can benefit from our insights and experiences.

Tao Zhang and Jingui Fang co-authored the first IAM article entitled "Effective First-Filing Approaches for International Inventor Teams".[1] Tao Zhang, Dian Fu, and Wenyu Zhou co-authored the second IAM article entitled "Building a High Quality Patent Portfolio in China and the United States".[2]

Authors are sincerely grateful to Dian Fu and Wenyu Zhou for their contribution toward many insightful discussions on how to build high quality patent portfolios and thank them here wholeheartedly.

1.1.4. *Ultimate purpose of the book — comparing China and US IP practices*

The purpose of this book is mainly threefold:

(i)   First, we want to help patent applicants constantly keep their ultimate objectives of patenting in mind throughout the entire patent

---

[1] "Effective Patent First-Filing Approaches for International Teams of Inventors", *IAM Magazine*, Issue 66, July/August 2014, Page 77.
[2] "Building a High Quality Portfolio in China and the United States", *IAM Magazine*, Issue 68, November/December 2014, Page 33 (*Featured Article*).

prosecution process. This way, they will more likely obtain high quality patents. Such approach is necessary in order to harvest the fruit of your diligent efforts and eventually generate the desired results for your company and yourself from your innovations.

(ii) Second, we want to guide the readers through patent monetization process, point out potential hurdles you may face, and share some possible solutions. This will prepare you well before you conduct any patent transactions which should in turn assist you more quickly accomplish "patent to money".

(iii) Last but not the least, we want to compare China IP practices with US IP practices and highlight any significant differences. This way, readers interested in Chinese/US patent prosecution or IP transactions are keenly aware of the key differences between these two systems and have a general guideline on how to best proceed forward.

It is no doubt that there is a huge demand within the US IP business, legal, and technical community to better understand China IP practices versus US IP practices. Currently, there are books on China IP practices or US IP practices separately, but very few cover both practices in comparative checklist format. This book will be among the few to compare the China and US IP practices side by side to point out their main differences, from the initial idea selections, through various intermediary processes, all the way till the eventual IP transactions.

Another key advantage is that this book provides first-hand guidance and lessons learned from invention conception to IP monetization with a consistent emphasis on patent quality. Readers interested in any particular area can dive in any sub-section to obtain related in-depth knowledge and benefit from it. You can also move backward and forward into other conjunct chapters or sections to gain insights on the entire IP cycle.

A third advantage is that by utilizing a checklist format, this book highlights best practices/key lessons learned comprehensively, and thus enables readers to more easily and quickly pick out portions helpful to reader's particular issues during daily IP work.

1.2. The Importance of IP

1.2.1. *Definition of IP*

Intellectual property (IP) generally means patents, trademarks, trade secrets, and copy rights. Each sub-topic has its own corresponding local laws and practices. This book will focus on patents, including idea generation, invention selection, patent application drafting, patent prosecution, using patents defensively as an IP shield, or using patents aggressively as an IP sword, and patent transacted for defense or monetization purposes such as patent acquisition, patent sales, and patent cross-licensing.

1.2.2. *Roles of IP — for US and Chinese companies*

IP, due to its potential significant impact on financial bottom lines, is increasingly important to companies large and small, domestic or international. Figure 1-1 depicts the composition of top US Fortune 500 companies. The study was made by OceanTomo and revised recently to include data up to January 1, 2015.[3] Open columns represent a company market value attributable to its intangible assets, while grey columns represent a company's market value attributable to its tangible assets. The data clearly show that successful US companies are increasingly relying more on intangible assets rather than on tangible assets in its market valuation. The compositions of top companies today, compared to top companies 40 years ago, have a complete reversal in the relative weight of intangible asset versus tangible asset allocation. By January 2015, top companies have an 80/20% intangible/tangible-asset proportion, compared to 1975 where top companies had a 20/80% intangible/tangible-asset proportion. Successful companies in today's environment are investing more in intangible assets. These intangible assets mainly consist of IPs.

In fact, IP strategy has become an integral part of corporate overall strategy to defend and support a contemporary company's business success,

---

[3] Ocean Tomo, "Annual Study of Intangible Asset Market Value from Ocean Tomo, LLC", March 5, 2015, can be found at http://www.oceantomo.com/2015/03/04/2015-intangible-asset-market-value-study/.

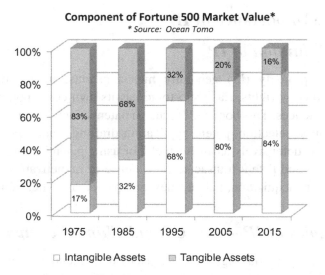

Figure 1-1   Evolution of the importance of intangible assets versus tangible assets.

R&D investment, and financial profitability. A strategically managed IP portfolio is a valuable asset which can help a technology innovator to defend its market leadership, a solution provider to thaw competitor's legal attacks, a new-entrance company to gain design freedom via patent cross-licenses (PCLs), or a strong IP portfolio owner to obtain licensing revenue.

Figure 1-2 "Smartphone patent war illustration" vividly depicts how companies use IP as a competitive weapon. The arrows represent pending litigations (solid lines), cross-licenses (dashed lines), and settlements (dotted lines). Dashed circles indicate which OS camp a company falls within. From the directions of clustered arrows, Android Camp and Windows Camp have mutual IP cross-fires at each other. Apple has IP cross-fire with both the Android Camp and Windows Camp. The now-dissolved RockStar Consortium funded by Apple, Blackberry, Microsoft, Ericsson, and Sony, launched IP attacks against companies in the Android Camp. These behaviors demonstrate that patent wars are often business wars, especially for the Smartphone industry.

US companies, compared with their Chinese counterparts, are usually more experienced at utilizing patent portfolios for offensive purposes in protecting their business market share. There are various offensive IP

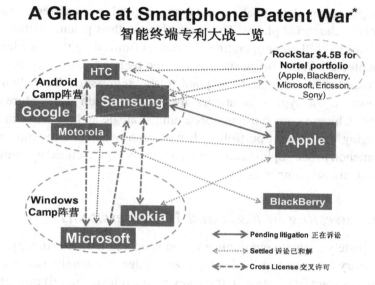

Figure 1-2   Smartphone patent war illustration (*courtesy of Wenyu Zhou).

motions and associated behaviors. The more aggressive motion involves suing competitors for patent infringement and seeking injunctive relief to prevent competitors from selling products in the patent protected jurisdiction. As a result, it disrupts the competitor's business operation and limits its revenue generation. Alternatively, the suing party may: (i) demand competitor paying a high royalty fee; and/or (ii) initiate patent litigations at courts seeking large damage awards by judges, intentionally increasing competitor's cost of goods substantially. Some patent licensing motions are more moderate, likely due to the fact that the asserting party merely wants to recoup its R&D investment or generate additional revenue via IP monetization and does not desire to escalate the activity to a long drawn-out litigation process unnecessarily.

Chinese companies, on the other hand, are more likely to use their patent portfolios for defensive purposes. The associated IP motions include the following:

(i) negotiating patent cross-licensing agreements with other operating companies to gain design freedom; or

(ii) simply accumulating patents in target geographies as a preparation to enter such market places. They may also use their patent portfolios as shields to chill other operating companies from suing them for fear of countersuit. When being sued or asserted by aggressors, they'll counterassert or countersue to respond to the aggressor's IP challenges. However, the typical behaviors are changing with time. More and more Chinese companies are becoming strategic and proactive in leveraging their patent portfolios. It will soon become a common phenomenon to see sophisticated IP strategies being practiced by both US and Chinese companies.

1.2.3. *Investing in R&D and IP process/tools*

To adequately protect your company, you need a holistic IP strategy. This is necessary for industries with a high percentage of intangible assets, and requires a strong foundation in three key areas, i) investing; ii) protecting; and iii) leveraging.

As shown in Figure 1-3, a holistic IP strategy must first start with INVESTING, i.e. allocating adequate investments in research and development as the basic foundation for IP creation to encourage innovations. In addition, it is necessary to also fund appropriate processes and IP tools to capture these inventions. Some corporations invest double digit percentage of their total revenue into R&D activities in order to continuously generate new ideas, invent leading-edge technologies, and develop untapped market segments. This is a "must have" in order to have a world-class IP portfolio.

In addition, resources are also required to support tools and processes turning ideas into protectable IPs, for example, enabling inventors and patent lawyers in capturing invention disclosures easily and timely.

1.2.4. *Protect by establishing a strong IP portfolio*

The second important aspect of a holistic IP strategy is PROTECTING, meaning that in order to protect company's R&D investment and defend business' market shares, companies need to build strong IP portfolios. This can be accomplished by organically growing one's IP portfolio through filing patents in US, China, and in other strategically important countries.

Figure 1-3   Establishing a holistic IP strategy to protect your company.

Alternatively, as a compliment approach to the above-mentioned internal patent prosecution, companies can strengthen their portfolios by acquiring patents in carefully chosen target areas. In addition, companies may also employ publications to establish prior art to prevent others from obtaining a patent for a particular technology.

1.2.5. *Leverage through strategic IP actions*

The third aspect and ultimate goal of a holistic IP strategy is **LEVERAGING**, i.e. to leverage the company's IP portfolio to protect the company's technology leadership and market share, or help shape certain technical spaces via Standards, new business models, etc. Other possible leverages of an IP portfolio include gaining freedom of operation through PCLs, generating additional revenue from patent assertions, patent sales, or technology transfers. An increasing number of companies realize that they need to further strengthen their IP portfolios to expand business into another country, file IPOs, defend themselves from unwanted litigations, or offensively file injunctive reliefs against competitor's products.

As can be seen, a strong patent portfolio plays an important role for large and medium enterprises as an integral part of their corporate strategies. Even for small or startup companies, investors demand a solid patent portfolio in order to better protect their financial investments. Therefore, it is not surprising that IP management is attracting more attention from executives of companies large or small. CXOs begin to set IP issues on their agenda and are more willing to be involved in IP management. To better meet each company's specific short-term and long-term needs, IP professionals should optimize their patent portfolio early-on during the filing process and strive to reduce overall risks while maximizing total ROI. It is your job and duty to help your company build a world-class IP portfolio.

1.3. Definition of a World-Class Patent Portfolio

To make sure you are working in alignment with your company's business strategy, you want to clearly understand possible deliverables by a world-class patent portfolio and be able to articulate the benefits to management. A world-class patent portfolio is defined as one that is *effective in enabling your company to successfully execute its worldwide business strategy.*

For each specific company, the criteria of a world-class portfolio may be very different depending on its own short-term and long-term business objectives. If a portfolio enables your company to carry out its business strategy successfully globally, then that portfolio is considered a world-class patent portfolio for your company even if it doesn't allow another company to execute its business strategy properly. Therefore, your first step is to thoroughly understand your company business strategy and keep it in mind all the time while you build and adjust your patent portfolio. Your IP strategy may need to be continuously modified as your company's business strategy evolves.

1.4. Patenting an Idea Does Not Equate to the Right of Practicing it

Considering that a patent is *an exclusion right* to prevent others from unauthorized making, using, selling, offering for sale, importing a product that uses your patented technology, you can exclude others from practicing your idea in their products or services. Needless to say, in order to effectively carry out such exclusion right, your patent must map exactly onto the target company's product. When you have a patent that corresponds with a competitor's product, you can rightfully exercise your IP right. For example, you may prevent a competitor from manufacturing their products in the patent protected countries; you can prevent a competitor from selling its products/services, or stop it from importing products into patented countries. You can also prevent a competitor's customers from using these products/services your ideas cover, which equates to preventing the competitor from selling these products/services since most companies provide indemnification to their customers.

However, many people confuse the exclusion right of a patent with the right to practice. They think that if you have filed a patent, you have a green light to practice the covered invention in your products or services. The reality is starkly different because *patenting an invention does not equate to having the right to practice the invention.* Such a misunderstanding could lead companies to a false sense of security and run into unexpected legal issues later.

Therefore, you must educate management and employees of your company that owning a patent does not necessarily entitle you to use that invention unless there are no other valid exclusionary rights for that invention. The reason is that a patent is often an improvement to existing technologies and built on top of other inventions. As a result, you may need to obtain a license to the other underlining technologies needed by your invention if these other technologies are covered by valid patents. If you don't obtain such licenses, the patent owners of the other underlining technologies may have the exclusion right to prevent your company from using your invention in your product or services.

Let's take a look at a hypothetical example. Assume somebody else first invented a completely new and revolutionary wireless charging mechanism which conveniently and safely charges up your phone. They file a group of patents to protect this idea. You then figure out an improved and non-obvious structure of such wireless charger so that the charging time is reduced significantly. Your company files a few patents to protect your improved fast wireless charger. Does this mean your company can start making such fast wireless chargers and sell to others? The answer is probably "NO". If the other party has filed patent claims covering the new wireless charging method and your fast charger uses their claimed idea as the underlining technology, you need to get a license from the other party for your products. In the same token, if the other company didn't come up your new fast charging structure and later wants to make a fast charger covered by your patent, they need a license from you in order to proceed.

Some may complain that the patent system is unfair because it allows people to sit on the sideline and watch for key technology breakthroughs. The minute they observe a major development in technology areas that might become important in the future, they can jump in and start patenting many various implementations of such new technology and then use them to extort money from others later. Non-practicing entities (NPEs) benefit from such practices and most operating companies dislike NPEs. Therefore, various patent reforms have been proposed to combat such "leeching" behavior.

On the other hand, the reality is that many clever and capable individual inventors also make good livings operating this way. They watch for technology trends and then come up with patents that solve future potential issues ("blocking patents"). Should they not be allowed to patent these ideas? If not, will they still be willing to share their good solutions with the public so that consumers can benefit from them? These are issues that patent reform bills face in their quest to fight NPEs. A possible solution lies with Patent Office of each country. If the Patent Office only allows patents with high quality, then the system is fairer because it provides both large companies and small individual opportunities to invent and benefit from high quality inventions. If a large corporation, with significantly more resources and manpower, can't come up with a better solution than an individual inventor, then that individual's invention is likely worth protecting.

Many were hoping and praying that the pending patent reform in the US congress will correct NPE related issues in the United States. Unfortunately, most proposed solutions address an issue but introduce a new set of other issues. As a result, effective patent reform is not expected in the near future. Therefore, operating companies need to anticipate possible behaviors from competitor as well as NPEs, and manage its technology development and patent portfolio smartly. Certain large corporations file indiscriminately, hoping to use volume to combat potential interferences from competitors or NPEs. This is costly and non-effective with very poor ROI. You could spend a lot of money filing the wrong patents, and then a lot more to maintain them, yet still missing the right target altogether. A wiser strategy is that operating companies need to think ahead, envision possible embodiments for their main technology developments and protect those as soon as possible. For some cases, companies may want to keep certain technologies as top trade secrets. Alternatively, they can publish some if cost is an issue. There are pros and cons to each approach and we'll discuss them in more detail in later chapters.

1.5. Benefits of a World-Class Patent Portfolio

Now let's take a look at your company's business strategy. If its goal is to expand globally into most countries in the world, you should make sure to build a high quality worldwide patent portfolio to protect your company's market share in those countries. This is the so-called offensive IP motion discussed in the previous sections, i.e. to prevent others from practicing your invention. If you are a leader in the industry or have made significant R&D investments in certain important technology areas, it is likely that competitors might need these technologies later. Then, you need to make sure to file patents and protect your ideas in all the countries that your competitors will operate with significant presence.

Perhaps your company doesn't plan to sell products globally. However, if you anticipate having aggressive competitors with global presence, your patent portfolio should cover those geographic areas where those competitors operate so that you can sue or countersue them when needed. In addition, if you need to access these competitors' technologies in the future, you can use this portfolio for cross-licensing purposes.

On the other hand, if your company has no plan to expand internationally and doesn't foresee global competitors or global IP threat in the future, a patent portfolio with only domestic patents might be sufficient.

Figure 1-4   Benefit of a world-class patent portfolio.

Some companies may want to leverage the patent portfolio to generate revenue and increase profits. Then their portfolios need to cover all the countries where potential licensees operate and have reasonable presence.

In summary, the benefits of world-class portfolio are tremendous. IP professionals need to communicate to management so that executives understand the importance of IP and thus allocate funding and strong support. We leverage the three-legged triangle structure in the previous section to illustrate this in Figure 1-4. The benefit of a world-class patent portfolio is mainly threefold:

(i)   It enables your company to capture the innovative ideas from R&D investments. These could be reflected via invention disclosures, patents, trademarks, trade secrets, etc.;

(ii) It protects existing and future product or business market share. These could be via patent cross-licensing agreements, defensive assertion or litigations in response to other's offensive assertion or litigations.

(iii) It can provide financial contribution to bottom line. This could be realized through technology transfer, licensing via standard pool, patent sales, patent license or trademark license.

1.6. IP Strategy as a Cornerstone of Business Strategy

The above benefits are precisely the reason why IP strategy must be seamlessly integrated into a company's business strategy in order for it to be an effective enabler. IP strategy should be a cornerstone of your company's overall business strategy.

Depending on whether your company business strategy is defensive, offensive, or IP revenue generation, your corresponding IP Portfolio should be built to enable such IP actions.

For defensive IP and business strategy, your portfolio should focus on enabling you to successfully negotiate PCLs, or counterassert/suit if being asserted or sued by other companies, which is shown as path #1 in Figure 1-5. For PCL purpose, it requires the patent portfolio to be at least negotiation grade quality, i.e. having some patent families that read onto target company's existing products or cover technologies that the target company is interested in licensing. For counterassert or countersuit, the portfolio needs to be litigation grade quality, i.e. maps well onto the target company's existing significantly important products without serious defects in the patent.

For an offensive IP and business strategy, you'll need to build a strong portfolio that enables you to successfully carry out offensive assertions and litigation, which is represented by path #2 in Figure 1-5. In addition, it needs to survive various invalidity or non-infringement challenges.

Path #3 in Figure 1-5 represents patent monetization strategy to generate IP revenue. This could be executed, for example, via patent sales or patent licensing. In the past, companies used to purchase patents to increase portfolio volume so quality could be overlooked. Nowadays most, if not all, buyers require high quality in the purchased patents. Similarly, patent licensing requires the patent quality to be essentially litigation grade quality and must be able to survive various invalidity challenges, such as *inter partes review* (IPR), covered business methods (CBMs) challenges, or post grant review (PGR) challenges.

In summary, regardless of whether your company's IP strategy is offensive, defensive, or IP revenue generation, you need to build a portfolio consisting of negotiation grade or litigation grade quality patents.

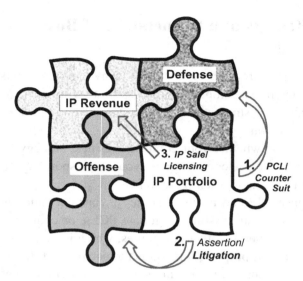

Figure 1-5   IP strategy must be a cornerstone of business strategy.

This book covers methodology from the initial idea generation to the ultimate IP transaction. We also discuss, in great detail, various approaches and provide relevant checklists on how to carry out such an IP strategy for US and Chinese markets.

1.7. How to Use This Book

This book can be used by inventors, lawyers, IP practitioners, and IP educational professions in both the US and China. It intentionally includes many figures to clearly illustrate authors' points of view. Readers are encouraged to cite these figures in presentation, provided that credentials are given to this book.

More importantly, this book tries to summarize key points for each main section in a checklist table so that readers can easily find and utilize needed information to assist their daily IP practices. For readers' convenience, we put US and China practices, for each particular issue, side by side so that readers can easily compare them to see the important differences. Table 1-1 illustrates the format these checklist tables utilize in order

Table 1-1   Checklist format to illustrate how to use the comparison tables in this book.

Issues to Consider	US Typical Approach	China Approach: (Similar), or Different
Key issue #1	• How does US IP practitioner typically resolve it	• (China's process is similar for Aspect #1) • Aspect #2 is different between the two systems. How you need to proceed differently in China to comply with China's special process or policy
Key issue #2	How does US IP practitioner typically resolve it	How you need to proceed to comply with China's special process

to help reader easily spot issues, and identify key differences between the US and China IP practices.

For example, US IP practitioners interested in understanding the China IP practice can benefit by scanning the relevant checklists to spot the ones that apply to their current IP situation. Maybe they are already familiar with US process for such IP situations, but can read the China process portion to see if they need to modify their strategy somewhat for their counterpart case in China. Similarly, Chinese IP practitioners interested in understanding US IP practice can search the checklist relevant to their particular IP situations, understand the corresponding US processes for such IP matters and proceed accordingly.

Chapter 2

Main Considerations/Differences in IP Practices Between US and China

2.1. Intellectual Property Trend in US

Due to recent changes in US patent law such as America Invents Act (AIA) and the proposed Patent Reform bills pending in the US congress, as well as US Supreme Court's increased number of rulings on IP issues such as *Alice v. CLS Bank*, compounded by the large percentage (80%+ at mid-2015) of patent invalidities by USPTO's Patent Trial and Appeal Board (PTAB), non-practicing entities (NPEs) are having a much harder time succeeding in generating IP licensing revenues. Even long entrenched licensing operations within operating companies report that they are seeing an increased cycle time in licensing negotiations. As a result, various IP intelligent sources are forecasting that IP actions will spread more quickly outside US into Europe, China, as well as other Asian countries with large sales revenue markets or manufacturing bases.

2.2. IP Trend in China

Many in US are still skeptical that China will become an active IP market. However, considering recent increases in damage awards for patent litigations in China such as *Netac v. Watertek* (~US$6.45M) and *Chint v.*

Schneider (~US$53.4M), there are ample signs that IP activities in China will pick up significantly. Moreover, China is a centralized system. If Chinese government believes that IP is important for the Chinese market and begins to implement more consistent IP policies, IP industry in China could overnight become a much more vibrant one.

We expect to see increasing patent transactions by Chinese companies in buying or selling patents or transferring technologies, and patent licensing activities for more advanced IP rich companies to collect royalty payments from those with very little R&D investments. We predict that patent litigation will become more common in China as Chinese domestic and international companies try to expand their business in Chinese market or globally and prevent others from copying their technologies.

As a result, companies who are interested in Chinese market need to understand China's IP policy and practice in order to be successful in China. This book keeps this objective in mind and tries to provide practical guidance at different stages of IP cycle to help those interested in Chinese IP market to avoid key missteps.

Some US companies may still hesitate to explore Chinese IP system; perhaps with an unsubstantiated belief that foreign companies are disadvantaged when they litigate in Chinese courts. IAM magazine Issue 76[1] recently published China litigation statistics, finding that Western companies are "too quick to write off Chinese patent system as a rigged game". Their compiled data indicate that foreign companies filed patent litigation suits in China 49 times, winning 35 of them, and were sued just 29 times. Foreign companies are significantly better off than Chinese state-owned monopolies which were accused of infringement in 14 suits and lost 11 of them.

Meanwhile, Chinese companies will become more IP savvy and start building their own patent portfolios either defensively or offensively. Those with global expansion plans would definitely need to look at their international IP strategies. For example, if your employer is a Chinese company wanting to sell products in US, you'd need to make sure to understand how does US patent policy and process work, how does it differ from that back home in China?

---

[1] Brian J. Love, "Patent Litigation in China: protecting rights or local economy?", IAM Magazine, Issue 76, March/April 2016.

This book takes US policy as the base to compare with Chinese IP policy, and thus is a good guide for Chinese IP practitioners to utilize if they are interested in conducting IP transactions in US. We'll describe the global differences of Chinese IP system compared to US IP policy in Chapter 2. For Chapter 3 and beyond, we'll go into more details of each relevant step of IP cycle and provide further comparisons between the two systems.

2.3. Antitrust in China and US

When comparing Chinese and US IP practices, antitrust practice relating to IP is "an elephant in the room" and should be addressed.

US law treats IP and antitrust separately, with IP protecting inventions, while antitrust ensures a level playing field for commercialization. IP and antitrust laws "share the same fundamental goals of enhancing consumer welfare and promoting innovation, working in tandem to bring new and better technologies, products, and services to consumer at lower prices", observed by US Federal Trade Commission (FTC) and Department of Justice (DOJ).[2] US IP industry in the past few years is particularly concerned with Patent Assertion Entities (PAEs). In the process of trying to balance inventor's right to exclude competitors while fostering open competition in the market, private and public sectors, including the White House, have been actively proposing bills to amend US patent law and modifying US legal practices. However, when FTC started looking into the PAE issue, questions arose as to whether PAE is a competition law problem or a patent system problem.[3]

China, on the other hand, has a more blurred line between the competition law and patent system. China's patent law was adopted on

[2] U.S. Department OJ & Federal TC, "Antitrust Enforcement and Intellectual Property Rights: Promoting Innovation and Competition at 1 (2007)", available at http://www.ftc.gov/reports/innovation/P040101PromotingInnovationandCompetitionrpt0704.pdf.
[3] Remarks of Maureen K. Ohlhausen, Commissioner, FTC, "Recent Developments in Intellectual Property and Antitrust Laws in the United States", June 17, 2013, available at https://www.ftc.gov/sites/default/files/documents/public_statements/recent-developments-intellectual-property-and-antitrust-laws-united-states/130617intellectualpropertyantitrust.pdf.

March 12, 1984, which was modified approximately every eight years thereafter (amended on September 4, 1992; then on August 25, 2000; and again on December 27, 2008; with a new proposal targeting to be implemented soon). A new proposed amendment is receiving public comments and should be adopted sometime in 2016. In comparison, China's Anti-Monopoly Law (AML) was established on August 1, 2008.

A recent paper by Yee Wah Chin[4] comprehensively explained China's antitrust practice. In principal, AML establishes a multilevel enforcement structure under China's State Council, which designates three existing agencies to share enforcement responsibilities: (i) the Ministry of Commerce (MOFCOM) which is mainly responsible for merger control and enforcing AML against anti-competitive conduct in international trade; (ii) the State Administration for Industry and Commerce (SAIC) which is assigned to enforce the AML regarding all other violations except for pricing conduct; and (iii) the National Development and Reform Commission (NDRC) which retains broad authority under the Price Law. There is only one provision in China's AML (Article 55) which expressly relates to IP right: "This Law is inapplicable to undertakings which use IP right according to the laws and administrative regulations relevant to IP, but is applicable to undertakings which abuse IP and eliminate or restrict market competition".

MOFCOM has imposed conditional approval of several transactions relating to IP issues, such as Microsoft's purchase of Nokia mobile phone business, due to concerns about Nokia abusing its control of standard essential patents (SEPs) without honoring fair, reasonable, and non-discriminatory (FRAND) commitments for SEPs and Microsoft using its large Android OS patent portfolio to disadvantage Chinese device manufacturers.

NDRC has investigated InterDigital and Qualcomm for abusing IP right and their monopoly positions, in the Qualcomm case for charging exorbitant license fees, fees on expired patents, tying coerced cross-licenses and grant backs, and refusals to license. It is believed that NDRC has also started investigating Dolby Laboratories, Technicolor SA, and Vringo.

---

[4]Yee Wah Chin, "Intellectual Property Rights and Antitrust in China", available at http://papers.ssrn.com/sol3/papers.cfm?abstract_id=2645171.

2.4. Patent Filing in China — The Changing Landscape

China's IP system is very young. The very first version of Chinese patent law was issued in 1984. Ever since then, a new revision or amendment was made at approximately 8 years interval. The first revision to Chinese patent law was made in 1992 after China joined international Patent Cooperation Treaty. The second revision was made in 2000, mainly focusing on compliance with WTO's Agreement on Trade-Related Aspects of Intellectual Property Rights (TRIPS). The third revision in 2008 shifts away from international alignment emphasis, but instead deals more with domestic legislative policies to shape a higher value-added economy. Currently, a fourth revision is being proposed and seeking public comment. We'll analyze the proposed fourth revision and their potential impacts as well as practical suggestions in Section 2.8 "Potential Changes to Chinese Patent Law".

2.4.1. *Chinese patent system versus US patent system*

The Chinese patent system is more similar to the European patent system, especially the German patent system. China's State Intellectual Property Office (SIPO) will grant a patent if the invention has novelty, inventiveness and practical applicability (Article 22).

The Chinese patent system, similar to the Germany patent system, grants utility model patents besides invention patents. The invention patent has a term of 20 years while the utility model has a term of 10 years. The Chinese invention patent has a similar substantive examination process as the US utility patent. The Chinese utility model patent is only subject to a format examination without any substantive examination. A Chinese invention patent takes about 3–5 years to grant, while a utility model takes approximately 6 months to grant due to recent government automation of the formality checking process.

2.4.2. *Chinese utility model versus US provisional application*

One might want to compare China's utility model to US provisional applications since neither undergo substantive examination, and both can quickly establish priority date. However, these two types of patents are fundamentally different. US provisional application is not a patent itself, automatically expires within a year, and must be converted to a US utility patent within a year of filing in order to be able to enjoy the priority date of the provisional application. The Chinese utility model, on the other hand, is deemed a granted patent and enforceable. One can enforce a utility model after requesting an evaluation report of patent (ERP) from SIPO. The Chinese courts, when considering damage awards, treat a utility model the same as invention patent. In *Ke Huizhong v. Zhouxinda Auto Parts Co. Ltd.*, courts awarded plaintiff a favorable amount of damage award based on a utility model patent.

Due to the lack of an equivalent to US' provisional application in the Chinese patent system, for shape and structure-related inventions, one can utilize Chinese utility model to fast track a patent application in order to lock down a priority date, with the added benefit of obtaining an enforceable patent as a result. With respect to the priority date claiming, a Chinese utility model patent application has the same characteristic as a US provisional application where a latter filed case must be filed within a year from an earlier filed case in order to claim priority to the early case. However, one notable requirement for the Chinese system is that if a later invention patent application claims the priority date of an earlier utility model patent application, the utility model patent application should be withdrawn according to Chinese patent law. This is significantly different from the US patent system under which the early utility patent application can provide priority date to a latter utility patent application, and the early utility parent/seed application can still be kept alive in parallel with the child application. Furthermore, the scope of subject matters protected by the Chinese utility model differs from the invention patent. According to Chinese patent law, utility model focuses on the shape or structure of a product (or the combination thereof) which means that utility model always produces an apparatus patent instead of a process patent. On the other hand, invention patent is not limited to just shape and structure. As a result, not all features of a product can be adequately protected by utility model. For example, software implementation invention can't be protected by utility model because it is not an improvement to the shape, structure, or the combination of the two aspects of the product at issue, even though a software implementation invention is embodied in a general computer. In comparison, the scope of patentable subject matter for both US provisional application and US utility patent are the same.

Chinese SIPO releases patent filing statistics regularly and it is evident that foreign companies seem to rarely leverage Chinese utility model patents. We think it is time to correct non-Chinese companies' unfavorable views on utility models. The following section takes a deeper look into Chinese utility model and its differences from Chinese invention patent.

2.4.3. *Chinese utility model versus Chinese invention patent*

As discussed in Section 2.4.1, both invention patent and utility model require **novelty, inventiveness and practical applicability**. However, it is generally believed that the patentability standard for utility model is lower than invention patent. The novelty and practical applicability requirements are the same for utility model and invention patent. The inventiveness standard, on the other hand, is different for these two types of patents.

According to Chinese patent law, the inventive step standard of an invention patent means **having prominent substantive features and representing notable progress**. In comparison, a utility model inventive step standard is **having substantive features and representing progress**. Furthermore, according to the guidelines for patent examination by SIPO for patent examiners (Chapter 6, Section 4, GPE 2010 version), the scope of analogous art (in the proximate or related technical field) and the number of prior art references used to assess the inventiveness have different requirements for these two types of patent applications. Usually, only references from the same art or technology field can be used to attack the inventiveness of a utility model patent application, unless the primary cited reference definitely teaches, suggests, or refers to another similar art to obtain the means to resolve the problem at issue. In addition, only one or two pieces of prior art can be used to attack the inventiveness of utility mode patent application. In comparison, there are no such limitations for an invention patent application.

In other words, the inventiveness of a utility model patent application is determined by using only **one or two pieces of prior art from the same technical field**. An invention patent, on the other hand, during substantive examination is subject to **more than two prior arts from adjacent or related technical fields in addition to the same field as the invention patent**.

To further illustrate these points, Figure 2-1 depicts the relative patent review standards under the Chinese patent system carried out by China's SIPO versus under the US patent system carried out by USPTO. The vertical axis represents the requirement in patent quality. Past patent prosecution data suggests that although China, in general, follows European patent system which is perceived by some to be strict, its relative standard on patent quality is neither higher nor lower than that of USPTO. Certain cases are allowed by USPTO but their Chinese counterparts are not allowed by China SIPO. On the other hand, there are other cases which are allowed by China SIPO, but their US counterparts are not allowed by USPTO.

We use Figure 2-1 to further illustrate the differences between Chinese patents and US patents. Along the patent quality axis (Y-axis), the direction of arrow indicates increasing patent quality:

(i) At the very bottom of the Y-axis lies a dotted line P_0 representing the lowest standard in patent quality with "no review" by the patent office. US Provisional patent application essentially falls within this category.

(ii) The next level up in patent quality along the Y-axis is U_0 representing the minimum patent quality for China's Utility Model patents. It has a slightly improved patent quality versus the "no review" level of P_0. China's SIPO carries out a preliminary examination of Utility Model patent applications. If the format check reveals no issues, the patent is granted. With recent improvement in process and procedures, SIPO is able to grant a Utility Model patent in 6 months. A significant difference from US Provisional application is that China's Utility Model patent is enforceable. However, Utility Model patent has a relatively short life time, at 10 years compared to the typical 20 year life for an invention patent.

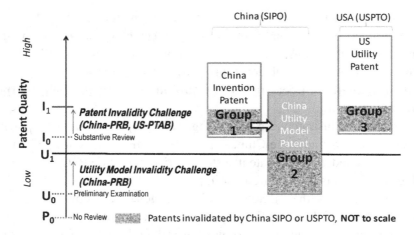

Figure 2-1   Difference between China and US patent system.

According to Rule 56 of Chinese Patent Law "Implementing Regulation of the Patent Law", after a utility model patent is granted, patent owner and any interested party may request SIPO to provide an Evaluation Report of Patent (ERP). The ERP can be used either:

 (i) in a future patent infringement litigation case before courts; or
 (ii) during the invalidation proceeding before SIPO's Patent Reexamination Board (PRB).

To some extent, the ERP for a utility model application can be regarded as the substantive examination which covers all the substantive patentability requirements for a utility model application, such as adequate disclosure, written description support, or whether the claim is indefinite, etc. As discussed in the above sections, SIPO examiners only look for two or less prior arts in the same technical field with respect to the inventiveness assessment for utility model application for the purpose of ERP. If the minimum requirement to pass the invalidity challenge (i.e. receiving a positive ERP indicating that the utility model patent meets the patentability requirements) is represented by U_1, it will be higher in quality than U_0. In Figure 2-1, U_1 line is extended horizontally to intercept with the box representing typical Chinese Utility Model patent distribution. As can be seen, the portion below the U_1 line is represented by shaded gravel pattern and labeled as Group 2. This Group 2 represents Utility Model patents with negative ERP results, or having been invalidated after going through the invalidity challenge. For simplicity, we'll also include in Group 2 those Utility Model applications that haven't gone through any ERP or invalidity challenge process. Those above the U_1 line represent the Utility Model patents that survived the invalidity challenge and thus can be enforced.

(iii) The next level up in patent quality is I_0 representing China's Invention patent review standard. As discussed in the above sections, Chinese SIPO examiners typically look for more than two prior arts from the adjacent or related technical field in addition to the same field as the Invention patent. As a result, the minimum requirement for China's Invention patent I_0 is higher than that of the Utility Model patent invalidity challenge minimum standard U_1. In the above section, we compared the US patent with its Chinese counterparts and concluded that the review standards between USPTO and Chinese SIPO are not consistently higher or lower when compared with each other. For simplicity, we'll assume USPTO grant standard during substantive review is the same as China SIPO's grant standard for invention patents during substantive review. Therefore, both USPTO utility patent and Chinese SIPO invention patent review standard are represented by I_0.

To invalidate either a US utility patent or a Chinese invention patent, one can initiate such invalidity challenges, to US PTAB for the US utility patent and to China's "PRB" for the Chinese invention patent. Again, for simplicity, we assume the quality standard for invalidity by both PTAB and PRB board is similar and represented by I_1. Since US PTAB adopts a higher standard than USPTO examiners and China's PRB adopts a higher standard than the Chinese SIPO examiners, I_1 is above I_0 in Figure 2-1 on the Y-axis scale.

For patents that have been granted by USPTO, when challenged at PTAB via IPR procedure, the current invalidity rate is 80%+ (as of mid-2015). We use the shaded gravel stone box Group 3 to represent the invalidated patents by US PTAB (not to scale). China's PRB utilizes a higher standard than SIPO substantive review during the invalidation procedure, with a reported typical invalidity rate for invention patent at approximately 28%. We use the shaded gravel stone box Group 1 to represent the invalidated invention patents by China's PRB. For Chinese Utility Model, the invalidity rate by China's PRB is reported approximately 35% represented by the shaded gravel box Group 2.

2.4.4. *Chinese utility model deserves attention — benefits and drawbacks*

As discussed in the above section, to invalidate a utility model, similar to an invention patent, you have to submit an invalidation request to SIPO's PRB. Because SIPO's PRB will use a lower standard for inventiveness for utility model than invention patent, the same invention could be invalidated as an Invention patent but survives as a Utility Model patent. Therefore, **Utility Model is considered harder to invalidate than Invention patent under China's patent system**.

Examining Figure 2-1 further, it is apparent that invalidated Invention patents in Group 1 that are deemed not valid by China's PRB as invention patents have a patent quality in the range from I_0 to I_1. They **ALL** have a higher patent quality than China's PRB invalidity standard for Utility Model patent U_1. Therefore, they **ALL** should survive the invalidity challenge as Utility Model patents and will be deemed valid by the same PRB when applied under the Utility Model patent initially. The patent applicant in this case would be wise, as permitted, to have filed this group of patents as utility model instead of invention patent represented by Group 1. This recommended strategy of changing the invention patent filing to utility model filing is shown in Figure 2-1 by an arrow pointing from Group 1 to the group of utility model patents that would survive invalidity challenges positioned above Group 2.

Similarly for the invalidated patents by USPTO PTAB indicated by Group 3, if they enter China via PCT or as a Chinese patent foreign counterpart, instead of choosing invention patent as the counterpart, it might be wise to consider the utility model patent as an option (provided the scope of invention falls within shape or structure). The interesting fact is that the majority of non-Chinese companies appear uncomfortable with utility model patents. In 2014, the number of total utility model patents applied by foreign companies in China was less than 1% of the total utility model applications in the year. Japan was the highest among foreign countries applying utility model in 2014, but still had less than 4000 utility model applications in total. US is the second highest foreign country applying Chinese utility model in 2014, with less than 2000 utility model applications, while Germany at the third place, with less than 1000 utility model applications in 2014.

In addition, although it might not be commonly practiced, but according to PCT definition, you should be able to file a Utility Model in China first, then enter other countries via PCT. PCT Article 2 Definition stipulates:

(i) "application" means an application for the protection of an invention; references to an "application" shall be construed as references to applications for patents for inventions, inventors' certificates, utility certificates, **utility models**, patents or certificates of addition, inventors' certificates of addition, and utility certificates of addition;

(ii) reference to a "patent" shall be construed as references to patents for inventions, inventors' certificates, utility certificates, **utility models**, patents or certificates of addition, inventors' certificates of addition, and utility certificates of addition.

Therefore, China's Utility Model can be used somewhat similar to US' Provisional patent application to lock down a priority date. If you then file a PCT within a year from filing the Utility Model, it will enable you to designate various countries to seek patent protections. The main difference between Chinese Utility Model and US Provisional is that the former is an enforceable patent while the latter is only an application which will expire in a year if not converted to a regular patent.

More importantly, Utility Model can be enforced the same way in court as an Invention Patent provided an Evaluation Report of Patent "(ERP)" has been obtained from China's SIPO. The *Chint v. Schneider* case mentioned in Section 2.2 had an award of ~$50M+ which is among one of the highest award amount for an IP infringement case in China. It was based on an infringement of a Utility Model patent.

Due to the fact that Utility Model doesn't require substantive review, and has a 10 year term rather than the typical 20-year life for invention patents, it is much cheaper to file, and lower cost to maintain.

In summary, compared to Invention patent, the benefits of filing Utility Model would be:

(i)   lower cost without the initial substantive examination but still enforceable;
(ii) more difficult to invalidate at China's PRB; and
(iii) entitled to similar damage award amount during litigation compared to invention patent.

However, there are limitations to Utility Model. It can only be used for inventions covering shape, structure, or their combination. Method claims or process steps are not allowed in Utility Model. As a result, Utility Model is typically only useful to protect hardware or physical products. In addition, Utility Model patent is only valid for 10 years compared to 20 years for Invention patent. As a result, Utility Model patent is more suitable for products or features with a short life cycle.

2.4.5. *Chinese patent priority claiming versus US provisional application*

Some inventors in China complain about Chinese patent system lacking an equivalent to US Provisional application and thus causing inventors to miss out on certain opportunities. For example, if an inventor in US needs to disclose a patentable idea within a short period of time, US Provisional application mechanism allows patent drafter to quickly put together the specification, graphs, without having to carefully draft the claims. This is particularly important where "first-to-file" is the law which applies to both China and US. In fact, for many US technology developments, if your development cycle is somewhat long, and you don't want lose the patenting to a competitor who might come up with similar ideas, you can file a Provisional application as soon as the first idea is enabled so that it is protected. Then, as you develop additional features or processes, you can file another Provisional application and repeat this procedure as soon as a new feature or process is enabled. At the end of the year, you can consolidate all these Provisional applications into one regular patent application. If the claims are included sufficiently in the first Provisional application specification, the regular patent will be able to claim priority date of the first Provisional application filing date. However, if the claims of the patent depend on the later Provisional applications or are a mixture of both the latter and the earlier Provisional applications, then priority date will be based on the later Provisional application filing date.

In China, one can utilize the priority claiming mechanism to obtain similar effect as the US Provisional application. For example, if you are in a hurry to file a patent application due to a required disclosure within a short period of time and worry about not having good claims supporting your idea, you can either utilize the first few months' time period of voluntary amendment to improve claims so that you have more time to work on the claims. If you need more time than a few months, the priority claiming mechanism works as well. In this case, you can cover any scope that a regular invention patent covers, and claiming earlier priority date, yet count the life time from the time of the second patent filing date. In this case, the first case is considered abandoned, and the 20 year life time counts from the time of the filing date of the second patent even though the second patent still claims priority date to the first abandoned patent. Figure 2-2 illustrates these differences in more details.

2.4.6. *Chinese design patent versus US design patent*

Interestingly, Design Patents are treated somewhat differently from other patents internationally, including in China and US. They are not included in the PCT definitions (see the PCT Article 2 "Definition" discussed in Section 2.4.4) and thus cannot register in various countries via PCT. However, US officially joined Hague Agreement international design registration system on May 13, 2015, enabling US applicants to obtain an international design patent, enforcing the corresponding rights in multiple

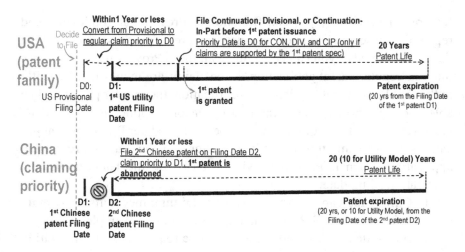

Figure 2-2   China priority claiming versus US patent family.

economies. The Hague Agreement allows an applicant to register up to 100 designs in 62 Hague member countries.

Another key point to note is that, as a result of joining the Hague system, US changed its Design patent term from previous 14 years to the Hague Agreement Design patent term of 15 years if filed on or after May 13, 2015. China has not joined Hague Union yet, so applicants in China still have to file design patent separately in various jurisdictions under the Paris Convention. On the other hand, since both United States and Japan signed Hague Agreement recently, it is expected that many other countries will follow soon. Currently, a few economically important countries are still not Hague members including Canada, Mexico, Brazil, Russia, India, China, and Australia. China has proposed to join Hague but possibly will take a few more years before making it happen. However, IP practitioners should become familiar with the Hague Design patent pros and cons in order to execute a solid long-term design patent strategy.

Another distinction, besides US design patent having a longer 15-year term, is that US design patent can protect either the whole design or partial design. For example, one can use a dashed line to exclude the portion not being claimed, and only protect the solid lined portion. In addition, US design patents undergo substantive review by USPTO examiners and thus have some quality control.

In comparison, Chinese Design patent term is only 10 years. In addition, Chinese patent law only allows design patent to protect the entire design, not partial design. With the increasing awareness of brand names, design patent in China has gained great popularity due to its low cost, fast to grant, and easiness in obtaining allowance because it is not subject to substantive review. Although Chinese design patent is generally considered to be low in quality, patent owner is allowed to recoup lost profit similar to that for a US design patent. Compared to utility patent in US or invention patent in China which typically protects a narrow function, design patent could cover the entire product. Therefore, damage award for design patent could be astronomically high. This is another attraction for filing design patents.

China has recently released its proposed Amendments to the Patent Law, which includes the proposal to:

(i) allow design patents for partial features; and
(ii) extend patent term to 15 years.

If these proposed changes are adopted, it will move China to complete synchronization with the international design patent system.

2.4.7. *Chinese government's subsidy to patent filings may end soon*

Chinese government believes that innovation helps driving its domestic economy toward higher rung of the food chain, and will create more high-paying jobs. As a result, it initiated a patent compensation program a few years ago under which for every patent application filed at PCT government will reimburse the patent applicant a substantial amount of money (speculated to be ~10,000 Yuan or ~US$1600). Some local governments at the state or city level started reimbursing even domestic invention patent or Utility Model. As a result, a lot of Utility Model patents were filed, many with little or very low value. An unverified source speculated that some cases were actual copies of other people's known ideas, with reshuffling of words to disguise the copying fact, for the purpose of obtaining reimbursement award from government. This is probably one of the main reasons why Chinese patent earned a reputation of having low quality.

A few foreign IP practitioners have been so frustrated with poor Chinese patent quality, to the point of recommending abolishing Chinese Utility Model all together. Authors believe such draconian measure is not necessary and uncalled for. The good news is that China believes that it has arrived at a reasonable number of patent filing quantities. Central government's compensation for PCT filings likely will come to an end soon. Hopefully this will prompt Chinese local state and city level government compensations for patenting to stop as well, which will help increase patent quality.

In addition, it costs money to maintain a patent regardless of whether it is invention patent or Utility Model. Low value patents are usually abandoned quickly. Therefore, by deactivating poor quality patents, the remaining active patent quality in China should be rising up to a reasonable level eventually.

2.4.8. *Checklist — differences between Chinese and US patent systems*

For reader's convenience, Table 2-1 lists key differences and some similarities between Chinese and US patent systems.

2.5. Comparing China and US IP Court Systems

2.5.1. *Differences in the court system — China's new IP Courts*

US IP system is a combination of common law (or case law), statutory law, and civil law. Therefore, US IP practitioners need to monitor new IP case rulings carefully. Plaintiff often utilizes International Trade Commission (ITC) to seek injunction of defendant's products because ITC cases can conclude in a year, much faster than suing through US

Table 2-1   Comparison of Chinese patent system versus US patent system.

Issues to Consider	US Typical Approach	China Approach: (Similar) or Different
Regular Patent — Utility — patent (US) v. Invention patent (China)	• *Patentable invention*: a useful, new, and non-obvious invention for a process, machine, manufacture, or composition of matter. • *Judicial exception*: law of nature, natural phenomena, abstract idea (unless claims amount to significantly more).	• *Patentable invention*: new technical solutions proposed for a product, a process or the improvement thereof. • *Judicial exception*: 1. Scientific discoveries; 2. Rules and methods for intellectual activities; 3. Methods for the diagnosis or treatment of diseases; 4. Animal or plant varieties; 5. Substances obtained by means of nuclear transformation; 6. Designs that are mainly used for making a pattern, color, or the combination of the two prints.
	• *Prosecution length*: typically 2–5 years. • *Patent allowance/grant*: after successfully passing Patent Office substantive examination. • *Term of the first granted parent patent in the family*: 20 years from filing date. • *Term of the child patent*: 20 years from the first granted parent patent filing date.	• *Prosecution length*: typically 3–5 years. • (same) • (same) • *Term of the child patent*: 20 years from the child patent filing date. The preceding patent from which the child patent claims priority from is considered abandoned.
	• *Priority date period derived from a foreign parent patent application*: 12 months • *Priority date period derived from a Provisional application*: 12 months	• (same) • No applicable

(Continued)

Table 2-1 (*Continued*)

Issues to Consider	US Typical Approach	China Approach: (Similar) or Different
	• *Priority date period derived from a domestic parent patent application.* The benefit claim of continuation application (CA), divisional (DIV), or continuation in-part application (CIP) to the parent utility patent application can be greater than 12 months provided CAs or CIPs are filed prior to the issuance of the parent utility patent.	• *Priority date period derived from a domestic parent patent application.* Divisional in some cases claim priority date to the time of its own filing date. There is also a separate priority claiming mechanism where the later patent application claims domestic priority to an early patent application, the early patent application will be considered abandoned, and the 20-year patent term is counted from the filing date of the later patent application rather than early patent application
	• *International patent filing*: (i) may designate other member countries after PCT filing with a 12 months priority date; (ii) may directly enter other countries via Paris Convention within the priority date period.	• (same)
	• *Country specifics*: pre-*Alice* observed significant percentage of patents being software and some business methods. Post-*Alice*, 80+% of challenged software patents have been invalidated. Even greater percentages have been invalidated for covered business methods. (CBMs)	• *Country specific*: very conservative on business methods and software patents. Has extremely strict requirement for amendments which are rejected unless directly supported by the specification => this is the reason why Chinese patent specifications often include literal recitations of all claims, and technical features known in the art.

(*Continued*)

Table 2-1   (*Continued*)

Issues to Consider	US Typical Approach	China Approach: (Similar) or Different
Utility Model Patent	• Not applicable	• *Patentable invention*: technical solutions proposed for a product's shape, structure, or their combinations, which are fit for practice use. • *Highly recommended*: hardware inventions with relatively short life cycle. • *Disadvantage*: not able to protect method or process inventions. • *Prosecution length*: ~6 month • *Patent allowance/grant*: after formality check. • *Term*: 10 years from filing. • *Enforceability*: anytime after grant, but the case is stronger after obtaining an Evaluation Report of Patent from SIPO. • *Invalidity standard*: harder to invalidate compared to Invention Patent due to the lower inventive step standard requirement. • *Damage award amount*: typically not different from that of an Invention Patent, but when the court adopts the statutory damages, it will consider the technical inventiveness or contribution of the patent. • *International filing*: similar to Invention Patent, may enter other countries via PCT with 12 months priority date. • *Special feature*: Utility Model patent may claim priority from an Invention Patent and vice versa. Applicant may file both an Invention Patent and Utility Model Patent for the same invention at the same time, but must choose one at grant.

(*Continued*)

Table 2-1   (*Continued*)

Issues to Consider	US Typical Approach	China Approach: (Similar) or Different
Design patent	• *Protection*: new, original, and ornamental design for an article of manufacture. Requires novelty, originality, and should be an article of manufacture. The design must be non-obvious. • *Country specifics*: partial designs are protectable. • *Term*: 15 years life (for application filed on or after December 18, 2013; 10 years for applications filed before December 18, 2013). • *International filing*: PCT is not available for design patents, but can enter other countries via Paris Convention with 6 months priority date.	• *Protection*: new designs of the shape, pattern of a product, or their combination, or the combination of the color with shape and pattern, which are rich in an aesthetic appeal and are fit for industrial application. • *Country specifics*: only full designs are protected. (However, the newly proposed amendment to patent law revises to cover partial designs as well.). • *Term*: 10 years life. (However, the newly proposed amendment to patent law revised to 15 years.). • *(same)*
Provisional (temporary) patent application	• *Nature*: a patent application, not a patent. • *Term*: expires in a year and loses priority date unless converted to a utility patent. • *Enforceability*: not enforceable unless converted to utility patent within a year and provides adequate support to claims in the utility patent. • *International filing*: may filing PCT within 12 months period claim priority from Provisional application.	• Not applicable
Government subsidies	• NA	• Chinese invention patent application, Chinese utility model (at local government level), US utility patent application, PCT patent application. • Subsidies are fading away.

courts. However, to bring a patent infringement case to ITC, plaintiff must satisfy the Domestic Industry requirement "the complainant in a patent-based 337 investigation must show that an industry exists or is being established (Economic Prong) and that the industry practices at least one claim of the patent at issue (Technical Prong)."

The Economic Prong can be met via three possible paths:

  (i) Significant investment in plant and equipment;
 (ii) Significant employment of labor or capital; or
(iii) Substantial investment in an IP right's exploitation including engineering, research and development, or licensing. Some additional facts include:

- Licensing alone can establish a Domestic Industry; and
- Five full-time licensing employees were sufficient to satisfy Domestic Industry requirement (*ITC Inv. No.337-TA-392,* 446, October 20, 1997).

The Technical Prong can be met by:

(i) Establishing that the domestic product practices one or more claims of the patent at issue either literally or under the doctrine of equivalents.

- Only need to show the Domestic Industry practices at least one claim of each patent; and
- Licensing of a patent can suffice if there is sufficient nexus. (e.g. *Inv. No.337-TA-630*, September 16, 2008, Tessera licensed a large portfolio to more than 60 companies, relied on its licensing activities and revenue related to Tessera Compliant Chip, or TCC, technology.).

In *InterDigital v. ITC* (January 2013), it was decided that NPEs may satisfy ITC's Domestic Industry requirement through substantial investment in domestic licensing activities, without any need to prove that any licensed products are produced domestically. In *In Certain Products Having Laminated Packaging* (March 2013), ITC ordered an early evidentiary hearing and initial determination as to whether the complainant has satisfied the economic prong of the Domestic Industry requirement.

In addition, on June 24, 2013, ITC announced a pilot program to expedite fact-finding on issues such as the existence of a Domestic Injury and will direct the presiding Administrative Legal Judge to issue an early initial determination within 100 days of institution. In May 2013, Samsung Display invested $25M to launch Intellectual Keystone Technology (IKT) in Washington D.C., possibly designed to satisfy ITC's Domestic Industry requirement.

Another path[5] is suing in federal courts to seek damages and potential injunction. Typical procedure is for plaintiff to initiate a complaint at district court after sufficient investigation to reasonably believe its rights have been damaged. The motion of complaint should be simple, clear, declares that the court has subject matter jurisdiction and personal jurisdiction, explicitly lists plaintiff's issue and requested remedy. Defendant after being served with the notice of complaint, must answer within 21 days or request extension. This is followed by initial disclosure, evidence investigation, claim interpretation (e.g. Markman hearing), expert report and evidence discovery. Then both parties typically request Motion for Summary Judgment. This may be followed by court hearing typically including 6–9 juries. The final verdict by Jury must be agreed by all to be effective. If a party doesn't agree with Jury's verdict, it can request judge to overrule by requesting Motion for Judgment as a Matter of Law. If a party doesn't agree with Jury's or Judge's verdict, they can also appeal at Federal Circuit. If not satisfied with the Federal Circuit ruling, a party can take the case to Supreme Court. Supreme Court has the freedom of deciding whether to take the appealed case. Typically, only when Supreme Court believes that the issue is important and the Federal Circuit possibly erred in its decision, then it will take the case to review.

China's IP policies follow the statutory law or civil law system which differ from US' mixture of common law, statutory and civil law for patent system. Therefore, earlier decisions do not bind other courts. However, lower courts in China in practice will follow the decisions made by the Chinese Supreme People's Court (SPC).[6] As a result, IP practitioners interested in Chinese market must closely observe the stipulations in the

---

[5] "美国专利诉讼-规则、判例与实务", 陈维国著, 2014.
[6] Richard Bird, "A Guide to patent PLitigation", 2013.

law, in the proposed revisions, and the decisions by the SPC as well as the Judicial Interpretation (II) of the SPC.

China has a two-track system consisting of:

(i) the patent infringement action; and
(ii) the invalidation action.

The patent infringement action is brought in front of the court; while the invalidity challenge final decision is made by SIPO according to the Administrative Litigation Act. This means that China's court can't determine the validity of a patent during patent infringement action. The defendant must separately file invalidation petition before the PRB of SIPO.

To start a patent litigation in China, one must find competent Intermediate People's Courts to hear the case. These competent courts are limited in number and most are located in Tier 1 or Tier 2 cities. For infringement proceedings, the plaintiff may choose an Intermediate People's Court in the state the defendant is located or where the patent infringement took place. Appeals may go to Higher People's Court, and then to Supreme People's Court. For validity proceedings, plaintiff will bring the case to China's PRB, whose decision can be appealed to the Intermediate People's Court in Beijing and then to Beijing Higher People's Court.

Recently, China added the new IPR Court (special court for IP rights or IPr cases) to handle patent-related disputes. This is great news because judges at the IPR Court will be more familiar with patent issues and thus make competent decisions. This will improve the litigation process significantly in the future.

Figure 2-3 is a chart depicting the simplified structure of Chinese court systems for patent infringement cases.

2.5.2. China's patent litigation procedure — lack of discovery process

In US, when filing a patent suit against an accused infringer, as discussed in Section 2.5.1, plaintiff needs to have reasonable believe that defendant

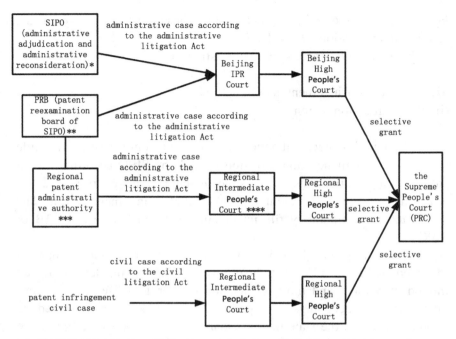

Figure 2-3   Structure of Chinese patent court system.

* The SIPO administrative adjudicative act including adjudication related to compulsory license and administrative reconsideration with respect to the some adjudicative acts during the procedure of patent application examination.
** PRB decision on the appeal of rejection of the claims during examination and the decision of invalidation procedure after the patent is granted.
*** The Regional patent administrative authority's administrative adjudicative act including investigating patent infringement and issuing injunction order, investigating or prosecuting passing off a patent, and false marking a patent.
**** For Beijing, Shanghai, Guangdong Province, the first jurisdiction court is Beijing IPR court, Shanghai IPR court and Guangzhou IPR court respectively, for other provinces and regions, the first jurisdiction court is the corresponding Regional Intermediate People's Court.

has infringed its IP. The US pending Patent Reform bill proposes to heighten the pleading requirement for plaintiffs by requiring more upfront work by plaintiffs such as providing claim charts of specific patent claims against specific products. By raising the bar in filing patent litigations, US Congress hopes to deter NPEs from abusing the court system. In the damage amount estimation, plaintiff often can use publically available product shipping or market share information, and later rely on discovery process to uncover more accurate information, such as source code information, revenue or profit data, and email communication, etc. Through such discovery process, some previous inaccessible confidential information can be uncovered. If the internal communications indicate that defendant knew about its patent infringement and still continued infringement act, plaintiff can then establish willful infringement and thus obtain up to treble damage (three times the damage amount). The bar for willful infringement has been raised recently such that it becomes more difficult than before to obtain treble damages (*re Seagate Technology*, 497 F.3d 1360 (Fed. Cir. 2007)). However, there are indications that such severe punitive damage award is making a comeback. In the oral argument of *Stryker Corp. v. Zimmer* and *Halo Electronics, Inc. v. Pulse Electronics, Inc.* (February 23, 2016), the U.S. Supreme Court signaled that it is inclined to discard the Federal Circuit's rigid test for awarding enhanced damages in patent cases. We will keep a close eye on the final ruling which is estimated to come out in June of 2016.

To sue a company for patent infringement in China, plaintiff needs to establish proof to a certain degree that defendant infringed and plaintiff suffered certain damage. This is a higher bar than that at the pleading phase for US cases. However, because there is no discovery process, plaintiffs have a hard time establishing clear evidence of use. For example, it is hard to obtain algorithms used by a software source code. It is also difficult to verify certain potential infringing features based on publically available sources, such as servers used in defendant's data room, test lab, etc. For product shipping information needed for damage estimate, there is scarce information available, especially for small and medium sized companies. Some plaintiffs resort to craftily obtaining information which may backfire on them. This causes a severe burden on plaintiff and is part of the reasons why there are very few IP litigations in China compared to US. This is also one of the reasons why China Patent Act provides statutory damages in lieu of damage award based on lost profit, infringer's profits, and reasonable royalty.

As discussed above, due to the lack of a discovery procedure in Chinese litigation process, it is difficult to produce the sales data, infringer profit data, and the evidence of use, or comparable licenses needed to establish reasonable royalty. Therefore, the Chinese court typically will adopt the statutory damages when patent infringement case is established. According to Articles 65 of China Patent Act, when it is difficult to determine lost profit suffered by the patent owner, profits infringer has earned, and reasonable royalty, the court may award damages in the amount of not less than RMB 10,000 Yuan and not more than 1,000,000 Yuan in light of factors such as the type of the patent right, the nature and the circumstances of the infringing act.

According to a study by a Chinese university, 97% patent damage cases from 2008 to 2012 adopted statutory damage rather than award damages. The average damage award amount for these cases is only 80,000 RMB Yuan.[7] However, current Draft Amendments to the Patent Act by the State Council Legislative Affairs Office proposes to increase statutory damages from the previous range of 10,000–1,000,000 RMB Yuan to a much higher range of 100,000–5,000,000 RMB Yuan. This would be a welcoming change cheered by patent owners and could impact the IP landscape in the future.

Although there isn't an exact counterpart to the evidential discovery process for US litigation system within Chinese evidence law or civil procedure law, the Civil Litigation Act of China, instead, provides court an avenue to collect evidences. According to Article 64 of the Civil Litigation Act of China, a court should investigate and collect evidences when the parties or their representatives (e.g. attorneys) are unable to collect needed evidences due to objective causes or there are evidences that the court considers necessary for adjudicating the case. In other words, Chinese court may collect evidences under two scenarios:

(i) Collection via application by the parties; or
(ii) Collection in *ex officio* manner.

The collection via applications by the parties only includes the following three scenarios:

(i) The evidence is held by relevant national department such that the parties and their representatives have no right to access the evidence;

---

[7] See http://www.chinapeace.gov.cn/2013-04/content_7329413.htm.

(ii) The evidence is related to national security, business security, or personal privacy; or

(iii) Other evidences that the parties or their representatives can't collect by themselves due to objective causes.

The *ex officio* collection includes the following five scenarios:

(i) Evidences related to facts that jeopardize national interests or public interests;

(ii) Evidences related to personal relationship;

(iii) Evidences related to environmental public interest lawsuit;

(iv) There is a possibility that the parties conspired maliciously to jeopardize other's legitimate rights and interest; or

(v) Evidences related to certain procedural issues, e.g. staying a suit, terminating a suit, or joining a party.

In addition, as discussed above, patent owners can also file a petition to Regional Patent Administrative Authority to handle the patent infringement case. In terms of evidence collection, the Regional Patent Administrative Authority has more rooms and greater power to investigate and collect infringement-related evidences. According to the proposals in "Evidence Guideline for the Administrative Enforcement of Patents (request for comments)",[8] the Patent Administrative Authority (an administrative branch of the government) will have more extensive investigation and collection power of evidences than Chinese courts. For example, it will be empowered to conduct various administrative investigation and evidence collections, including accessing and copying the account, agreement, or records related to a party's business or manufacture; as well as carrying out interim seizure of the products. Therefore, for the purpose of efficiency and speed, the Administrative adjudication route is more favorable to patent owners. The disadvantage of the Administrative adjudication route, however, is the lack of availability of its jurisdiction on

---

[8] http://www.sipo.gov.cn/tz/gz/201603/t20160304_1246757.html "Evidence Guideline for the Administrative Enforcement of Patent (request for comments)" (promulgated March 4, 2016).

damages. Therefore, a plaintiff's main purpose of utilizing the Administrative branch is to leverage its evidentiary capacity and its injunctive power upon the establishment of patent infringement.

It is noteworthy that with the great fortune of companies going public, more Chinese companies are trying to get listed on public stock exchange in China, Hong Kong or US. Such action of going public requires them to disclose product, shipment volume and brings much greater transparency. This will enable plaintiffs to more easily obtain information than before. In *Netac v. Watertek* case (US$6.45M), the litigation was initiated at the time Watertek filed for IPO, and the damage award was likely better established due to this fact.

2.5.3. *Difference in privileged communication and work product*

Some of the significant differences between US and Chinese legal systems include the degree of protection relating to attorney–client privilege and attorney work product. Attorney–client privilege means the right to prevent disclosure of certain information in court, especially when the information was originally communicated in a professional or confidential relationship. Attorney work product means qualified immunity of an attorney's product from discovery or other compelled disclosure. The tests used are substantial need and undue hardship.

In US, because there is discovery procedure, attorney–client privilege is extremely important in protecting confidential communications between the attorney and his client. This way, client can share his point of views which may not be correct legally in his lawyer's opinion without fearing that such information will be deposed during deposition or discovery process. However, under certain circumstance, judges can compel production of certain privileged communication. As a result, many attorneys, as a precaution, recommend clients to communicate sensitive information verbally. For example, when technical teams evaluate whether a prior art reads onto their own products, often attorneys recommend them to call the lawyer rather than writing comments down in email or other written format. Technical interpretation of a patent claim may be incorrect which affects technical assessment of whether a product infringes or not. Some misinterpretation may cause the technical team's conclusion to be wrong or inaccurate. In any event, companies wouldn't want such false internal opinions to be used against them later in courts as admission of willful infringement. Therefore, such precaution makes good sense.

There isn't a counterpart principal or doctrine in Chinese IP law system that's the same as US' attorney–client privilege protection due to the lack of a general evidence discovery in the Chinese legal system. When a party initiates a patent litigation in China, the burden of producing evidence rests with the party and discovery is unavailable. Therefore, one might argue that there is no need for attorney–client privilege which is designed mainly to counter the side effect of discovery process.

A special area to pay attention to is that under certain circumstances, even US system doesn't necessarily provide the attorney–client privilege protections. It is very important to understand these cases, summarized below, so that clients don't lose unintended sensitive communications during court discovery process while all along falsely believing that those were privileged communications.

(i) Non-US attorneys, such as Chinese attorneys, don't necessarily enjoy privileged protection for communications with clients. In a few cases, such as Apple v. Samsung, Court ruled that the communication with a non-US attorney was not protected. Such evidence was used partly to establish willful infringement and contributed toward the large damage award by jury.

(ii) US attorneys not specifically hired for the relevant case might not have sufficient nexus to provide the needed privilege. Some clients need advice or help urgently, but the specific lawyers or law firms hired for the case are not available. Under such scenarios, clients may want to simply invite another US attorney not involved with the specific case to participate in a communication, hoping to obtain the privileged communication protection. However, such case may be viewed unfavorably by a court under some circumstances and thus the judge may declare that the written communication is not privileged because the attorney was not hired by the client for the specific purpose. Therefore, clients should be cognizant of this issue and take proper measures to protect themselves.

(iii) Written communications between two team members simply copying the attorney might not be considered attorneya–client privileged communication and thus not adequately protected. Some clients may conduct elaborate discussions with each other via email, simply copying the attorney passively, on topics that they don't wish to be discovered later. Such emails might lose privileged protection if not handled properly.

In summary, attorney–client privilege and attorney–work product privilege play an important role during evidence discovery process in US system. However, Chinese legal system doesn't recognize attorney–client privilege so clients need to be keenly aware of such differences between these two systems.

The following Table 2-2 compares the extent of protection provided by Attorney-Client privilege in the corporate context between the US and China. If parties are disputing patent infringement cases in China, such lack of privilege may not have a significant impact on either parties because there is a lack of evidence collection process by courts. The Administrative Authority's evidence investigation and collection power will usually not extend to the communication between a client and the attorney. In addition, it is noteworthy that attorney–client privilege is not recognized in US patent litigation system for Chinese Attorneys in preventing discovery of evidences during the course of patent preparation and application.

Another related area is attorney work product. Attorney's work while working on a case is typically exempt from court discovery. For example, lawyers may develop internal claim charts that they want to use for licensing discussions. However, until it is ready, they may not want others to get hold of it in case others use the defects in the analysis against them in court. As a result, attorneys often label their work "attorney work product". In China, attorney work product is not protected.

IP practitioners must be keenly aware of these differences between US and Chinese legal systems, and advise their clients on such differences to best protect their clients' interests.

Table 2-2 Comparison of attorney–client privilege between China and US legal systems.

Legal System	Discovery Procedure Exists?	Privileged or Protected? (e.g. Communications Protected by Attorney–Client Privilege or Attorney Work-Product Privilege)		Comments
		In-House Attorney/Agent	**Law Firm Attorney**	
US	Yes	• Attorney: YES (for US attorney, NO for Chinese attorneys working with US clients) • Patent Agent: depends on the court. Different courts adopt different approaches. Most courts recognize the Agent's privilege. However, even if Agent's privilege is acknowledged, its scope is usually narrower than that of an Attorney. A CAFC's recent decision affirmed the Patent Agent's privilege but limited it to "as far as the Agent is allowed to ethically practice before the Patent Office".	Yes	Attorney–client privilege law varies by state.

(Continued)

Table 2-2   (*Continued*)

Legal System	Discovery Procedure Exists?	Privileged or Protected? (e.g. Communications Protected by Attorney–Client Privilege or Attorney Work-Product Privilege)		
		In-House Attorney/Agent	Law Firm Attorney	Comments
China	NO (1) Court has limited evidence investigation and collection power. (2) The Patent Administrative Authority has greater power than court in evidence investigation and collection for patent infringement cases. (3) PRB of SIPO will NOT conduct evidence investigation and collection for patent invalidation.	NO (1) NO for patent infringement proceedings before the court, the Administrative Authority, or during the patent invalidation proceedings before SIPO's PRB. (2) The evidence investigation and collection power of the court or the Administrative Authority usually will not extend to communications between the client and attorney.	NO (1) NO for patent infringement proceedings before the court, the Administrative Authority, or during patent invalidation proceedings before SIPO's PRB. (2) The evidence investigation and collection power of the court or the Administrative Authority usually will not extend to communications between the client and attorney.	Attorney–client privilege does not exist in China although attorneys still have a duty of confidentiality to client. (This lack of privilege system may not have significant impact on the parties **in China** because Chinese courts are unlikely to honor US privilege law without also adopting US discovery law.).

This case may have impact on future district courts' decisions.[9]

[9] *In re Queens University* (Fed. Cir. 2016).

2.5.4. *IP infringement damage award*

In US, damage award could be very high. Table 2-3 shows a list of the top 10 largest initial adjudicated damage awards from 1995 to 2013.[10]

As a result of such astronomically high damage award in US, patent owners are highly motivated to go to court and sue for infringement. However, AIA introduced PTAB and implemented new patent invalidation programs such as IPR, CBM, post grant review (PGR). PTAB has been aggressively invalidating patents, with invalidity rate as high as 80%+ as of mid-2015. It has earned a nickname "death squad". Therefore, it will be more difficult in the future for NPEs because defendants will immediately turn to the IPR proceeding as soon as they are asserted or sued to invalidate the asserted patents. If NPE's core patents are mostly

Table 2-3   US top 10 largest initial adjudicated damage awards: 1995–2013.

Year	Case Name	Technology	Award (in US$MM)
2009	Centocor Ortho Biotech v. Abbott Laboratories	Arthritis drugs	$1,673
2007	Lucent Technologies v. Microsoft	MP3 technology	$1,538
2012	Carnegie Mellon v. Marvell Technology Group	Noise reduction on circuits for disc drives	$1,169
2012	Apple v. Samsung Electronics	Smartphone software	$1,049
2012	Monsanto Company v. E.I. Dupont De Nemours	Genetically modified soybean seeds	$1,000
2010	Mirror Worlds v. Apple	Operating system	$626
2005	Cordis v. Medtronic Vascular	Vascular stents	$595
2004	Eolas Technologies v. Microsoft	Internet browser	$521
2011	Bruce N. Saffran v. Johnson & Johnson	Drug-eluting stents	$482
2008	Buce N. Saffran v. Boston Scientific	Drug-eluting stents	$432

[10] "2014 Patent Litigation Study", pwc, 2014.

invalidated, it essentially destroys the NPE because it will take too long and is too costly to appeal while not earning revenue on these patents. Therefore, some patent litigation defendants wishfully hope that this means US IP pendulum is swinging toward favoring patent infringers. However, with the anticipated likely lowering of bar for willful patent infringement in the upcoming rulings by US Supreme Court (*Stryker Corp. v. Zimmer* and *Halo Electronics, Inc. v. Pulse Electronics, Inc.*), plaintiff in the future may more easily obtain treble damage judgment against the defendant and thus obtain a high award amount again provided its patents survive invalidity challenges. Therefore, it is possible that the US IP pendulum is actually swinging back a bit toward favoring litigation plaintiffs.

Regardless of which way the IP pendulum is swinging and how far it will swing before turning back, damage award in the tens of millions US dollars are still common. Considering that the typical litigation cost is US$3–5M per year, we expect patent litigation and patent assertion activities in US to continue. In addition, based on the speculated trend toward relaxing the tests for enhanced damage award in patent infringement cases (*Stryker* and *Halo*), patent owners are likely to more easily obtain larger damage awards without the need to meet the previous high standard in proving willful infringement.

China's damage award for patent infringement has been low, typically in the range of 1 million Chinese Yuan, which corresponds to US$160K. Since legal fees alone could exceed this amount and combined with the fact that foreign companies feel that they are disadvantaged in Chinese court, US companies typically don't want to venture along this path.

However, China's legal system is evolving quickly and Chinese government is beginning to take IP seriously. Recently, the statutory damage award amount for trademark infringement has been increased to 2 million Chinese Yuan. Patent infringement statutory damage award amount hasn't been revised yet, still staying at a low amount. However, with the increased awareness of IP and Chinese companies' greater accumulation of patent portfolios, as well as improved patent quality from Chinese companies, we expect the law to change quickly.

Table 2-4   Comparison of China and US court systems.

Issues to Consider	US Typical Approach	China Approach: (Similar) or Different
Patent Law	• Common law system. Although federal statute is the first authority, CAFC's decisions are important to study because they have precedence value to subsequent cases.	• Civil law system. Precedence is not binding to other courts but courts in practice follow the Chinese Supreme People's Court decisions. The judicial interpretation of Supreme People's Court also controls and is the authority on specific cases.
Litigation	• Court could judge both validity and infringement. • Patent invalidity can also be filed at USPTO.	• Two-track system. Infringement at Intermediate People's Court, patent invalidity at SIPO-PRB.
Discovery Process	• Court can compel defendant to produce evidence such as source code.	• No discovery process and difficult to obtain direct evidence (recent IP practice might make info access easier).
Attorney Client Privilege	• Protected for both in-house attorney and outside law-firm.	• Not protected.
IP Damage Award	• Could be US$1B+.	• Typically US$160K, but recently damage award reached up to US$50M.

2.5.5. *Checklist — differences between the court systems*

Table 2-4 is a checklist listing main differences between China and US court systems and some similarities for reader's convenience.

2.6. Patent Box — Lower Tax Rate for Income from Patented Products

"Patent Box" means a box on the form to check for patented products, and upon checking such a box, the associated products enjoy a lower tax rate compared to non-patented products. China is among one of nine countries (Belgium, China, France, Luxembourg, Netherlands, Spain, Switzerland,and the UK) in the world that set up incentives for companies to innovate. Such tax savings could be significant for companies. For example, in France, the tax rate can be dropped from a typical 33% to 15%. Others provide tax exemption for certain percentages. China's Patent Box, on the other hand, covers more than just patent. It provides lower taxes to firms that spend at least 3–6% of gross revenue on R&D, 60% revenue comes from core IP (invention patents, utility model patents, software, copyrights, proprietary layout designs and new plant varieties), 30% of employees have a college degree, or 10% employed in R&D or higher tech occupation.

2.7. Differences in Patent Eligibility for Software and Business Methods

We'll now take a look at the differences between US and Chinese IP systems regarding patent eligibility for software and business method inventions.

2.7.1. *Comparison of IP law for software*

US IP law stipulates that an idea that is new, useful and non-obvious is generally entitled to a patent, provided that the subject matter is a process, machine, manufacturing, or composition (PMMC). Recently, however, under the US Supreme Court's *Alice* ruling,[11] further evaluation is required on patent eligibility, such as whether the patent claims seek to tie up the judicial exception, i.e. law of nature, natural phenomenon, or abstract idea (LNA). Therefore, even though it does not treat software separately or call it out specifically, many software patents are subject to increased scrutiny due to the perception that they are closely associated with abstract ideas.

---

[11] *Alice Corp. v. CLS Bank International*, 573 U.S. __, 134 S. Ct. 2347 (2014).

Chinese IP law, on the other hand, deals with software patents from a slightly different angle. Chinese patent law Article 25 declares that patent rights shall not be granted for any of the following (in addition to four other categories):

(i) Scientific discoveries; and
(ii) Rules and methods for mental activities.

In addition, Article 2 states: for the purpose of this law, invention creations mean inventions, utility models and design, where:

(1) Inventions mean new technical solutions proposed for a product, a process or the improvement thereof;
(2) Utility models mean new technical solutions proposed for the shape and structure of a product, or the combination thereof, which are fit for practical use; and
(3) Design means a new design of a product's shape, pattern or the combination thereof, or the combination of its color and shape and/or pattern, that is aesthetically pleasing and industrial applicable.

As can be seen from (1) and (2) definitions, technical solution is the material test for the patent eligibility of invention and utility models. Technical solution is an aggregation of technical means applying the laws of nature to solve a technical problem. Usually, technical means are embodied as technical features. A solution that does not adopt technical means to solve a technical problem and thereby does not achieve any technical effect in compliance with the laws of natures does not constitute a subject matter as defined in Article 2.

Although the two jurisdictions of US and China adopt different mechanisms or approaches to determine the subject matter eligibility, the inherent and essential nature is similar behind the Articles, Rules, Laws, Rulings, or Regulations, which is to exclude subject matters unsuitable for patent protection from the patent regime.

For US Patent Law, after *Alice*, the scope of the eligible subject matter for patenting has gotten closer to that of the Chinese Patent Law.

2.7.2. *Subject matter eligibility comparison*

However, from practical perspective, there still exist some significant differences between US and Chinese jurisdictions in terms of the subject matter eligibility test. We'll discuss the key differences in the following.

(1) Generally speaking, the United States adopts a more general, flexible and open test on the eligibility issue. However, *Alice* and *Mayo*[12] cases substantially restricted the scope of eligible subject matter as compared with the previous standard going back at least to 1998 represented by the *State Bank*[13] case. *State Bank* was considered the seminal case that opened the door to business method patent. In comparison, China adopts a relatively more specific and practical test, i.e. the "technical solution test" for the subject matter eligibility issue.

(2) Even with *Alice*, the scope of the specific eligible subject matter in US is still broader than that in China, as described in Figure 2-4 (graphically) and Table 2-5 (categorically). In Figure 2-4, region I represents subject matters that are eligible for patenting under both US and Chinese law. Region II represents subject matters that are eligible under US law, but not eligible under Chinese law. Region III represents subject matters that are eligible under Chinese law, but not eligible under US law. As can be seen region II is greater than region III, which attempts to convey that China eligible scope is somewhat narrower than the US scope. As shown in Table 2-5, some types of subject matters are patentable in US but still excluded from the patent protection in China, for example, computer readable media CD and VCD.

Specifically as shown in Figure 2-4, China and the United States have a large overlapping area of commonly eligible scope, i.e. Region I. Moreover, as depicted by Figure 2-4(a) before *Alice*, there was also a large

---

[12] *Mayo v. Prometheus*, 566 U.S. —, 132 S. Ct. 1289 (2012).
[13] *State Street Bank & Trust Co. v. Signature Financial Group*, 149 F.3d 1368 (*Fed. Cir. Jul.* 23, 1998).

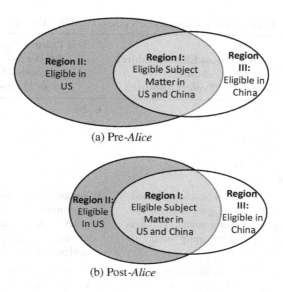

(a) Pre-*Alice*

(b) Post-*Alice*

Figure 2-4   Depiction of patent eligibility scope between China and US patent laws.

Region II under which subject matters were eligible in US but not in China. However, as indicated by Figure 2-4(b) after *Alice*, although there are still differences in subject matter eligible scope between the two jurisdictions, the gap between the two jurisdictions, represented by Region II (and III), have decreased significantly because US and Chinese law are becoming more synchronized in terms of subject matter eligibility. In addition, with US Supreme Court's recognition of "solving a technological problem" test as one of the exceptions to the patent ineligibility in *Alice* compared to China's "technical solution" test, the subject matter eligibility tests in China and US are merging.

However, some cases are still ineligible under Chinese law but are eligible under US law, which are represented by Region II in Figure 2-4. These are the cases that fail the "technical solution test" stipulated in Article 2.2 of the Chinese Patent Act and thus are ineligible subject matter under Chinese law. On the other hand, they are able to pass either the Step 1 test in *Alice*, e.g. not an abstract idea, and/or Step 2, i.e. the "significantly more" or "inventive concept" test. Computer readable CDs and

Table 2-5   Comparison of China and US patent eligibility testing standards.

Issues to Consider	Is it Patent Eligible Subject Matter? — US Typical Approach	Is it Patent Eligible Subject Matter?— China Approach: (Similar) or Different
Pure business method	• No	• No
Pure software	• No	• No
Program product (CD, VCD, etc.)	• Yes	• No
Computer implemented business method	• No for business method running on common or general computer, unless "significantly more".	• No for business method running on common or general computer, unless meeting technical means resolving technical problem and achieving technical effect.
Computer implemented algorithm	• No for algorithm performed by common or general computer, unless "significantly more".	• No for algorithm performed by common or general computer, unless meeting technical means resolving technical problem and achieving technical effect.
Data structure	• No for per se (pre-*Enfish*) • Yes (post-*Enfish* if improving computer related technology).	• No for per se, unless meeting technical means resolving technical problem and achieving technical effect.
Signal	• No	• No

VCDs belong to this region. With the recent decision on *Enfish*[14] by US Court of Appeals of the Federal Circuit, there have been speculations about whether it represents a reversal in direction toward pre-*Alice* era, i.e. a slight expansion in Region II. However, *Enfish* will likely pass the eligibility test in China as well, i.e. it is eligible both in US and China, and thus falls within Region I. As a result, the shapes in Figure 2-4 does not change much after *Enfish*.

Similarly, there are other cases that are ineligible subject matter under US law but eligible under Chinese law, which are represented by Region III in Figure 2-4. This region exists mostly in theory with a narrow range.

---

[14] *Enfish, LLC v. Microsoft Corporation, et al.*, 2015–1244, CAFC (issued on May 12, 2016).

Under US law, *Diehr* [15] addresses "solving a technological problem" principal which was acknowledged in *Alice*. There are some subtle differences between *Diehr* "solving a technological problem" and the Chinese "technical solution" test. In the rare scenario where a case fails *Diehr* but passes the Chinese "technical solution" test, it would fall within Region III. However, due to the fact that subject matter ineligibility rejection in China either in the examination proceeding or during invalidation proceeding based on the ground of Article 2.2 is relatively uncommon compared to the large number of §101 rejections in US IP practices (especially post-*Alice*), Region III is not completely non-existent. The examples we provide below for Region III are not necessary the result of differences between Chinese and US IP law, but more due to how IP practices are currently empirically implemented in China.

More specifically, under Chinese Patent Law, if a novelty point relies only on the business or commercial mode, usually the invention will be rejected on the ground of ineligibility subject matter. In China, at times, the ineligibility rejection is made after prior art searches. If after comparing the examined invention with the searched prior arts, the distinguished features are merely directed to business concept of non-technical feature, then it will be rejected. Similarly, if the distinguished features identified from the prior art are in the background, or the description of the application without consulting a new searched prior art is not directed to technical features or aspects, then the subject matter will be rejected under the ineligibility category. This test is similar to a combination of "the point of novelty test" and "the technological arts test" established by US case law. [16]

Table 2-5 further summarizes and compares the differences between China and US patent subject matter eligibility testing standard by categorys. For example, US law allows CD or VCD program product as a patentable subject matter while Chinese law does not. US law requires a

---

[15] *Diamond v. Diehr*, 450 U.S. 175 (1981).
[16] *Parker v. Flook*, 437, U.S. 584 (1978), *Ex parte Carl A. Lundgren*, Appeal no. 2003-2088, Application 08/093,516 April 20, 2994, *In re Bilski*, 545 F.3d 943, 88 U.S.P.Q.2d 1385 (Fed. Cir. 2008).].

computer implemented algorithm to add "significantly more" in order to be patent eligible, while Chinese law requires technical means, solving technical problems, and achieving technical effect in order to be patent eligible.

In the following, we'll provide some additional examples for the purpose of further illustrating the similarity and differences in the eligibility subject matter tests between US and Chinese law from a practical perspective rather than only in theory.

(i) Example #1: a game machine for displaying advertising information, comprising:

a storage, configured to store game program;

an advertising data receiving means, configured to receive updated advertising data in a predetermined time interval, with the received updated advertizing information stored into the storage; and a processor, configured to execute the game program stored in the storage and output display data corresponding to the updated advertising data according to the game program.

The above claim could pass the US patent eligibility test according to pre-*Alice* or pre-*Bilski*[17] Standard, but is likely to be rejected under the new *Alice* eligibility test because the claim only uses a standard processor and a memory to perform the steps of receiving, storing, and displaying data.

Under Chinese law, in comparison, the claim will also likely be rejected on the ground of ineligible subject matter under Article 2.2 of Patent Act,[18] because it is not directed to a "technical solution" and does not solve a technical problem.

---

[17] Here, *Alice* and *Bilski* both refer to the Supreme Court cases, i.e. *Bilski v. Kappos*, 561 U.S. 593 (2010) and *Alice Corporation Pty. Ltd. v. CLS Bank International, et al.*, 134 S.Ct. 2347 (June 19, 2014).

[18] Article 2.2 of patent Act states invention' means any new technical solution relating to product, a processor improvement thereof. GPE Part II, Chapter 1, section 2 (2010) further states" a technical solution is an aggregation of technical means applying the laws of nature to solve a technical problem, technical means are embodied as technical features. A solution that does not adopt technical means to solve a technical problem and thereby does not achieve any technical effect in compliance with the laws of nature does not constitute a subject matter as defined in Article 2.2."

ii) Example #2: a method of identifying a message, comparing:

receiving, on a second computer, a digital content identifier created using a mathematical algorithm unique to the message content from at least two of a plurality of first computer having digital content ID generator agents;

comparing, on the second computer, the digital content identifier to a characteristic database of digital content identifiers received from said plurality of first computers to determine whether the message has a characteristic; and

responding to a query from at least one of said plurality of computers to identify the existence or absence of said characteristic of the message based on said comparing.

iii) Example #3: an apparatus for filtering an email message, comprising:

a receiving module, configured to receive a digital content identifier created using a mathematical algorithm unique to the message content from at least two of a plurality of first computers having digital content ID generator agents;

a comparing module, configured to compare the digital content identifier to a characteristic database of digital content identifiers received from said plurality of first computers to determine whether the message has a characteristic; and

an identifying module, configured to identify the existence or absence of said characteristic of the message based on said comparing in response to a query from at least one of said plurality of computers.

The above #3 exemplary claims is likely to be rejected on the ground of "pure software" test under US law in accordance with *Allvoice*,[19] because the claimed subject matter is not one of the four statutory categories under 35 U.S.C. §101.

In China, however, following the Chinese law, example #3 will not be rejected as "pure software per se". Instead, such format of

---

[19] *Allvoice Developments US, LLC v. Microsoft Corp.* (Fed. Cir. 2015).

Table 2-6 Summary of eligibility test outcomes under US and Chinese law for three exemplary cases.

Examples	US Law (*Pre-Alice* Test) Pass or not Pass (with High Probability)	US Law (*Post-Alice* Test) Pass or not Pass (with High Probability)	Chinese Law (Technical Solution Test) Pass or not Pass (with High Probability)
Example #1	• pass	• not pass	• not pass (as it is directed to how to display a newly retrieved data in a game terminal, not resolving a technical problem, and achieving a technical effect.
Example #2	• pass	• not pass	• pass
Example #3	• not pass	• not pass	• pass

claims will most likely be examined according to GPE Part II, Chapter 9 (2010) and accepted as software invention with the scope covering only software implementation without any hardware implementation.

Table 2-6 summarizes the differences between US and Chinese eligibility tests based on the above three examples.

2.7.3. *Information disclosure statement requirement comparison*

According to Article 36(2) of Chinese Patent Law, when an applicant for an invention patent requests substantive examination, applicant shall submit the reference materials relating to existing prior art for the invention up to the date of the patent application. If an application has been filed for an invention patent in a foreign country, the patent administration department under the State Council may require the applicant to submit, within a specified time period, materials concerning any search made for the purpose of examining the application in that foreign country, or materials concerning the results of any examination made in that country. In the event of the applicant's failure to comply with this rule within the specified time period without legitimate reasons, the application shall be deemed to be withdrawn.[20]

Although there is a mandatory requirement to submit the reference materials relating to an invention, the requirement is only imposed at the time when the applicant for an invention patent requests substantive examination. This is different from US practice where such submission requirement is expected during the entire examination period until the patent is granted. In other words, for Chinese patent system, there is not a mandatory obligation to submit relevant materials which the applicant becomes aware of after the applicant submits the substantive examination request. Furthermore, there is no legal effect of non-disclosure of any reference materials relating to an invention known to the applicant. For China's patent prosecution practice, there are no reported cases where a patent application was voided, invalidated or withdrawn due to non-disclosure of any reference materials relating to the inventions. Therefore, in reality, there is hardly any mandatory requirement for the invention reference disclosure in China and little consequence for failure to disclose.

However, if during the examination, the examiner requires the applicant to submit, within a specified time limit, references or materials of the counterpart application in another country, the applicant has the obligation to submit the related references or materials as per the requirement of the examiner. Otherwise, the application shall be deemed to be withdrawn. On the other hand, there is an exception to this rule so that the application is not deemed as withdrawn. It applies when the applicant for an invention patent cannot furnish, for justified reasons, the documents concerning any search or results of any examination specified in Article 36 of the Patent Law. In that case, he or she shall make a statement to the patent administration department under the State Council and submit them later when said documents become available.[21] The withdrawn outcome suggests that there will be adverse consequences if the applicant doesn't meet SIPO's search

---

[20] Article 36 of Chinese Patent Act (2008 Amendment).
[21] Rule 49 of the Implementation Regulations of the Chinese Patent Law Act.

material submission requirement within the time limit. These materials should cover any search made for the purpose of examining the application during the patent prosecution process in the country where the counterpart was filed. However, SIPO rarely takes initiatives requiring applicants to make such submissions. Even if SIPO starts enforcing such submissions, the bar of the requirement is easily met by applicants compared to US' stringent disclosure requirement because the submitted material only covers the search and examination result. Table 2-7 summarizes the differences in informational disclosure requirement between the two systems.

Table 2-7   Comparison of information disclosure submission between US and China

Issues to Consider	US Typical Approach	China Approach: (Similar) or Different
Does the Applicant have general reference disclosure obligation?	• Yes. • The disclosure obligation applies during the entire prosecution period until patent is granted for each individual application. (See 37 CFR and USPTO's MPEP for detailed regulation and guidelines on the disclosure submission).	• No. • But the Applicant has two specific obligations including (1) initial submission during search and examination period; and (2) submission by examiner's requirement. • There are no detailed rules, regulations, or guidelines for the disclosure submission in China except the two provisions (Art. 36 and Rule 49). In addition, there are no judicial decisions found to address this issue.
Are there any adverse consequences for non-disclosure?	• Yes. • It may result in a need for affirmative defense, e.g. equity defense of inequitable conduct which will render the patent unenforceable when meeting the following three conditions: materiality, knowledge of materiality, and a deliberate decision to deceive as ruled in	

(Continued)

Table 2-7   (*Continued*)

Issues to Consider	US Typical Approach	China Approach: (Similar) or Different
	Therasense.[23] Alternatively, it could lead to patent misuse affirmative defense,[24] or unenforceable declaration judgment; or may result in the antitrust counterclaim or declaration judgment, i.e. the *Walker Process* claim[25]; or may cause fee-shift (§285 exceptional case),[26] and also may pierce the attorney–client privilege if it constitutes a crime or fraud exception to the.[27]	• Mostly No. • At most will render the patent application withdrawn during prosecution, if the Applicant does not respond to the examiner's requirement to submit the search result or examination result conducted for the counterpart patent application in other countries. No other penalties are available for breaching the disclosure duty under the Chinese patent law system. There are no equity defense, equity affirmative claim, fee-shift consideration, etc based on the current statute and judicial practices in China.
Specific disclosure requirement by the examiner?	• Usually the examiner will not initiate or require the Applicant to submit the reference disclosure. Instead, the obligation is fulfilled by the Applicant's own accord.	• Except for the submission duty when Applicant requests the substantive examination, the obligation is mainly triggered by the examiner's requirement during the course of the substantive examination.

---

[22] *Therasense, Inc. v. Becton, Dickinson & Co.*, 649 F.3d 1276, 1290 (*Fed. Cir.* 2011) (en banc).

[23] *Daryl Lim, "Patent Misuse and Antitrust Law", Pages 136–137 (2013).*

[24] *Walker Process Equip. v. Food Mach. & Chem. Corp.*, 382 U.S. 172, 173–741 (1965).

[25] 35 U.S.C§285. *Brasseler, U.S.A. I., L.P. v. Stryker Sales Corp.*, 267 F.3d 1370, 1380 (Fed. Cir. 2001).

[26] *In re Spalding Sports Wordwidel Inc.*, 203 F.3d 800, 807 (*Fed. Cir.* 2000); *Therasense, Inc. v. Becton, Dickinson & Co.*, 649 F.3d 1276, 1290 (*Fed. Cir.* 2011) (en banc).

2.7.4. *Comparison of third-party pre-issuance submission process*

Beginning from September 16, 2012 under the US law, anyone is deemed to have standing to submit documents related to a pending patent application to USPTO. In comparison, according to Rule 48 of Implementation Regulations of the Patent Act of China, any person, from the date of the publication of a patent application for an invention until the date of announcing the grant of the patent right, may submit his opinions to the administrative department under the State Council, with the reasons why the patent application is not in conformity with the Patent Law.

According to the US law, a third-party's pre-issuance submission statutorily must be made for a patent application before the earlier of: (a) the date a notice of allowance (NOA) under 35 U.S.C. §151 is given or mailed to the Applicant; or (b) the later of (i) 6 months after the date on which the application is first published under 35 U.S.C. §122 by the Patent Office, or (ii) the date of the first rejection under 35 U.S.C. §132 of any claim by the examiner during the examination of the application. In other words, if the NOA has been issued, you may not file a third-party submission. If the NOA has not been issued, and as long as the first rejection has not been issued or the application has not been published for 6 months, you may file a third-party submission. This time window is more restrictive than that of the Chinese practice. For Chinese patent applications, the Applicant must submit the challenge from the time of publication until the issuance of the patent. In addition, there is no reference type limitation for Chinese patents. In contrast, the pre-issuance submission in US can only include patents, published patent applications, or other printed publications. However, the protest or appeal mechanism under CFR §1.292 provides a broader scope of using any kind of information or documentation to attack the patentability of a patent application.[27]

A third-party patent submission, whether in China or US, will not result in estoppels effect, and can be made anonymously. This is a good tool to use to devalue a competitor's patent portfolios in a proactive manner, especially when discovering that the competitor's patent may

---

[27] MPEM 1901.02 Information Which Can Be Relied on in Protest [R-08.2012].

potentially impact your company's product development and deployment. You can study relevant patents among competitor's newly filed cases by monitoring competitor patent portfolios regularly or on ad hoc basis when performing internal clearance searches.

Although the two jurisdictions have similar mechanisms to permit third-party to challenge pending applications, there are some significant differences worth noting and are summarized in Table 2-8.

2.8. Potential Changes to Chinese Patent Law

The following are detailed discussion of the draft amendment to the current Chinese Patent Law proposed by China's State Council (version sent for approval on December 2, 2015). The proposed changes involve multiple aspects. We only highlight here a few key areas that have significant impact on foreign companies in China or patent holders who are interested in potential patent enforcement in China, such as administrative protection of patent holder rights, the employment invention, indirect patent infringement, and internet service provider (ISP) liability for patent infringement, and standard essential patent (SEP) issues.

The following are highlights of key relevant sections in the Proposal of the Amendment to the Patent Law of China submitted by Chinese SIPO to the State Council.

2.8.1. *Chinese administrative authority in protection of patent right*

Prior to the proposed amendment, under the current patent law, Chinese Patent Administration department has jurisdiction over patent infringement cases and may issue injunctive order upon establishment of patent infringement during the course of its investigation proceeding. However, the proposed patent law further strengths the power of the Patent Administration Department's ability to enforce patent law in both the administrative enforcement power as well the breadth of its jurisdiction scope. Under the current law, Chinese Patent Administration Department executes the administrative adjudication on patent infringement cases

Table 2-8   Comparison of third party pre-issue submission.

Issues to Consider	US Typical Approach		China Approach: (Similar) or Different
	Pre-Issuance Submission Under CFR §1.291	Protest Under CFR §1.292	
Time frame for filing third party pre-issue submission	• Before the earlier of: (a) the date NOA; or (b) the later of (i) 6 months after the date on which the application is first published, or (ii) the date of the first rejection of any claim.	• Prior to the date the application was published under §1.211, or the date a NOA under §1.311 was given or mailed.	• After the publication of the patent application up until the announcing of the grant of the patent right. According to the guideline for patent examination of the SIPO (*Chapter 8, Section 4 of GPE 2010 version*), submissions filed after the NOA will not be considered.
Content permitted to be filed	• Only includes patents, published patent applications, or other printed publications and concise description of relevance, e.g. claim chart without including arguments and conclusions against patentability.	• Not only cover patents, published patent applications, or other printed publications, but also items of other information for attacking the patentability, (for example, information relating to inventorship, or information relating to sufficiency of disclosure or failure to disclose best mode, or any other information demonstrating that the application lacks compliance with the statutory requirements for patentability, or information indicating "fraud" or	• Not clearly specified in the Rules and *GPE* guideline, but in practice, submission should mainly cover patents, published patent applications, or other printed publications, and the reasons or arguments and conclusions against the patentability.

	"violation of the duty of disclosure" or information about fraud or other inequitable conduct issues), and concise explanation of the relevance may include argument and conclusions against patentability.	
Whether to reveal identity of submitter.	• Yes, but only for the actual submitter, not for the behind-scene real party in interest.	• No.
Whether need local agent to file the submission for foreign submitter	• Likely Yes.	• No need for local agent for foreign submitter.
Fee requirement	• Yes, a third party must submit the required fee for every ten documents listed or fraction thereof, there is a fee exemption subject to certain conditions, e.g. a submission of three or fewer documents, provided it is the party's first such submission and the party files a "first and only" statement.	• No fee.
	• NA	

upon applications by the patent owner or a party of interest (for example, exclusive licensee). In contrast, according to Article 3[28] and Article 60[29] of the proposed bill, the Patent Administration Department's jurisdiction scope shall extend to *ex officio* initiated patent infringement investigation. This has significant impact on intentional patent infringements that disrupt the market order, such as consortium infringements or repeated

---

[28] Article 3 states that the Patent Administration Department under the State Council shall be responsible for the administration of patent-related work nationwide. It shall accept and examine patent applications in a uniform way and grant patent rights in accordance with law, be responsible for performing patent-related market supervision and administration, investigating patent infringement and passing off of patent having significant impact, establish public patent information service systems, promoting patent information propagation and utilization. The patent administration departments under local people's governments shall be responsible for patent-related work, implement patent administrative enforcement, and provide public patent services within their respective administrative areas. The aforementioned patent administration departments under local people's governments mean provincial level, city districts level, and authorized by under laws and regulations county level patent administration departments under local people's governments.

[29] Article 60 of the proposed law states that if a dispute arises as a result of exploitation of a patent without permission of the patentee, that is, the patent right of the patentee is infringed, the dispute shall be settled through consultation between the parties. If the parties are not willing to consult or if consultation fails, the patentee or interested party may take legal action before a people's court, and may also request the patent administration department to handle the dispute. Where the patent administration department deems, when handling a dispute, that an infringement is constituted, it can order the infringer to immediately stop the infringement. If the infringer is dissatisfied with the order, he may, within 15 days from the date of receipt of the notification of the order, take legal action before a people's court in accordance with the Administrative Procedure Law of the People's Republic of China. If the infringer neither takes legal action at the expiration of the time limit nor ceases the infringement, the patent administration department may file an application with the people's' court for compulsory enforcement. The patent administration department shall investigate and handle intentional patent infringements that disrupt the market order, such as group infringements and repeated infringements. The patent administration department may confiscate or destroy the patent-infringing products as well as the components, tools, molds, devices, and other means used to produce patent-infringing products or apply infringement methods. For repeated patent infringers, the patent administration department can order a fine, where the unlawful business income reaches or exceeds RMB 50,000, a fine equal to one to five times of the unlawful business income may be imposed; where no unlawful business income has been generated or the income is less than RMB 50,000, a fine for less than RMB 250,000 may be imposed.

infringements. In addition, according to Article 3 and 60 of the proposed bill, the Patent Administration Department will enjoy a wider range of administrative patent enforcement measures including confiscating or destroying patent infringing products as well as the components, tools, molds, devices, and other means used to produce patent infringing products or applied to the infringing methods. Furthermore, the Patent Administration Department shall have administrative penalty authority to order: (i) a fine equal to one to five times of the unlawful business income when the unlawful business income reaches or exceeds 50,000 RMB; or (ii) a fine for less than 250,000 RMB when no unlawful business income has been generated or the income is less than 50,000 RMB.

Moreover, the Patent Administrative Department will also have the authority to investigate and fine internet users who use internet service to infringe a patent. It shall notify the ISP to take necessary measures to stop the infringement by the internet users. If an ISP received the notice but failed to take necessary measures, it shall be jointly liable with the internet user for the extended damages.

Compared with the United States ITC, Chinese Patent Administration Department has a wider scope of authority and jurisdiction on patent cases with a power not limited to importation action across boarder with foreign countries, but include almost all other patent infringement-related activities. Table 2-9 compares US ITC with the Chinese Patent Administration Department.

2.8.2. *Choice of patent enforcement forum in China*

How to choose a forum to enforce patent right in China is an interesting issue worth careful strategizing. You will need to take into consideration of various factors, such as time taken to obtain reliefs, cost of the proceeding, final goals to be accomplished, etc.

In the United States, US companies who own Chinese patents seem to have more leverage than Chinese companies to enforce its patents in China. Patent owners should consider filing complaints to the Chinese Patent Administration Department to adjudication their patent infringement case. This may generate better results than complaining to US ITC, which only has jurisdiction regarding imported goods.

Table 2-9 Comparison of US ITC with China's patent administration department.

Issues to Consider	US ITC	Chinese Patent Administration Department (Under the Current Law) : (Similar) or Different	Chinese Patent Administration Department (Under the Proposed Bill): (Similar) or Different
Jurisdiction	• Limited to importation.	• Any kind of patent infringement as provisioned in patent Act, not limit to importation.	• Any kind of patent infringement as provisioned in patent Act, not limit to importation.
Threshold of investigation	• The complainant must establish three elements: 1. Importation 2. Domestic industry; and 3. Infringement of a valid US patent.	• Almost no special requirements.	• Almost no special requirements.
Ex officio investigation	• No	• No for patent infringement, but yes for passing off a patent.	• Yes for both patent infringement (e.g. for willful patent infringement) or passing off a patent.
Relief	• Temporary Exclusion Order (TEO), Permanent Exclusion Order (PEO) including general exclusion order and limited exclusion order, and Cease and Desist Orders.	• Injunction order for stopping patent infringement; • Seizure or seal and detention of the products proved to be passing off.	• Injunction order for stopping patent infringement; • Confiscate or destroy patent-infringing products as well as the components, tools, molds, devices; • Order a fine; • Seizure or seal and detention of the products proved to be passing off.

2.8.3. *Employment-related invention*

The new proposed Article 6 of patent law stipulates that "[a]n invention-creation that is accomplished in the course of performing the duties of an employee shall be deemed an employment invention-creation".

The new proposed provision deletes the second portion of the current employment invention definition and thus narrows the scope of the employee owned invention. The present law covers two situations under which an invention should be assigned to the employer. However, the proposed act deletes one of them, i.e. "mainly by using the material and technical conditions of an employer", and takes such scenario out of the employer owned invention definition. This means that under the new proposed law, even if an inventor makes an invention by mainly using materials and technical conditions of an employer, as long as there is no agreement about the ownership of the invention between the inventor and the employer, the title and ownership of the invention should go to the inventor.

Special attention should be paid to the determination of which invention is accomplished in the course of performing the duties of an employee. Although this definition was already included in the current Chinese patent law and the proposed change does not affection this portion, we still desire to address this issue in the following sections merely trying to alert foreign applicants to pay particular attention to this existing clause.

First of all, one may wonder what is considered an invention that is accomplished in the course of performing the duties of an employee. The answer is not very clear.

In US, different states have different practices according to the specific state common law. Most Jurisdictions limit the employer owned inventions to those by inventors "hired to invent" or "hired to resolve a particular problem" or "served the employer in a fiduciary role". For example, an inventor is hired for the specific purpose of making the invention, or is directed, after being hired, by his employer to make the invention.[30]

---

[30] *Standard Parts Co. v. Peck, 264 U.S. 52 (1924); Houghton v. United States, 23 F.2d 386, 389–390 (4th Cir. 1928), cert. denied, 277 U.S. 592 (1928).*

According to Chinese judicial practice in applying this clause, the description of "accomplished in the course of performing the duties of an employee" appears to be broader than the description of "hired to invent" or "hired to resolve a particular problem" utilized by most states in the US. Therefore, even though the proposed change to Chinese patent law narrows the scope for employer owned invention; the Chinese patent law defined employer owned invention scope is still broader than those of most US states' law.

However, such broader scope seems to only make sense under the circumstances in which the invention is made in China, or the employment relationship of the involved inventor is established in China. As to the invention originated from a foreign country and the employment relationship is created in the foreign country, this broader clause is inapplicable. The rationale is that the applicable law to such invention should be the law governing the employment relationship, e.g. the employment contract. China has no conflicting law at the statute level to address such an issue as to the applicable law for the initial title and ownership of the invention. However, according to the commonly adopted rules governing this issue by main IP countries, such as US, EP, as well as the judicial practices in China, the initial title and rights to the invention is governed by the law that governs the contract or relationship (see §311 of "Intellectual property principles governing jurisdiction, choice of law, and judgments in transnational disputes" provides the application of law for the initial title to registered right, and Article 60 EPC). Therefore, this proposed change will not affect inventions originated from foreign countries, because in those cases most of the employment relationship is also governed by the invention originating country.

In addition to the proceeding broader employer owned invention definition by Chinese law compared with US law, Chinese law does not give the employer a non-exclusive and non-transferrable royally-free license (no "Right-to-Use" by employer) even though employee developed the invention using employer's materials, resources, or facilities. Such Right-to-Use doctrine was judicially created by US common law to limit the employee's right to the patent if the invention was not developed fully independently. Under the US Right-to-Use doctrine, if an employee uses materials, resources, or facilities of the employer to develop the invention, the employer will have the right to use and implement the employee's patented invention.

In the proposed change to Chinese law, when an employee mainly uses the material and technical conditions of an employer to develop an invention, the statute no longer treats such invention as employer owned invention. Instead, the employee may retain the ownership to the invention, provided there does not exist an employment agreement between the two parties.

The material issue here is whether and how to apply the "Right-to-Use" law. Should you treat it as an element of the initial ownership issue, or separate the "Right-to-Use" from the initial ownership issue. Under the proposed changes to Chinese law, it is unclear how to apply the new law to the Right-to-Use question. One possible approach is that if the invention was made in China under local employment, then Chinese law governs the initial ownership of the invention and there may not be a Right-to-Use by the employer. On the other hand, if the invention originated from US and was developed further in US where the employment occurs, then US law governs the initial ownership of the invention and there is a Right-to-Use. Otherwise, the Right-to-Use issue is complicated and depends on which law is being applied.

2.8.4. *Indirect infringement and ISP liability*

The new Article 62[31] of the proposed law creates two similar categories of indirect patent infringement, one being contributory infringement and the other induced infringement, similar to 35 U.S.C. §271(c) and §271(b) of

---

[31] Article 21 of "*the supreme people's Court Interpretation on Several Issues Concerning the Application of Law in Trial of Cases of Patent Infringement Disputes (II)*" (issues on March 22, 2016, and shall take effort on April 1, 2016) states: where one knows that a product is a material, component or intermediate for implementing a patent, and, without the permission of the patentee, provides the product to others to carry out acts that infringe the patent, and the patentee claims that the providers conduct is conduct helping others to commit an infringement under Article 9 of the Tort Liability Law, the people's courts should support it. where one knows a product or process is covered by a patent, and, without the permission of the patentee, actively induces others to carry out acts that infringe the patent, and the patentee claims that the inducer conduct is conduct helping others to

the US patent law. Prior to this proposed law, neither Chinese patent law, the Implementation Regulations of the Chinese patent law, nor the Supreme People's Court Interpretation[32] provisions cover indirect patent infringement. A few Chinese courts, such as Beijing High People's Court, applied indirect patent infringement principle in an adapted manner in coordination with Chinese tort liability law to patent infringement cases. However, the application of indirect patent infringement is not broadly accepted in China and is controversial in several aspects. For example, it is contentious regarding the scope of the indirect infringement application, or how to coordinate with joint tortfeasor with respect to the mental mind requirement in Chinese judicial practice.

In addition to the indirect infringement, the proposed law further introduces a brand new Article 63 [33] imposing liability on ISP (such as Amazon, eBay, and Alibaba). If an ISP provides online market place for

---

commit an infringement under Article 9 of the Tort Liability Law, the people's courts should support it.

[32] Article 62 of the proposed bill states: "those who know that a product is raw materials, intermediates, components or equipment that is especially made for use in practicing a patent, and provide the product to others to carry out acts that infringe the patent, without the permission of the patentee and for production and business purposes, shall be hold joint and severable liability with the infringer. Those who know that a product or method is patented but induce others to perform acts infringing the patent without the patentees permission and for production or business purposes, shall be hold joint liability and severable with the infringer."

[33] Article 63 of the bill states: "internet Service Providers know or should have known internet user uses its internet services to infringe or pass off a patent, and failed to take timely delete, block, or disconnect the infringing product's links and other necessary measures to stop the infringement shall be held jointly and severable liable with the internet user. Where the patentee and the interested party have evidence to proof the internet user uses internet service to infringe or pass off its patents, the patentee and the interested party may notice the internet service provider to take the aforesaid necessary measures to stop the actions of the infringement or passing off. Where the internet service provider received the qualified notice but failed to take necessary measure timely, it should be jointly and severable liable with the internet user for the extended damage. Where the patent administrative department found the internet user uses internet services to infringe or pass off a patent, it shall notify the internet service provider to take the aforesaid necessary measures to stop the actions of infringement or passing off. Where the internet service provider failed to take necessary measure

any third party retailer to sell products, it is held responsible if the sold product infringes or infringed a Chinese patent.

Although the bill provides a "safe harbor" under certain situations to ISPs similar to those under the copyright law context, this change is still considered to be extremely severe to the ISPs, as commentaries criticized.

Under copyright law, the determination of whether infringement exists is relatively easy. However, under patent law, the determination of infringement is complicated and controversial because the ultimate decision is usually based on detailed and sophisticated technical and legal analysis made by the technical experts concurred by the presiding judge. The proposed new provision may encourage patent holders to abuse the notice provision and take measures to prevent availability of "safe harbor" to ISPs. They can accomplish this goal by claiming liability exemption defense and thus will seriously impact e-commerce transactions and may even incapacitate the entire e-commerce industry. The reason such scenario could happen is that the proposed change to law does not include misrepresentation liability by the involved parties which help to trigger and provide the "safe harbor", similar to the DMCA situation in US.[34]

Furthermore, the proposed provision is considered to be more favorable to the patent holders rather than to the ISPs. Article 63 does not merely introduce a liability exemption provision; it also creates a separate statutory patent infringement liability especially for ISPs in addition to the general indirect patent infringement. Thus, if it is eventually enacted to law, it will actually provide convenient avenue to help patent holders to enforce their patents in China more effectively. Most infringement cases in China are difficult to identify because there are many scattered small retailers providing the infringed products. Chasing after them one by one to collect damage award is impractical. On the other hand, going after a large ISP who hosts these small retailers is much easier.

However, the proposed new law puts too great a responsibility and liability on ISPs. In addition, a problem of how to coordinate the general indirect patent infringement with the special ISP liability will arise.

---

timely, it should be jointly and severable liable with the internet user for the extended damage."

[34] 17 U.S. Code §512 — Limitations on liability relating to material online.

In contrast for US, neither the federal statute nor common law creates a separate type of liability for the ISPs except for applying the conventional direct infringement (35 U.S.C. §271 (a)) and indirect infringement evidence (35 U.S.C. §271 (b) and (c)). Furthermore, neither the federal statute nor common law sets up a counterpart to "safe harbor" rule in the patent law context as provided in 17 U.S.C. §512 of copyright law.

In US, the Court of Appeals for the Federal Circuit ("CAFC") precedent cases have not yet addressed ISP's liability for patent infringement under a specific type of ISP liability, nor have applied the counterpart of "notice to take down" rule to the patent infringement defense regime. US courts usually apply direct infringement (35 U.S.C. §271 (a)); or indirect infringement (35 U.S.C. §271 (b) and (c)) analysis to address ISP's patent infringement liability combined with the conventional defense rules, rather than China's approach of creating a new type of patent infringement liability and specific "safe harbor" for the ISP.

Last year, the district court of western district of Washington in the United States addressed the ISP issue and concluded that, according to the evidences, Amazon was not liable for several online retailer defendants' selling products through Amazon's online marketplace platform.[35] The case applied conventional direct infringement under 35 U.S.C §271(a) to determine whether Amazon should be liable by violating the "sale" or "offer to sale" right rather than using an ISP specific liability rule.[36]

US companies should pay special attention to the indirect infringement, ISP liability, and "safe harbor" issues as created by this bill if it is ultimately enacted to law. Anticipating potential enactment of the proposed law, parties on each side should plan and strategize to better protect itself in China. From a patent holder's point of view, it will have a legitimate right to seek remedies directly from ISPs, such as e-commerce platform provider (eBay, Amazon, etc), if any accused products are sold or provided via the platform. On the other hand, from the ISP's

---

[35] *Milo & Gabby, LLC v. Amazon.com, Inc.*, 2015 WL 4394673 (W.D. Wash, July 16, 2015).

[36] This case didn't determine whether Amazon should be liable under the inducing infringement, possibly due to the plaintiff has not alleged induce infringement.

perspective, it should take more active actions to avoid the joint tortfeasor liability.

2.8.5. *SEP issue*

The enforcement of the SEP is a hot topic in the past two years both in academic communities and among IP circles regarding appropriate adjudication/judicial practice. The controversial issue concentrates on three key questions:

(1) whether a patentee with FRAND encumbered patent can seek injunctive relief;
(2) how to determine the FRAND rate and terms; and
(3) in what situation will the patentee's enforcement of SEP be considered an antitrust issue.

As to the first question, two cases are good representations of the US Federal Court's position on this issue:

(i) The first case is *Microsoft v. Motorola*[37] which addresses this issue in a contract breach suit. *Microsoft* filed a lawsuit after receiving *Motorola*'s patent license offer letter asking for a high royalty rate (2.25% of the price of the end product covered by Motorola's 802.11 and H.264 SEP); and
(ii) The second case is *Apple v. Motorola*[38] which addresses the issue in the context of patent law and adopts the *eBay* framework[39] decided by US Supreme Court as a normal non-SEP case.

The US ninth circuit court affirmed in the first case to prohibit Motorola from seeking injunctive relief for its SEP in a contractual suit. The US Court of Appeals for the Federal circuit (CAFC) in the second

---

[37] *Microsoft Corp. v, Motorola, Inc. et al.,* Case No. 14-35393 (9th Cir. July 30, 2015) (Berzon, J.).
[38] *Apple Inc. v. Motorola, Inc.,* Nos. 12-1548, 12-1549 (*Fed. Cir. April* 25, 2014).
[39] *eBay, Inc. v. MercExchange, LLC,* 547 U.S. 338 (2006).

case affirmed the district court's denial of issuance of injunction based on *eBay*'s equity test in a patent suit. It is noteworthy that in the second case, CAFC made dicta that an injunction may be justified where an infringer unilaterally refuses a FRAND royalty or unreasonably delays negotiation to the same effect. However, an alleged infringer's refusal to accept any license offer does not necessarily justify issuing an injunction, noted CAFC. For example, the license offered may not be on FRAND terms (see *Apple v. Motorola*).

US courts have not completely reconciled the various considerations in the two different situations: (i) the first situation is in the affirmative claim of contractual breach or antitrust for prohibiting SEP holder's seeking of injunction; and (ii) another situation is in the defense of injunction in a patent litigation case. For example, if it is determined that the SEP holder may seek an injunction (or the SEP holder is not prohibited from seeking an injunction by an US authority entity such as courts or administrative agencies), can the injunction be automatically granted by the patent infringement suit without performing the *eBay* equity test? They are separate issues and should be treated differently using different criteria. As to the issue of whether SEP holder can seek injunctive relief compared with the issue of whether to grant or issue an injunction, Figure 2-5 summaries related timeline.

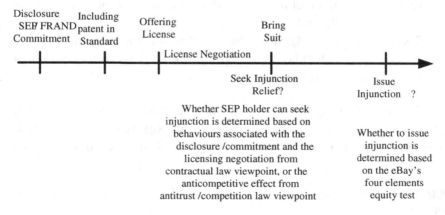

Figure 2-5   Timeline related to SEP and injunctive relief.

The two jurisdictions between US and Chinese IP systems take differentt approaches in the remedy law concerning patent infringements. In China, injunction will usually be issued automatically after establishing patent infringement. In US, in comparison, according to *eBay* rule, the issuance of injunction for a typical case needs to meet a four-element equity requirement even if patent infringement is established.

Therefore, from patent law perspective, some believe that in US it is not a pressing matter to resolve the SEP-based injunction issue by revising the US law. Just like any other typical patent case, the court has a chance to make equity balance in determining whether to issue injunctions. In addition, US as a main common law country, even if there were no rules or precedence to be used to resolve the SEP issue, US court still may use judge's law-making system to address this new issue. Table 2-10 lists issues related to injunctive relief by SEP holders.

In China, however, as a civil law system, statutory law (including statute and regulation/rule, and SPC's judicial interpretation) constitute the main authorities for court in adjudicating cases. Therefore, there is an urgent need to establish an applicable statutory rule on this issue for the courts to adopt. Due to the particular situation in China, both *The Interpretation (II) of the Supreme People's Court on Several Issues*

Table 2-10   Whether SEP holders should seek injunction and related issues.

	Can SEP Holder Seek Injunctive Relief?	Issue Injunction or Not?
Criteria	SEP holder's' behaviors associated with the disclosure/commitment and the licensing negotiation from contractual law viewpoint; or anticompetitive effect evaluation from antitrust/ competition law viewpoint.	*eBay*'s four elements equity test
Yes/No	If the answer is "no"	No (without performing the four elements equity test)?
Yes/No	If the answer is "yes"	Directly/automatically issue or still separately perform the four elements equity test?

concerning the Application of Law in the Trial of Patent Infringement Dispute Cases" (hereafter referred to as "Interpretation (II) of the SPC") and the proposed patent bill address this specific and important SEP issue. But it should be cautioned that the statute should not provide a rigid and specific provision on this issue, but rather provide an equitable and general principle, or provide a test equipped with certain considerations or elements.

Article 85 is a brand new provision of the bill to address the SEP implementation problem.[40] However, it is unclear what specific issue the expression "[p]atentee who failed to disclose its owned standard essential patent during participating standard setting process with the national standard-setting body, is **deemed to have licensed such patent to the implementer of that standard**" was intending to solve. It might be targeting to resolve the nondisclosure issue through pressuring SEP holders to commit to a compulsory license of their SEPs to any implementer at certain royalty rate, if SEP holders fail to disclose their SEPs. Alternatively, it might mean to prohibit any SEP-based injunction issuance through compelling the SEP holders to grant a license of its SEP to any implementer with certain royalty rate if the SEP holder fails to disclose its SEP, which treatment is similar to the implied license doctrine. Obviously, the latter meaning is both unreasonable and inequitable.

From the language of the bill itself, it is more likely to be interpreted as only covering the commitment to license its SEP to any implementer at certain royalty rate if the SEP holder fails to disclose its SEP. The bill does not address the issue of whether SEP holders can seek injunction. In other words, the option of committing to license its SEP under fair royalty rate, e.g. FRAND, is operated by the law instead of SEP holder's active action in the event of SEP holder's omission of its SEP disclosure during

---

[40] Article 85 of the proposed bill states: "[p]atentee who failed to disclose its owned standard essential patent during participating standard setting process with the national standard-setting body, is deemed to have licensed such patent to the implementer of that standard. The license royalties shall be negotiated by both parties, where an agreement cannot be reached, the parties may petition to the patent administration department under the State Council for a decision. Where the party is dissatisfied with the decision, that party may appeal the decision to the people's court within 15 days of the receipt of the notice of the decision."

the standard setting process. Whether the patentee could seek injunction in this situation should be treated as an additional and separate issue, which is similar to the normal situation in which the patentee himself committed to license under FRAND during the standard setting process.

The opposite scenario seems to support the above interpretation as well. For example, if the SEP holder has already disclosed its SEP during the standard setting process, then this provision is inapplicable. If this provision in the new bill attempts to address SEP-based injunction, it should not differentiate disclosure from non-disclosure. Thus, the provision is more likely to be interpreted to only cover the non-disclosure issue.

However, the amendment provides its own explanation of this proposed provision[41] and offers an interpretation that the proposal of the added new provision is to address the general SEP injunction issue instead of only covering the committing FRAND operated by the law in the condition of the patentee's non-disclosure. Such an interpretation will naturally result in a non-commitment of SEP licenses. In comparison, the first interpretation produces a relatively better outcome where the prohibition of SEP injunction only covers the cases where SEP holders fail to disclose their SEPs. Nevertheless, there are other problems for the first interpretation. Therefore, in the case where the SEP holder has already disclosed its SEP, there is no such implied license. In addition, this proposed new provision only applies to the behaviors in relation to national standard setting which should not include industry standard setting and regional standard setting.

Article 24 of *"The Interpretation (II) of the Supreme People's Court on Several Issues concerning the Application of Law in the Trial of Patent Infringement Dispute Cases"* (hereafter referred as to *"Interpretation (II) of the SPC")*[42] already went into effect on April 1, 2016. It also includes a

---

[41] See http://www.sipo.gov.cn/zcfg/zcjd/201504/t20150402_1096196.html, it provides the explanation of the proposed Article 82 (the Article 85 of the version of submission to approval) in the "Explanation regarding 'Proposals for the Amendment of the Patent Law of the People's Republic of China, PRC (request for comment version)'".

[42] Article 24 of *"the Interpretation (II) of the Supreme People's' Court on Several Issues concerning the Application of Law in the Trial of Patent Infringement Dispute Cases"* (as adopted at the 1676th Meeting of the Judicial Committee of the Supreme People's Court on January 25, 2016, is hereby issued and shall come into force on April 1, 2016) states: "[w]here the recommended national, industry or regional standard explicitly indicates to

provision to prohibit SEP holders seeking injunctions. A main condition of such prohibition is met when patentee intentionally violates the FRAND obligation. Other conditions set by the provision include non-disclosure committed by the patentee during the standard setting process, or intentionally failing to achieve an agreement of the essential patent license <u>and</u> the accused infringer is not obviously at fault during the course of negotiation. This condition is completely different from the condition of SEP injunction seeking prohibition set forth in Article 85 of the proposal law described above. The *Interpretation (II) of the SPC* focuses on the behaviors of the SEP holder and the accused infringer during the SEP license negotiation. In addition, Article 24 of the *Interpretation (II) of the SPC* only applies to recommended national, industry, or regional standard which explicitly implicates an essential patent. As for the compulsory standard or recommended national, industry, or regional standard which does not explicitly implicate an essential patent, Article 24 of the *Interpretation (II) of the SPC* does not apply.

---

implicate an essential patent, the people's courts generally should not affirm the non-infringement defense by the accused infringer based on that the standard implementation needs not to get the permission from the patentee. Where the recommended national, industry or regional standard explicitly indicates to implicate an essential patent, in the course of the negotiation between the patentee and the accused infringer of the essential patent license condition and term, the patentee intentionally violates the Fair, Reasonable and Non-Discriminatory (FRAND) obligation which the patentee commits during the standard setting process and thus resulting in failing to achieve an agreement of the essential patent license, and the accused infringer is at no obvious fault in the course of the negotiation, the people's courts generally should not grant the injunction claim by the patentee for stopping the standard implementation action. The essential patent license condition and term as mentioned in clause 2 of this provision should be negotiated and determined by the patentee and the accused infringer. Where failing to achieve the agreement of the essential patent license after fully negotiating between each other, the parties may petition the people's courts to determine the essential patent license condition and term. When the people's courts determine the essential patent license condition and term, the people's courts should overall consider the factors of the innovation degree, the contribution of the patented technology to the standard, the technical area, the nature of the standard, the scope of the standard implementation and the related licensing condition and term, etc., according to the FRAND."

Chapter 3

For Inventors and Patent Review Committees (Relating to Idea Generation)

3.1. Driving Force for Inventions — The Important Role Played by Portfolio Managers

Many inventors are R&D scientists or engineers working for companies, universities, or non-profit organizations. Some inventions are produced by individuals not associated with any organizational projects. As discussed in Chapter 1, Section 1.1.3, generating patents and building a strong patent portfolio based on organizational or individual funding should not merely be a passive outcome of their R&D efforts. Patent applicants should always keep in mind the objectives of obtaining these patents, and then file patent applications accordingly. Otherwise, they most likely will be wasting time, money, and missing opportunities. However, it is difficult for inventors to be fully abreast of their company's intellectual property (IP) objectives. Companies need to communicate better with inventors.

For medium and large organizations, there is typically an IP Portfolio Manager (PM or PortfolioM), as shown in Figure 3-1, represented by the grey colored box in the middle. The PM is responsible for a company's IP Strategy and IP Portfolio management. In the top half of the figure above the PortfolioM box, displays various functions (each represented by a

Mining Ideas for Diamonds

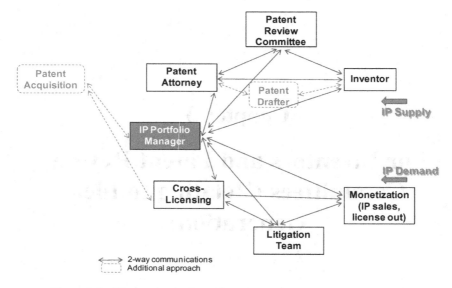

Figure 3-1   IP team interactions — each function plays an important role.

corresponding box) responsible for generating **IP Supply**. In the bottom
half of figure below the PortfolioM box, lists various functions (each represented by a corresponding box) responsible for generating **IP Demand**.
On the right-hand side of the PortfolioM box are functions to "organically"
generate IP Supply to meet the IP Demand via **internal idea generation**.
On the left-hand side of the PortfolioM box is a box representing the function to generate IP Supply "non-organically" via external avenues such as
by **patent acquisition**. It is the Portfolio Manager's job to ensure IP Supply
is adequate relative to IP Demand, and there is an appropriate balance
between internal inventions versus external patent purchase.

3.1.1. *Cross-functional team collaborations are needed*

The PortfolioM must communicate timely with various departments or
teams in the IP Demand area to understand their short term and long term
needs. These teams include Cross-Licensing team, Litigation team, and
Monetization team (e.g. Patent Sales, Technology Transfer, Patent Licensing,

Standards Licensing, Brand Licensing) that generate IP Demands based on company's IP strategy. For example, if the Cross-Licensing team is anticipating a negotiation with a few target companies in the next few years, the PortfolioM should make sure that his patent portfolio has a reasonable amount of high quality assets for the negotiation team to use.

More specifically, for the portfolio to be effective in IP negotiation or (counter) assertion/litigation, the quality of patent assets need to be high and read onto target companies' products. Since a company's products usually change with time, some of the target company's products will be obsolete in a few years while others may become much more important compared to just a short period of time ago. Therefore, the Portfolio Manager must ensure his patent portfolio is refreshed timely and ready to support the negotiation team whenever called upon. For example, Litigation team might suddenly be thrown into "fire-fighting" mode upon receiving a patent infringement notice from an unexpected party. If the plaintiff is an operating company, the PortfolioM needs to help the Litigation team to quickly find a dozen high quality patents that potentially read onto the plaintiff's products. Similarly, if Patent Sales team receives a request from an eager purchaser to buy patents that read onto the purchaser's competitor's products, the PortfolioM should be able to help Patent Sales team identify potential candidates for the proposed transaction. If none are found, the Portfolio Manager should take notice and consider whether to treat such shortfall as a gap in his patent portfolio.

In other words, the PortfolioM needs to build his company's IP Portfolio according to currently known and anticipated future IP Demands. He should have a solid understanding of the status of his Patent Portfolio including the strength, weakness, gaps as well as future likely sources and pipelines to augment his portfolio. For urgent short term needs and gaps in his patent portfolio, the PortfolioM may need to resort to Patent Acquisitions to fill certain gaps in his IP Portfolio in order to meet such IP Demands in a timely manner. On the other hand, in the long run, it can be more cost effective and with better process control by generating needed IP internally. The key to success is making sure that the internal IP Supply providers produce the targeted patents in alignment with your company's IP Strategy. Thus, it is crucial that the PortfolioM communicates effectively with the IP Supply side.

For large, medium and even some small companies, after inventors come up with ideas, those ideas typically go through a review by the Patent Review Committee (Committee) which determines whether to file a patent application based on business needs and budget constraint. After an idea is approved to file, internal or external patent attorneys draft the patent application and submit to USPTO (or SIPO for Chinese patent). Some companies utilize an external patent drafter to write the patent application while the in-house patent attorney simply acts as a program manager and coordinates between the Committee and the drafter. As will be seen in the following discussions, regardless of whom a company uses to draft its patent applications (utilizing external or internal resources), effective communications between the PortfolioM, Inventor, Patent Review Committee, and patent drafter are extremely important to a company's success in its IP strategy defensively or offensively.

3.1.2. *Innovation-driven IP strategy*
versus IP-driven innovations

In order to build a world-class patent portfolio, the function teams shown in Figure 3-1 must collaborate seamlessly with each other. For example, Inventors and the Patent Review Committee should try to proactively reach out to the PortfolioM to understand their company's IP strategy, which helps in deciding the technology areas to file more patents for, and patents mapped onto which target company's products are needed to meet company's IP Demands. Inventors should try to work on inventions that align with recommendation from the PortfolioM. The Committee should approve to file more inventions that help to achieve the objectives set by the company's IP strategy. Only by working in such a coherent manner, a company's IP strategy can be successfully carried out.

Even for individual inventors, similar approach should apply. The inventor will need to take up simultaneously the role of Inventor, Patent Review Committee, IP PortfolioM, and sometimes even its own patent attorney or patent drafter if the inventor doesn't use an outside patent agent/attorney. In such a scenario, the Inventor should constantly keep in mind what is his final objective for his IP Portfolio as well as the IP demands he is trying to meet, and then invent according to these objectives or IP demand requirements.

Some people argue that R&D and innovation should drive IP strategy, while others insist IP strategy should drive innovation. We believe that a sophisticated IP strategy is likely somewhat different from the R&D strategy, or the two at least at certain point in time do not completely overlap due to their differing purposes. As shown in Figure 3-2, circle #1 represents R&D strategy which depends on team members, their capabilities/experiences, directives given to them, and resources provided to them. Circle #2 represents product offering and product strategy. Due to supply availability, customer reception, pricing, and competitive landscape, the product strategy may not completely overlap with the R&D strategy. Circle #3 represents a company's IP/Patent strategy. Similarly, this circle likely does not completely overlap with the other two circles, indicating that IP strategy differs from R&D or product strategies because a forward looking IP strategy must take into consideration future long-term competitions while at the same time protect the business for the short-term challenges. A holistic company Business Strategy is represented by Circle #4 which comprises a combination of R&D strategy, product strategy, and IP strategy.

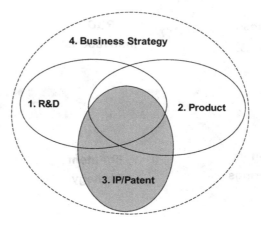

Figure 3-2   Interceptions of R&D, product, IP and business strategies.

To further illustrate our points, we'll use a typical innovation cycle as an example represented by the outer circle in Figure 3-3. At the early stage of the cycle, it is common that R&D strategy drives most of the corporate business strategy. IP protection is largely a result of the R&D strategy at the beginning of the innovation cycle, to protect your ideas and prevent others from copying your technology. After the idea is reasonably protected, product based on the technology can be released to the market. Thereafter, based on market reception to the product, business strategy will be adjusted or modified, which then drives refinement or change in R&D strategy.

On the other hand, the inner circle represents the advanced phase of an innovation cycle. During this stage, business strategy is more mature and largely directs product roadmap. To protect your company's product market share, IP strategy during this phase plays an important role defensively and offensively. These are some of the IP demands mentioned earlier. To meet these IP demands via organic growth, innovations need to be created in alignment with such IP strategy. Business strategy will take into consideration of these innovations, which then drives product offerings. Therefore, in such scenarios, innovations are actually driven by the IP strategy. However, this does not mean that all R&D activities are

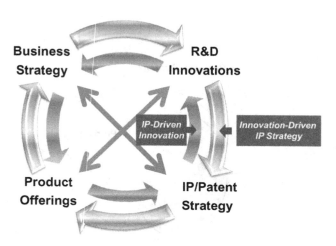

Figure 3-3   Innovation, IP strategy, products and business strategy influencing each other.

completely relying on IP demand. R&D teams need to innovate on the product side in order to lead, enable, and support its company to build a successful business strategy. As your company's products evolve continuously, innovation and product will influence each other, business strategy and IP strategy will also affect each other.

Therefore, R&D strategy and IP strategy may differ from each other due to different considerations, yet they are constantly entangled with each other. They may have greater overlaps for certain technology sectors such as pharmaceuticals, and less overlaps for other technologies such as big conglomerate commodities. Innovation and IP strategy may take turns as the driving force of the other, and their roles could flip at different phases of an innovation cycle.

3.1.3. *Jumping S-curve and finding the next disruptive technology*

Another example is the frequently talked about "jumping S-curve", discussed in depth by Paul Nunes and Tim Breene of Accenture. Nunes and Breene assert that companies must reinvent continuously, "climbing and jumping from one S-curve to the next S-curve" in order to maintain a high performance.

As shown in Figure 3-4, a hypothetical company has developed the First Industry Leading technology/business through innovation and investment. As Accenture's researches indicate, most business cycles follow the "S-curve" phenomena where the company goes through an initial infancy phase, then undergoes growth phase as adoptions broaden, but will enter maturity phase as market begins to saturate, and finally declines when the initial idea becomes obsolete. Such technology or business life cycle is inevitable.

In the initial infancy phase, many highly innovative or breakthrough inventions are being generated. If your company is the industry leader, it is critical to protect your leading technologies and therefore innovation strategy drives IP strategy. However, after the company experiences huge growth and enters mature phase, there are less innovative ideas in the technology area available because most inventions have been discovered

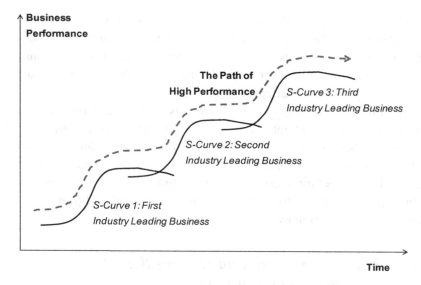

Figure 3-4   Accenture (Nunes & Breene)'s climbing and jumping the S-curve illustration.

already. As a result, inventions are mostly minor improvements. Inventors and Patent Review Committee need to decide whether it's worthwhile to protect these ideas. In addition, to better protect their existing market share and mature business, they need to anticipate competitive IP threats, prevent new market entrance companies to take over technology leadership or market leadership.

Typically, the number one market leader has invested lots of money to pioneer and develop a new market. It is costly because many mistakes are made on the way to find the right ingredient and finally educate customers on the new technology. The second or third place market players can leverage these learning's without putting the same amount of investment, and thus will have a much easier path to success by simply following the leader's footsteps. Therefore, market leader often has strong incentives to use its IP to attack and block new entrance companies to prevent unjust enrichment. As a countermeasure, new entrance companies would want to build its own IP to counterattack the market leader. However, after market adoption there will be fewer highly innovative inventions available. Therefore, new entrance companies need to look for minor improvement yet patentable inventions to block the market leader. Similarly, the market leader would want to prevent new entrance companies from filing first and thus will need to develop a solid blocking strategy accordingly. During these phases, often IP strategy drives innovation.

In addition, as indicated in Figure 3-4, companies should start looking for the Second Industry Leading business that is in alignment with their long-term strategy before the mature phase of the First Industry Leading Business. This way, the company can jump from S-curve 1 to S-curve 2 so it goes through another round of S-curve and experiences another growth cycle. This is often called "jumping the S-curve" and referred to by an IP analytics guru, Hoo-min Toon, as "finding the next disruptive technology".

A good question to ask is how to find the next disruptive technology that's most suitable for your company so that you are more likely to succeed than others? What makes your company unique in this technology or business area so that you have more stamina than your potential competitors to eventually take the leading market share and seize greater profit? If your competitors have a greater advantage in leading this particular disruptive technology and you don't have an effective path to prevent them from surpassing you, should you still invest and enter into this particular disruptive technology, or should you instead find another more advantageous disruptive technology? This is where IP strategy can potentially guide your company to wisely choose a disruptive technology that leverages your unique strength the most and offers you the best opportunity to lead to great success.

For illustration purposes, assume your company was a start-up being the leader for an industry leading business, and has successfully experienced at least one S-curve cycle, for example S-curve 1 in Figure 3-4. Consequently, at the end of the S-curve cycle, your company may have grown into a mid-sized company staffed with a reasonably large technical team and support resources. In other words, your company has built certain leading strength and expert competency in specific domain areas and has advantages in those domain areas compared to other companies. This strength could be technology related (e.g. a unique secure encryption technology, a new smart phone user interface, etc). However, competitive advantage is not limited to merely technical leadership. Many companies beat competitions through non-R&D driven competency, for example, through superb supply chain logistics, sustainable low cost with high quality, strong marketing program, etc. Regardless of the type of your company's competency, it is much more likely for your company to reproduce its previous technology/business success if it effectively leverage its strength for the next chosen disruptive technology. In the following, we focus on helping technology (compared to business model) leaders in searching for its next disruptive technology.

A well-developed IP strategy cans assist you in identifying the next disruptive technology that is most suitable for your company based on your company's specific strength and weakness relative to your competitions. A proper IP landscape analysis should be performed taking into consideration of your technology strength. By analyzing technical areas that relate to and leverage your expertise, it can reveal gaps and weak spots in the industry. These are the so-called "white spaces". If marketing analysis indicates that one of such white spaces has a huge commercial prospect, then you have potentially identified a target disruptive technology. However, you should take different actions based on the specific situation. The following is a non-exhaustive list of possible scenarios and recommended strategies:

(i) If an IP landscape analysis reveals that your existing strong patent portfolio is applicable to another technology area not well developed yet with very little seminal patents (i.e. a "white space"), you should direct your R&D resources to invest in this space, build seminal patents, and produce products. Your existing technology strength should enable you to quickly lead the market share, and your IP strength can prevent competitors from copying your new product features. You may even want to spin-off the patent portfolio with a competent team so that they can move fast with a razor sharp focus to unleash this new disruptive technology area and lead it.

(ii) If you discover that your target next disruptive technology is already overly crowded with patents and your potential competitors can easily lead that market but haven't entered the "white space" for various reasons, then you need to pause and analyze carefully whether this is an area you still want to invest in. If you have speed and size, you might be able to occupy the "white space" with a "first mover" advantage. You may also be able to stay as one of the top leaders for a while due to your size. However, if competitors' seminal patents can easily stop your business, then you may want to first seek freedom of operation via a patent (cross) license or avoid this space until you have also established a strong IP portfolio that can be used against your competitor.

(iii) If IP analysis indicates that there are only a few seminal patents in your target disruptive technology area and the patent holders are relatively small-sized companies, then your company may consider whether to acquire those small companies.

In the above scenarios of searching for the next Disruptive Technology, IP strategy could help your company narrow down which technology area(s) to invest and innovate in order to successfully jump onto the next S-Curve. Therefore, one might call such a scenario as "**IP driven innovation**". However, in order to succeed during the next S-Curve cycle or the next Disruptive Technology, it requires a technology leader to come up with highly innovative ideas, which puts Innovation back into the driving force. In this case, IP strategy will function more as a supporting role, which is regarded as "**Innovation driven IP**". Such role changing dynamic will occur continuously as a company reinvents itself repetitively along the path of high technology/business performance.

3.2. How to Ensure High Patent Quality

As will be made abundantly clear in Chapter 6, Section 6.6.3, high patent quality is a "must" for a world-class IP portfolio. To ensure high quality, one needs to implement process control at each step from idea generation, invention selection, application drafting, patent prosecution, until final patent grant. As an analogy, patent quality is like a chain of links connected in series, with every link representing each of these steps. If one of the links/steps is weak, the chain becomes weak, i.e. the patent quality is poor because others may disarm your patent by attacking such a weak spot. Therefore, organizations must ensure that **strict quality control exists at each step** in order to produce high quality patents.

3.2.1. *Step A — selecting and approving invention disclosures*

During the initial phase of a patenting process which we'll designate as "Step A", inventors, Patent Review Committee, and the patent attorney need to work closely with each other to make sure that patent office (USPTO for USA, SIPO for China) will grant a patent (with desired claims) and the granted patent will survive invalidity challenges.

3.2.2. *To do prior art search or not*

To intelligently assess whether PTO (USPTO or SIPO) will allow the desired claims to be granted requires strong domain expertise and/or proper prior art search to ensure the patented claim is not anticipated by other patents, publications, and the idea is not obvious.

Figure 3-5 illustrates a range of approaches adopted by various companies in the US when deciding whether to conduct prior art searches. On the left-hand side is the most liberal end of the spectrum where companies allow inventor and attorney conduct thorough prior art searches. This is the most effective way to ensure that inventions selected for filing patents are not easily invalidated. On the right-hand side is the most conservative approach where companies don't allow either the inventor or the patent attorney to conduct any prior art searches for fear of being accused

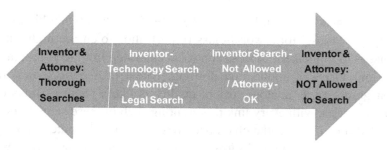

Figure 3-5   Various company policies on whether to perform prior art searches.

of willful infringement. An ulterior motive is avoiding the burden of having to determine which discovered pieces of prior art are relevant to the invention and obligated to report to USPTO. In the middle of the spectrum are intermediate approaches. Company policy may allow inventor to only perform technology searches while the patent attorney performs legal searches. Alternatively, attorneys are allowed to do prior art searches but inventors are not. We believe that in order to survive various patent invalidity challenges, relying solely on domain experts' knowledge of prior arts in a technology area is not sufficient. Certain controlled prior art searches are necessary. If being potentially accused of willful infringement is a concern, you may need to hire an external prior art search company to supply and analyze relevant prior arts.

In China, as a comparison, there is no discovery process and thus difficult to establish willful infringement. As a result, companies who require high quality patents typically resort to diligent prior art searches. Please see Chapter 2 for a detailed discussion on the attorney-client privilege differences between China and US.

3.2.3. *Implement pre-screening process*

One of the issues inventors face is that they tend to focus on technical implementation details, and have a hard time articulating the novelty point of their invention. For companies that fully or partially restrict inventor's prior art search activities, inventors have an even harder time clarifying the inventive aspect of their idea compared to prior arts to which they are forbidden of full access. As a result, some inventors have to go through many iterations of presentation and revision of invention disclosures submitted to the Patent Review Committee. Yet, their inventions are still being rejected repeatedly due to insufficient prior art identification. This discourages inventors from engaging in the future and may cause your company miss important inventions from being filed and protected. Therefore, you should take actions to prevent such outcomes.

Patent Review Committee and Patent Attorneys should act more as enablers, rather than inhibitors for their company's inventions. Instead of simply rejecting ideas that are not clearly defined, they should offer guidance to inventors and assist in refining inventors' invention descriptions to clarify the novelty points. In addition, they should help inventors in due diligence searches to distinguish from prior arts and improve subsequent patent drafting quality. This should be done before inventors present to Patent Review Committee and thus is called "pre-screening" process.

In US, pre-screening under a lawyer's guidance may reduce the risk of future willful infringement allegations if conducted under the attorney-client privilege or attorney work product protection. It also enables proper handling of prior art submission as part of the mandatory disclosure obligations to USPTO.

In both China and US, pre-screening helps inventors in learning about what's important. It helps train the inventors to become more IP savvy. Through such a continuous Inventor/Patent Review Committee/Attorney interacting/learning process, your company will build a powerful "invention engine" that can continuously crank out high quality "diamond" patents to strengthen your IP portfolio.

3.2.4. *Step B — drafting and prosecuting patent applications*

The above discussion of Step A covers how to ensure that only useful ideas are selected by asking the correct questions and align well with company's IP strategy. However, even if one selects top quality ideas, if your patent attorney or patent engineer doesn't pay enough attention to the case during drafting or prosecuting, he/she can turn a great idea into a piece of useless paper. Therefore, it is extremely important to pay attention to the subsequent Step B, i.e. drafting and prosecuting your patent applications. We'll first provide specific methodologies for Inventors and Patent Review Committees in the following section, and then discuss patent drafting and prosecution in more details in Chapter 4.

3.3. Recommended Methodology for Inventors and Patent Committee

To increase the patent quality in a portfolio, one must begin with sound criteria combined with solid process in determining whether to file a patent application in the pre-patent filing phase in order to systematically weed out low quality ideas. Afterwards, one must continue its patent quality control effort during the application drafting/prosecuting phase in order to generate high quality patents. The associated specific requirements may vary with countries due to local laws and practices. In this book, we focus on US and China based on authors' experience with them.

In the following few sections, we'll revisit Step A mentioned above and walk you through a few specific steps on how to spot potential "diamond" ideas and make them into high quality patents so they become effective IP "tools" for your company.

3.3.1. *To file or not to file?*

In their efforts trying to file only high quality patent applications to improve ROI and reduce overall patent maintenance cost, many companies use various complicated matrix to evaluate an invention or pending application. Some of the commonly used parameters include: (1) technology innovativeness, (2) number of applicable industries, (3) claim broadness, (4) file history estoppels, (5) ease of infringement detection, (6) potential work-around, (7) number of products affected and associated dollar amount, (8) litigation history, (9) forward citation, (10) backward citation, (11) prosecution length, (12) number of claims, (13) length of independent claims, (14) enablement of the specification, (15) inventor proliferation, (16) whether the case has continuations, (17) foreign counterparts, (18) size of the existing patent portfolio, (19) strategic alignment to company's roadmap, (20) relevance to standards, etc. Some rank as many as 15 factors and rely on the total score of these chosen parameters either in evaluation of a granted patent, or in the initial idea evaluation for the purpose of determining whether to file the case and the amount of external/internal legal resources in filing the corresponding case. The higher the total score, the more resources and attention will be paid to prosecuting the case.

However, some of the parameters being scored could be seriously misleading and thus diverting precious resources to wrong cases. For example, companies often use a score of how "Innovative" an idea is, say from 0 to 10. The higher the Innovation score is toward a perfect "10", the more likely the idea would be approved to file for a patent application. On the other hand, if the score is low, say lower than a "5" because the idea is a small incremental improvement, then the idea is likely dropped. This approach could cause serious issues of dropping off ideas that are only minor improvement in functionality but read onto competitor's products square on. Consequently, companies will miss the opportunity of obtaining a valuable patent which could be used offensively or defensively against the competitor.

Another problem with focusing too much on high Innovative score is that it doesn't take into account the time-frame that the idea may be used in an actual product. One could have a brilliantly innovative idea that is utmost revolutionary and forward looking by decades. However, if nobody would ever possibly use this brilliant concept in the life time of the patent (typically 20 years from the priority date), then the huge amount of resources put into filing the patent would be a waste of company's time and money. It is especially alarming for industries where most innovations are incremental. In this case, one may find a lot of patents reading onto competitors' products even though the inventions are minor improvements.

Therefore, when deciding whether to file a patent application or not, the answer should be a simple "Yes" or "No". It is not efficient to calculate a total score based on many factors. A streamlined process is necessary to help inventors better understand what is important and reduce probability of inadvertently not file patents for valuable inventions. We believe that the fundamental issues regarding whether a patent is worth filing or not boil down to two key questions:

(i) Is the PTO likely to grant a patent for this invention (with the desired claims)?
(ii) Are others likely to use this invention significantly between 2 and 20 years?

The rationale for choosing the above two questions in making patent filing decisions, and the due diligences required for answering each of the questions, are explained in detail below.

3.3.2. *Is the patent office likely to grant a patent?*

The first question to ask should be "Is the patent likely to be granted by the patent office?" In particular, will the key claim that is the core invention of the patent be allowed by the patent office? Answering this question requires strong domain expertise or proper prior art search.

A patent doesn't have to be highly "Innovative" in order to become a high value patent. One of the necessary requirements for a high value invention is to be able to receive PTO's allowance as a valid patent. It is also important that the patent is unlikely to be invalidated later. If an invention meets the requirements of PTO and gets granted rightfully, its value is no longer affected by its innovativeness. When evaluating a valid patent, we mainly focus on how big a market its claims cover, not how innovative its embodiments provide. In other words, a patent has a binary status, "valid" or "not valid". As a result, it is inconsistent to attach many different values to the Innovative factor when deciding whether to file a patent application or not. We can simplify this question to "whether PTO likely will grant a patent".

To determine whether PTO will grant a patent, USPTO requires the invention to be a patentable subject matter, useful, new, and non-obvious. Similarly for a Chinese patent, two factors need to be examined carefully: (a) is the invention a patentable subject matter; and (b) does the invention meet the requirement of novelty and obviousness? For large enterprises, this requires that the company's invention evaluating committees be equipped with technical experts who are familiar with technology developments in their subject matter areas, and can readily make a sound determination. Otherwise, proper prior art search is necessary in the initial evaluation of an idea.

It is interesting to note that companies have vastly different philosophies and practices regarding whether to conduct prior art searches before filing a patent application. As discussed above, some require thorough prior art searches before filing. Others forbid inventors from conducting any prior art search for fear of either potential wilful infringement risks later or mandatory disclosure requirement by PTO (or both). There is a mid-way approach involving conducting a controlled prior art search where clear boundaries are set, for example inventors only conduct searches for publically available literature while legal counsels conduct legal searches. Alternatively, search is performed entirely by patent attorneys instead of inventors themselves. We believe a proper prior art search is an absolute "must" in order to generate high quality patents. Companies can adopt various measures to control their legal risks, but the saying that "quality comes from knowledge" definitely holds true for patent applications.

One also needs to be familiar with PTO's prior art search process and prosecution practice in order to better judge whether a case is likely to grant. In addition, one should monitor the patent appeal board's decisions carefully to determine whether a patent might be invalidated later. For example, software patents have encountered an increasing resistance in different countries lately. Washington Post in September of 2013 stated that "The patent troll crisis is really a software patent crisis". Many countries declare software patents unpatentable. In US, previous practice was that patent patents are patentable if they meet the *Bilski* machine-or-transformation (MOT) test. However, the US Supreme Court reviewed a few patent cases and issued corresponding decisions, such as *Alice v. CLS Bank*, that significantly changed requirements on software patents. In addition, a patent patent deemed patentable in US may not be patentable in other countries. For example, a computer-readable medium claim is explicitly excluded as a patentable claim in the Guidelines for Examination by China's SIPO.

Based on such a country-specific standard on patent quality, one needs to make an educated determination whether an invention is likely to be allowed by the PTO or not. If it is unlikely that PTO will allow a patent due to highly crowded prior arts in the specific technology area, it is probably not worth the effort and money to file the patent application. On the other hand, if it is likely that the applicant will receive a grant, then one should look at the second factor, i.e. whether others likely will use the invention, and then decide whether to file the application.

3.3.3. *Are others likely to use the invention significantly in the next 2–20 years?*

When deciding whether to file a patent application for an invention, the second question one should ask is whether anyone likely will use this invention between two to twenty years from filing. More specifically, you want to know "whether others may copy your product and profit unfairly, or invent independently and then file injunction against your product". In addition, you must also look into whether there are enough market values to you to pursue the patenting process.

If a feature improves the product performance and customer experience significantly, it is likely many people will want to adopt it so it would be wise to file the patent application. Moreover, if a patent maps onto a mandatory Standard feature, it is almost inevitable that products conforming to the standard will use the patent so you should also file a patent application to exclude others from using your idea.

Other companies may use your invention by simply copying your product feature after hearing your idea. Alternatively, someone may have independently developed the same technology as you have done but hasn't made any public announcement on its upcoming product yet. They may have already applied for a patent on this idea or may file soon after hearing about your idea. As a result, they may be able to file a patent suit against you and stop your product shipment. Therefore, in these scenarios, you should file a patent application to retain the option of excluding others from using such an invention and/or preventing others from stopping your own product shipment.

In addition, you should also take into consideration product life cycle in making your decisions. For example, if an invention has an extremely short life cycle compared to the patent prosecution period (typically 2–5 years in the US), then perhaps there is no reason to file a patent application for this short lived feature because it will be obsolete by the time the patent is granted. Similarly, if the invention is too expensive or too complicated to commercialize within the patent life time of 20 years, there is no reason to file a patent application either.

Some company will consider factors such as market size, infringement detectability, etc. In Authors' opinion, these factors are important when determining how high the value of the granted patents, but not fundamental factors for initially deciding whether to file a patent application on an invention or not. When the Patent Review Committee was initially trying to evaluate an invention, they don't even know how the claims will be written and whether the claims will be granted AS IS or severely modified. The same invention when drafted by different lawyers will have different degree of detectability. Some use wording or phrases that are hard to detect, while others draft smartly from the very beginning. For the same idea, your patent drafter can enable or kill the case without your realizing it, unless you pay attention.

Another example is that most patents used in recent litigations between smartphone companies were filed before 2000. It is evident that the inventors, at the time of filing, didn't anticipate the extreme high value of these patents. It was too difficult even for these experienced experts in industry-leading companies to determine, at the time of patent filing, the market size and product type of the smartphones used today. If every market success is foreseeable, there would be no opportunity exist for latecomers to catch up with leading companies. That is why the authors believe that the practical approach when deciding whether to file a patent is to omit these unpredictable factors such as market size. Instead one could take a look at the total possible impact the patent might have on the potential infringer. Even if the market size is always going to be a niche area with very little revenue potential, if the technology sector is extremely strategic to the potential infringer, such invention could still be an effective weapon against this infringer and thus should be patented. Therefore, we use a qualitative description "whether the idea will be used **significantly**" to address this aspect.

Some companies put too high a value on inventions that are used in their own products. In fact, one common question asked to inventors during the invention review meeting is "are there any plans to use the feature in our own company's products?" This is not the correct approach unless the inventing company is the leader in the industry such that others likely want to copy this company's products. The correct question should be "is it likely that third parties will use this feature in the future?" A patent is highly valuable when it reads onto other's products, but not useful reading onto your own product unless others also use your idea in their products. One possible scenario is that an invention is used in your own product and the product is made by an OEM manufacturer. This OEM manufacturer not only makes product for you but also for other companies. There is a greater probability that other companies will use the invention in the future, because the OEM manufacture may learn from the invention and make proposals to a third party to use the invention.

3.3.4. *Deciding whether to file a patent application*

Once you've answered the above two fundamental questions, you are ready to decide which IP action to take. In Figure 3-6, we propose actions you should take depending on the answers to the above described two key questions.

(i) As shown in Figure 3-6, the horizontal axis and vertical axis represent each of the two questions, respectively. The X-axis addresses whether the PTO for a specific country will likely allow your key claims for the patent. The Y-axis addresses whether others likely will use your idea significantly within 2–20 years time frame from patent filing.

(ii) As shown in the upper-right quadrant, when the answer to both questions is a "Yes", one should definitely file a patent application. This scenario means that the invention is likely to be granted by the PTO as a patent. In addition, it is likely that other companies would want to use this invention after seeing this idea or could independently develop a similar idea on their own. In this case, it is necessary to file a patent.

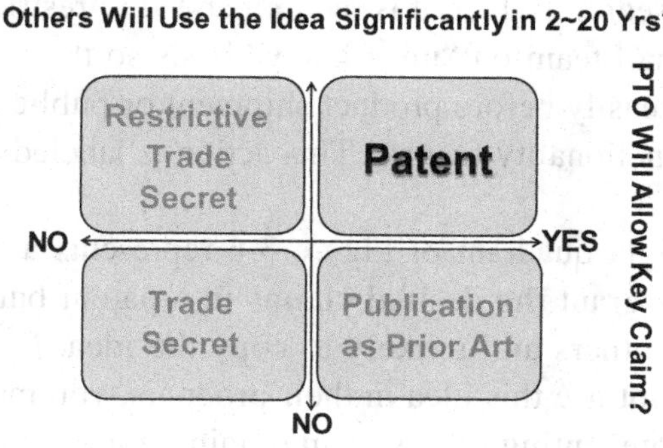

Figure 3-6   Recommended matrix for determining whether to file a patent.

One should bear in mind that this decision may vary based on the countries you are filing in. If you are filing in the US, you need to look at how likely USPTO will grant such a patent. On the other hand, if you are filing in China, you need to look at China SIPO's customary practices. Different PTOs have different policies and patterns for different industries. For example, many pharmaceutical companies often avoid filing patent applications in China because it is very difficult to obtain a grant patent for that industry.

It is also noteworthy to mention that when considering whether a third party will use your invention in their products, besides considering whether they'll incorporate your inventive feature into their products in the country of question, you should also consider whether they may sell, offer to sell, import, manufacture, use such a product in that country.

To summarize, it is clearly worthwhile to file a patent application for the specific invention when (i) you are likely to get a patent granted; and (ii) your competitor will likely use the invention for a product within 2–20 years.

If at least one answer to the two questions is a "No", it is not necessary trying to protect the invention by filing patent applications. Instead, other approaches are probably more cost effective. For example, as shown in the upper-left quadrant of Figure 3-6, when an idea is unlikely to get PTO allowance, there is no point filing a patent application. However, if someone else might want to copy the idea after they hear it, then one should protect the idea from leaking out inadvertently by keeping it as a trade secret. In fact, it is recommended to restrict the information within a small team on "must know" basis so that others can't get hold of the idea easily before product shipment or public announcement of the related functionality/feature. This action is labeled as "Restrictive Trade Secret".

The lower-right quadrant of Figure 3-6 represents a scenario where PTO is likely to grant the desired claims in a patent but the feature is so peculiar that others are unlikely to copy the idea. Even if someone else likely will not use this idea in their products, you may still want to take actions in preventing others from obtaining a patent if you plan to incorporate this feature into your products. The recommended action is publishing the idea to establish a prior art so that no patents can be obtained on this particular feature and thus preventing others from stopping your product shipment in the future. This is much more cost effective than filing a patent and maintaining the patent.

The lower-left quadrant of Figure 3-6 depicts an idea that is unlikely obtain PTO allowance as a patent and unlikely be used by others in their products. In this case, keeping the idea as a trade secret should suffice.

With inventors and patent review committees all asking the same questions and screening for high quality ideas, next step is paying close attention to high quality patent application drafting. We'll dive into a detailed discussion on patent application drafting in Chapter 4.

3.3.5. *Inventor and patent review committee checklist*

In Table 3-1, we list key factors to consider for inventors and patent review committees when deciding whether to file a patent to protect an idea and how to select the best ideas among many choices.

Table 3-1   Comparison of factors inventor and patent committee should consider.

Issues to Consider	US Typical Approach	China Approach: (Similar) or Different
Questions to confirm when deciding whether to file a patent.	• Is USPTO likely to allow the claim? • Will others likely to use the idea in US significantly within patent life time?	• Is SIPO likely to allow the claim? • Will others likely to use the idea in China significantly within patent life time?
Is the invention patentable (provided it is patentable subject matter)?	• Yes, if the invention is useful, new, and non-obvious.	• Yes, if the invention meets the requirement of novelty and non-obviousness.
Is the invention likely to be used significantly within patent life time?	• 2–5 years for US utility patents.	• 3–20 years for Chinese invention patents. • 0.5–10 years for Chinese utility model patent.

3.4. Effective First-Filing Approach

Although it is extremely important to pay attention to the Step B (drafting and prosecuting your patent applications) to ensure high quality patents, the first decision is deciding where to draft and file your patent applications. Patent Review Committee typically consists of leaders from R&D, domain experts, in-house IP legal counsel, and possibly business team leaders to jointly determine what inventions are worth company's investment to obtain the optimum ROI. Besides determining whether to protect an idea, the Committee also needs to decide where to first file the patent application to best reduce risks and meet company's strategic IP needs. Inventors should understand this issue thoroughly upfront to enable easier handling of the situation later on. The following section will cover this area in details.

Companies with R&D operations in both China and the United States can choose the best jurisdiction in which to file their initial patent applications. This can have a major impact not only on priority and grant dates, but even on the quality of the initial patent application drafting.

3.4.1. *The increasing international characteristics of IP*

As companies try to expand globally, R&D work often are conducted in various international locations to meet local needs. As a result, an invention could be the outcome of collaborative efforts by team members from multiple countries, for example, between US and China, or other combinations of countries. In certain circumstances, ideas could be the result of inventors visiting team members in another country.

One of the issues such teams face is where they should file their patent in order to comply with the local IP laws while ensuring a cost effective process. This issue may look minor but could affect the portfolio quality if not handled correctly. Proper procedure will prevent potential future problems regarding patent ownership or patent validity, and reduce legal risks down the road. In this chapter, for illustrative purposes, we focus our discussions on a common scenario where inventor teams include members located in US and China. We'll compare relevant US IP laws with Chinese

IP laws, and point out how to establish an effective strategy guiding the decisions on which country to first file your patent in order to satisfy both sets of law and align with your strategic IP goal at the same time. Teams with members from other countries will need similar detailed analysis of the specific IP laws in those countries.

3.4.2. *Factors in selecting first-filing country*

Where to first file your patent application is typically determined by where the invention was made. However, there are a few key factors you must consider during the entire process. First, you need to clearly identify the invention, and who are the inventors for this invention. Second, you need to figure out which country did the inventor make the invention in. Then, you choose which country to first file based on your overall international patent filing strategy.

In the following, we look individually at: (a) who is deemed the inventor; (b) where is the invention made; and (c) how to optimize your filing approach to align with your overall strategy. We discuss in detail various scenarios, possible actions to take under these scenarios, and the pros and cons of each action. The examples include cases where an invention is made by an employee who works internationally, but more focus will be on inventions made collaboratively by multiple international inventors within a team.

3.4.3. *Identification of inventor(s)*

First, let's take a look at "inventor" definitions under the US and Chinese law. US law defines the inventor as one who conceived the invention. Conception does not mean simply suggesting an idea of a result, but clearly disclosing the invention to enable one skilled in the art to reduce it to practical form without the exercise of extensive experimentation or the exercise of inventive skill.

Chinese law, on the other hand, defines an inventor as a person who made creative contribution to the substantive features of an invention creation. It doesn't include personnel responsible for organizational work, or who only offers facilities for making use of material and technical means, or who only takes part on other auxiliary functions. In other words, inventor's supervisor or scientist's technicians are not inventors unless they contributed to the invention creation.

For an international team, if multiple individuals contributed to the idea conception and made creative contributions to the substantive features of the invention, they are deemed co-inventors of the invention. To decide which country to first file their patent application, we need to next take a look at where the invention was made.

3.4.4. *Determination of the location where invention was made*

Under US Law, to determine whether an invention was made in the USA, one needs to examine where the invention was reduced to practice which could be actual reduction or a constructive reduction. Proof of a constructive reduction to practice requires sufficient disclosure under the "how to use" and "how to make" requirements. Actual reduction to practice, on the other hand, was established by a two-pronged test in one of the interference proceeding's case (*Eaton v. Evans*, 2004):

(i)   the party constructed an embodiment or performed a process that met every element of the interference count; and
(ii) the embodiment or process operated for its intended purpose.

In addition, US law requires that an invention made in US must be filed first in US except when authorized by a license obtained from the US Commissioner of Patents. There is an expedited process to obtain such a license.

In parallel, according to Chinese IP law, an invention is considered made in China when the substantive contents of the technical solution were made within the territory of China.

For inventions made in China, inventor must file first in China except when authorized by a license obtained from China authority. This process could take several months and will be discussed further in the following sections.

However, sometimes at first brush, it is not straightforward to determine where the invention was made. For example, an inventor may have conceived the initial idea in China but traveled to US to conduct experiments, made substantive contents of the technical solution and reduced the idea to actual practice in US. Here, even though he came up with his idea in China first, his invention would be deemed to be made in US according to both Chinese law and US law. Similarly, even if an inventor conceived the initial idea in US, but if he made substantive contents of the technical solution and reduced the idea to practice in China, then his invention would be deemed to be made in China.

When there are several international co-inventors collaboratively coming up with an invention, one may want to separate those inventions made in US from those made in China which makes the decision on where to first file easier. However, sometimes the inventions are not divisible into made by US or China. For example, when a person working in US collaborates closely with another person working in China to come up with an idea, the invention would be considered made in both US and China if the person in US reduced to practice while in US, while the person in China made substantive contents of the technical solution in China. In this case, deciding which country to first file the patent application becomes a bit complicated. According to the US law, this patent application should be filed in US first, unless a foreign filing license is obtained from US Commissioner of Patents. Meanwhile, according to Chinese law, the application should be filed in China first, unless a foreign filing license is obtained from Chinese government.

The following sections will discuss different considerations and treatment as well as pros and cons of each approach.

3.4.5. *Optimization of first-filing decisions under various scenarios*

In general, for inventions made in US or China, one should file the patent application first in the country where the invention was made, regardless of where the inventor came from or what nationality he/she is, provided that export license is not a consideration for the particular invention.

However, for inventions made collaboratively in both US and China, there are various approaches to take. The most common approach is to look at where was the main invention made and file patent applications in that country. However, this may not be the most optimal approach, especially with US' adoption of "first-to-file" under the new AIA where timely filing becomes critically important compared to before. If two (or more) inventors came up with a similar invention independently, the one who filed first will be rewarded with a granted patent while all the other inventors will be complaining bitterly about having missed the opportunity to protect their hard work and investment in the invention. Therefore, it is worthwhile to investigate what options one has when filing patent applications and associated consequences. We'll address each of these approaches in detail by taking a look at the factors that affect our decision on where to first file.

3.4.6. *Time period to obtain the permit of foreign filing license → to file first in China provides an earlier filing date, but the disparity may be temporary*

One important factor to consider is how quickly you can obtain your License for foreign filings. US Licensing and Review stated that their process of petitions for expedited license is within 3 business days of receipt. In limited cases, license may be processed even quicker upon a showing that a bar date is imminent.

In China, Rule 9 states that patent administration department under the State Council will promptly issue a notification of confidentiality examination of the application, and promptly make a decision on whether the invention or utility model is required to be kept secret. The advice is applicants may proceed to filing in a foreign country or an international application if it fails to receive a decision within 6 months of filing the request. In practice, it takes about <u>3 months</u> after your petition to get the permit. One noteworthy comment is that if one files PCT directly, it also implies a petition and thus a separate petition is not needed.

Figure 3-7 is a comparison of patent prosecution process when selecting various paths. First of all, for a regular US patent application, it takes approximately 2–5 years of going through the Examination Process after filing to get a granted patent. The Examination consists of waiting about 1–2 years to receive your first Office Action (OA), another 3 months to respond to the OA, an additional 3–6 months to receive the second OA (which often is the final OA), then 3 months to respond to the OA, appeal, or file a Request for Continued Examination ("RCE"). Within One year from the priority date, you should file PCT or enter other countries directly. After grant, US patents under the new America Invents Act ("AIA"), are exposed to potential patent review processes such as Post Grant Review, Inter Partes Review, Covered Business Method, etc. The patent is ordinarily valid for 20 years after the filing date, subject to paying maintenance fees.

China's Invention Patent goes through a similar but slight longer process of 3–5 years. The Examination process consists of requesting

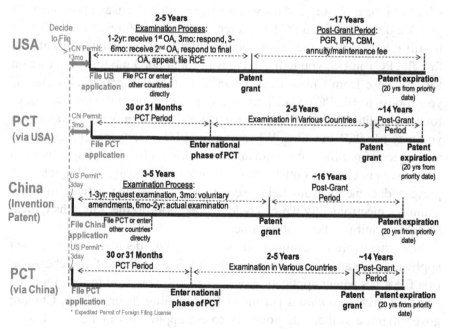

Figure 3-7   Comparison of patent prosecutions in China and US via different paths.

examination in 1–3 years, voluntary amendments in 3 months, and actual examination within the next 6 months to 2 years. One can also file PCT in US or China. Figure 3-7 depicts a PCT process via US or China which is first subject to a 30 to 31 months PCT period, followed by entering national stage, with the remaining process similar to that of the national-ized country.

For an invention made in both US and China, regardless of whether you are filing first in US or China, you should first obtain a permit of foreign filing license from the non-first filing country. How fast you are able to get such a government permit will affect your filing date. As shown in Figure 3-7, if you are first filing in US (whether filing a regular US patent application or PCT in US), you will need to wait and seek a permit of foreign filing license from China's patent administration department under the State Council which typically takes 3 months. However, if you file your patent application in China first, you'll first need to seek and obtain a permit of foreign filing license from US Commissioner of Patents which can be as fast as 3 days when an expedited license is petitioned. If you decide to first file a PCT in either US or China, foreign filing license is still required from the other country. Figure 3-7 illustrates that if you first file PCT in US, you will need to wait for about 3 months for a foreign filing license from China, then file PCT with an US office. However, if you choose to file PCT via China office, you only need to wait for 3 days for an expedited foreign filing license from US government first, and then you may file PCT in China. When you file PCT specifying Chinese SIPO as the receiving office, it is equivalent to asking a foreign filing license to file patents in countries other than China. You should avoid filing eFile to prevent documents from being sent to PCT receiving offices in other countries electronically which could happen prior to the 3 months typical foreign permit license waiting time.

In other words, assuming on January 1, you decide to file a patent application for an invention made in both US and China. If you choose to first file a US patent application or PCT in US, you need to wait until the end of March to obtain a permit of foreign filing license from Chinese government, and then file your US patent application or PCT in US on April 1. On the other hand, if you instead chose to first file a Chinese patent application or a PCT application via China, you'll only need to wait until January 4 or so to obtain a permit of foreign filing license from US government, then file your Chinese patent application or PCT application in China on January 5. <u>For the same invention, the filing date could differ nearly 3 months depending on which country you first file your patent application, in this particular case your earliest filing date will be April 1 if filing first in US, or January 5 if filing first in China.</u>

Therefore, for inventions that are time-sensitive, you may want to first-file in China to get the nearly 3 months earlier filing date than first filing in US. After US law changed from "first-to-invent" to "first-to-file" for patent applications filed on or after March 16, 2013, early filing date becomes a "race against the clock" and could determine whether you are entitled to a granted patent or lose out the right to another inventor who filed before you. The advantage of filing first in China than filing in US is that it can be much faster to get the permit of foreign filing from the US government than from the Chinese government. One may argue that such time difference is temporary and may change in the future. For example, when both US government and Chinese government synchronize their approximate timing required in granting the foreign patent filing licenses, such filing date discrepancy between the first filing in these two countries will disappear. However, until that day, you should be aware of the current differences, consider pros and cons of other key factors as well as the timing, and choose which country to first file your application.

Some patent practitioners may point out that first file in US provides the opportunity to file Provisional Patent application. A Provisional application is popular because it locks in an early priority date at a low cost and has a much simpler documentation requirement on the part of the inventor/patent-attorney when filing the Provisional Patent applications, while China doesn't have a Provisional Patent application process available.

3.4.7. *Time to grant → file first in US provides generally an earlier grant date*

Depending on the technology of the invention, the purpose of your particular patent filing, and the overall strength of your existing portfolio, there might be additional benefits in obtaining an earlier patent grant date. As shown in Figure 3-7, a typical patent application in US takes about 2-5 years to grant, which in China takes about 3–5 years to grant. Therefore, if you desire to have a granted patent as soon as possible, then first filing in US would help you reach your goal faster.

In addition, USPTO offers various accelerated patent grant program, such as "TrackOne". With an upfront fee, the patent time to grant could be reduced to about 6 months or 1 year, significantly shorter than a Chinese patent's 3 to 5 year time-to-grant.

For the case where an extremely important patent was deemed invented in both US and China, besides wanting to lock down a priority date early, one may also desire to obtain a granted patent as soon as possible. In such a situation, one could adopt the following approach to achieve both these objectives the same time:

(i)   first seek an expedited US permit of foreign filing license which takes 3 days;
(ii) file a patent application in China right away; and
(iii) then immediately make a direct filing of the US counterpart patent application under the Paris Convention.

This way, the applications in both China and US will prosecute in parallel. The US patent application will be able to enjoy the early priority date of the China patent application due to the Paris Convention. At the same time, the US application can also enjoy and leverage the accelerated patent grant programs (e.g. TrackOne) offered by USPTO.

3.4.8. *Quality of application drafting → file first in US generally yields a higher quality patent application drafting*

For a well-managed patent family, extra special attention is usually given to the first patent application within the family because it "lays the foundation" for the rest of the family members. The quality of the first patent application has a strong influence on the quality of subsequent child patent applications. The following sections discuss two aspects of patent quality: (a) initial patent application drafting quality; and (b) jurisdiction requirement to support subsequent priority claims.

As far as patent application draft quality is concerned, at the present moment, there are still noticeable differences in the typical patent drafting quality made in China versus those made in the US. China's patent system is much younger than US with relatively less experienced IP professionals available for high quality patent drafting required to establish a strong global patent portfolio. Therefore, filing first in US will likely provide you with a better drafted patent application, with a faster grant date. If you need your patent to truly add value to your IP strategy, high quality is an important factor to focus attention on. Paying close attention to patent quality no matter where the patent is first filed will pay dividends in the long run.

On the other hand Chinese patent law, similar to the European patent law, imposes more restrictive criteria than that of the US patent law for the initial written specifications to support the after filing amendments or any future priority claims. As a result, filing patent applications first in China usually provides a well-written specification with a large set of varying alternative embodiments and details due to China's restrictive jurisdiction requirements. Such well drafted specification will allow more flexibility in later amendments and stronger support for foreign counterpart applications or child patent applications within the family. From this consideration, first filing in China provides certain advantage for a patent family quality.

3.4.9. *Other considerations such as overall portfolio management*

There are additional factors to consider when choosing which country to first file. You must optimize your portfolio in alignment with your overall IP strategy. As a result, what technology areas should the patent read onto, how important is the technology area to your company, how do you want to use your IP, what is your overall worldwide patent distribution strategy are all important factors to consider when you manage your patent portfolio. Table 3-2 summarizes the above analysis.

Table 3-2   Key factors affecting first filing strategy for inventions made in both US and China.

Key Factors	File First in China as CN Application	File First in China as PCT Application	File First in US	File First in US as PCT Application
Impact to Patent Filing Date	3 days to petition US for expedition	3 days to petition US for expedition	~3 months to obtain China permit	~3 months to obtain China permit
Time to Patent Grant	3~5 years	2.5 years + national prosecution length	2~5 years	2.5 years + national prosecution length
Patent Quality	Generally Lower	Somewhat Higher	Generally Higher	High

3.4.10. *Conclusion — effective patent application first filing is important to your IP strategies*

A well-developed patent first filing strategy is increasingly important to a company's overall IP strategy, especially with the trend of continuous expanding R&D activities globally. More and more inventions deemed made in multiple countries will require extra attention to prosecute properly. In particular, America Invents Act with the new "first-to-file" IP law makes locking in an early priority date critical and current mechanisms favor filing first in China. However, patent quality is generally higher for applications drafted in the US. In addition, USPTO generally can grant a patent faster than China SIPO.

3.4.11. *First filing strategy checklist*

In summary, IP practitioners working with an inventor team that either consists of members from US and China, or team members who travel frequently between US and China should carefully consider where to first file their patents. For readers' convenience, we summarize in Table 3-3 the above points in a comparison table format.

Table 3-3   Comparison of first filing strategies for China versus US.

Issues to Consider	US Typical Approach	China Approach: (Similar) or Different
When filing patents with multiple international inventors:	• Avoid to automatically first file with US PTO.	• Avoid to automatically first file with China SIPO.
• Check who are the inventors.	• Inventor is the one who conceived the invention. Conception means clearly disclosing the invention to enable on skilled in the art to reduce to practical form without additional inventions.	• The person made creative contribution to the substantive features of an invention creation.
• Determine where was the invention made.	• The invention is deemed made in US if the invention was reduced to practice, either actual reduction or constructive reduction to practice in US.	• The invention is deemed made in China when the substantive contents of the technical solution were made within the territory of China.
If invention is deemed made in multiple countries:		
• If priority date is critical.	•	• Request expedited foreign filing license from US Licensing and Review (3 days), then file a Chinese patent or PCT specifying SIPO as the receiving office (avoid eFiling).
• If getting a granted patent quickly is desirable.	• US typically takes 2–5 years go grant. Seek foreign filing license from China patent administration department under the State Council, then file a US patent or PCT specifying USPTO as the receiving office (avoid eFiling).	• China typically takes 3–5 years to grant.
• If the initial patent draft quality is important.	• First file in US generally has a higher quality patent drafting.	• Patent applications drafted in China often have more solid jurisdiction requirement support to subsequent priority claims.

3.5. Whether to Accelerate or Decelerate Your Patent Prosecution

Both USA and China have procedures to help speed up and slow down the patent prosecution process. Depending on your specific situation, you should utilize them intelligently to meet your IP strategy. For example, you may want to accelerate a patent application prosecution because this application reads onto a competitor's product and you need a granted patent to use against this competitor. On the other hand, at times you may need to utilize deceleration when you are in a situation where there is a need to wait for a competitor's product to come out first. You can then map your patent application claims better onto specific features in such a product. Similarly, you may wait for a standard specification to finalize in order to map your patent application claims better onto such a standard. In the following, we'll cover these scenarios in more detail.

3.5.1. *Acceleration*

The Leahy-Smith America Invents Act ("AIA") was passed by the US Congress and signed into law by President Barack Obama on September 16, 2011. It introduced a TrackOne procedure for applicants who want to speed up their patent prosecution process. Typically, a utility patent application in US takes 2-5 years from patent filing to patent grant. In certain circumstances, you may want to speed up or accelerate the process to obtain a granted patent as soon as possible. By paying an upfront fee (~US$4000), your case is moved ahead of other pending cases, and USPTO will provide a first OA within several months and a case may be granted as short as in 6 months. Some people claim that cases going through TrackOne have a greater probability of obtaining grants. Whether this is due to the fact that most people only file TrackOne for cases that are generally higher quality or because USPTO treats TrackOne cases more favorably requires additional data to ascertain. However, several companies report that they actually save money by going through TrackOne because they receive less OAs from USPTO and thus save money on the OA responses. As a result, some companies file as high as 50% of their cases via TrackOne.

However, there are some drawbacks to filing via TrackOne. Some restrictions or inconvenience include:

(a) Application must be complete at the time of filing, including inventor oath or declaration, and fee;

(b) No more than four independent claims are allowed, and the maximum number of total claims is set as 30. No multiple dependent claims are allowed;

(c) First filing (whether filed directly at USPTO or entering US via PCT at national stage), continuation, continuation-in-part, and divisional are eligible for TrackOne, but reissue applications are not;

(d) Request for TrackOne for utility patent applications must be filed using USPTO's electronics tool, EFS-Web.

(e) There is an upper limit of 10,000 granted requests for TrackOne and prioritized examination for the RCE request. Therefore, TrackOne requests submitted after reaching the 10,000 limit will not be permitted.

You must determine whether a case is TrackOne or not at the time of filing. If you have a case that is being prosecuted and you think it will take another 1+ years to get allowances and you desire to obtained allowances sooner, you can file a continuation with exactly the same material under TrackOne, and abandon the original case at the same time to avoid double patenting. An alternative approach is to simply file a continuation including those claims that you believe are grantable and TrackOne the continuation while still keeping the parent case alive.

In summary, companies can choose TrackOne for the following reasons and to leverage their advantages. Depending on the specific objectives, they may take the following corresponding actions.

(i) One or more of your claims read onto a competitor's product and you want to obtain an enforceable case as soon as possible:

=> Therefore, you should file TrackOne for the same case and abandon the original application.

(ii) Your patent application reads onto a competitor's product and you believe only a couple of claims will get allowance:

=> Therefore, you should file a continuation under TrackOne including only those few allowable claims.

(iii) You want to save money overall by utilizing TrackOne compared to standard process:

=> Therefore, you should file more cases via TrackOne.

There are other ways to accelerate your cases. If an examiner is willing to allow a few claims but rejects the remaining ones, you may simply drop the remaining claims in the original application to enable allowance, and at the same time file a continuation to include the remaining claims.

In China, there are various acceleration processes allowing prioritized examination of certain types of inventions. These types include important applications relating to energy conservation, environment protection, new generation IT/biotech/high-end equipment manufacture, new materials, new energy automobile; important applications promoting the development of green technologies; applications for the same invention first filed in China and then in other countries or regions; and other applications which materially affect national or public interests and require prioritized examination.

The accelerated examination in China will conclude within 1 year. However, because only certain categories of invention patent applications are eligible for fast tracking system in patent examination, it is not commonly utilized.

3.5.2. *Deceleration*

Under other circumstances, you may want to decelerate your patent prosecution process. For example, if your patent is targeted to read onto a standard, but the standard specification is not finalized yet, then you'd want to slow down the patent prosecution so that you can keep amending your claims to read onto the final standard specification more precisely. You may also have an application that pre-dates another company's up-coming products. Then, you would want to slow down the prosecution to revise your claims until the target product is released so that your claims read squarely onto the other company's released product.

In US, you can pay extra fee to extend the response time to an OA, to a maximum of 6 months from the OA letter date. Some also refuse to concede to examiner's recommendations and continuously argue for certain points to avoid allowance. Other ways include filing RCEs to keep the case alive. If you desire a longer prosecution period at the beginning of your patent filing process, you may file a provisional patent application first, then convert to a regular utility patent in a year, and follow the standard prosecution process thereafter. Another approach is to file PCT at the beginning or at the time of converting from provisional application to a regular patent, and then wait for 31 months before deciding whether to nationalize.

In China, there are similar ways to decelerate a case. You can pay a fee to extend the response time one-time for two months.

3.5.3. Comparison checklist — acceleration or deceleration of patent prosecutions

For reader's convenience, Table 3-4 summarizes the key similarities and differences between China and US in acceleration or decelerating patent prosecutions.

Table 3-4   Patent prosecution acceleration/deceleration for China versus US.

Issues to Consider	US Typical Approach	China Approach: (Similar) or Different
Acceleration in obtaining a granted patent	• "TrackOne" program prioritizes examination: available for regular utility patents provided applicant pays ~$4K and may get a granted patent in 6 months. • If some claims are allowed when others are not: Drop non-allowed claims to enable allowance, and pursue dropped claims in continuation cases.	• Prioritized examination is only available for certain special types of inventions. • If protecting shape and structure, apply for Utility Model patent which typically grants in 6 months. It isn't subject to substantive examination, but plaintiff needs to provide a technical search report prior to litigate in court (see Chapter 2 for details).

(Continued)

Table 3-4   (*Continued*)

Issues to Consider	US Typical Approach	China Approach: (Similar) or Different
Decelerate patent issuance	• Extend response time to an OA by paying extra fees up to 6 months. • Continuation or RCE to keep the case alive. • File Provisional patent application. • File PCT at the beginning or at the time of converting from Provisional application to regular patent.	• Pay a fee to extend the response time to an OA one time for 2 months.

Chapter 4

For Patent Drafters and Prosecution Managers (Relating to Idea Capture)

4.1. How to Ensure High Quality Drafting of Patent Applications

Chapters 1 and 3 discussed extensively the rationales for only filing high quality patents. As emphasized, patent quality depends on both the usefulness of the inventor's idea as well as the quality of the patent application drafting. Therefore, to effectively capture a good idea and turn it into a powerful "diamond-like" intellectual patent (IP) weapon or a strong shield for the patent owning company, you must pay close attention to both areas carefully.

We use a graphic depiction as shown in Figure 4-1 to analogize patent as being similar to a protective Ring (the grey shaded ring) encircling your inventive Technology (the white circle in the middle). When a patent is used in negotiation or litigation, the party being asserted or sued would try everything possible to show that their product is different from your protected Technology (i.e. their product does not completely overlap or fall within your Technology circle). They'll also argue that your patent is invalid by looking for the weakest spot in your protective Ring and try to break the Ring from the weak spot so that the Technology is no longer protected.

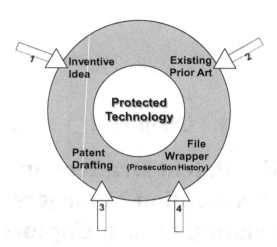

Figure 4-1   Defendant will attack each weak spot in your patented invention.

We'll address in the following sections of Chapter 4 how to prepare, during patent drafting and prosecution process, for such potential invalidity challenges. We'll also discuss how to prepare potential challenger's non-infringement arguments and related topics in Chapters 6 and 7.

As shown in Figure 4-1, your granted patent, represented by the shaded ring, enables you to exclude others from practicing the Protected Technology unless they obtain your prior permission. Parties being asserted will attack every aspect of your patent, such attacks are being represented by arrows. For example, Arrow #1 represents attack of your inventive idea, using 35 U.S.C. Section §101, as non-patentable subject matter. Arrow #2 represents attack from prior art perspective, claiming your idea is anticipated under Section §102, or obvious under Section §103. Arrow #3 represents attack of your patent drafting as being non-supportive to the claims, and thus indefinite. Arrow #4 represents attack of your communications with the patent examiner documented in the application prosecution history (a.k.a. file wrapper) which may serve as *estoppels*. Each of these attacks could successfully crack through your protective Ring and invalidate your patent.

Therefore, you must take measures upfront to ensure your teams are fully aware of each possible attacks in future patent invalidity proceedings. They must work closely with each other to ensure that there are no weak spots in any steps so that the final granted patent has true high quality.

4.2. Company or Patent Applicant Should Motivate Inventors to Invent and File High Quality Ideas

To build high quality patents, one must start with high quality invention disclosures. Many engineers and scientists are very busy with their immediate deliverables, and often are unable or unwilling to spend time on submitting quality invention disclosures. Therefore, Portfolio Managers, in-house attorneys, and patent drafters may need to request their companies take specific measures to motivate inventors. Some successful companies accomplish this by building an innovative culture. Such approach works well top-down by upper-level management being excited about, proud of, and reward inventions. Timely intellectual property training of new employees is helpful as well. Some in-house attorneys go as far as to give out company T-shirts to those that submit ideas. Others give out "inventor of the year" jackets embellished with company logo for the inventor to wear and promote inventions. Google reportedly gives out fancy puzzle pieces for each invention and a large amount of pieces form interesting shapes.

However, quantity is not enough, quality is more important. A good patent drafter needs to make sure that he understands the novelty point clearly, has a keen sense about possible prior arts in the space, competitor products and their future roadmaps, so that he can write the claims accordingly.

4.3. Should You Use Outside Law Firm for Patent Drafting?

In today's environment of seeking high quality patents, drafting the initial patent application well is extremely important. Having in-house attorneys drafting patents based on their own company's technology usually produces higher quality patents because of the following reasons:

(a) In-house attorneys have the incentive to write a high quality patents from the beginning to the end if they believe they have to live with the consequence of the final granted patent. This will be amplified if the company judges employee performance taking into consideration of the final granted patent quality and whether the patents have been useful in negotiation or litigation situations. Company can further promote such positive behavior by rotating in-house attorneys from patent prosecution to IP litigation (and vice versa) so that attorneys can personally experience the pain of poorly written patents.

(b) In-house attorneys can improve and self-adjust continuously based on prior writings and internal learning from other attorneys or inventors. They can eventually become domain experts for their own responsible business units which will improve the quality and speed of their drafted patent applications. Such re-use of knowledge is more prevalent for in-house attorneys compared to law firms which frequently use client cases to train new associates.

(c) In-house attorneys have the advantage of being able to participate in Patent Review Committee discussions. They can more easily consult or even befriend inventors. They also have access to Patent Portfolio Managers so are more in tune with company's IP strategy. Thus, their drafted patents should be in better alignment with company's IP needs.

Unfortunately, many companies have to outsource patent drafting to outside law firms due to increased number of patent filings, and not enough internal patent attorneys to draft the large volume of patent applications. In addition, in-house attorneys don't want to handle docket issues related to meeting statutory date of United States Patent and Trademark Office (USPTO). In fact, most organizations within a company would not be interested in dealing with the docket system due to potential legal risks. As a result, many companies hire outside law firms to take on such risks where outside law firms buy insurance to cover legal malpractice suits.

However, outside law firms' objectives are largely focused on making profits, their interests are not necessarily completely aligned with your interests. As a result, many poorly written patent applications have been produced. It is not unusual to see claims written by outside law firms that are unnecessarily narrow or don't even reflect the invention itself.

How to deal with this issue is an unsolved problem. Operating companies tried various approaches, such as paying the outside law firm a fixed cost for each patent, or paying hourly rates. Unfortunately, law firms are familiar with all such schemes, and will usually want to make sure that they come out ahead and make a profit with the smallest investment. A common complaint from operating companies is that law firms often use clients to train their new associates. It was even speculated that a patent drafter went as far as intentionally not getting his client's case granted at the first Office Action (OA) but with a minor modification to earn the fee charged for the second Office Action response drafting, and then get the patent granted afterwards. Some firms want to show good statistics of granted patent percentage. They may modify a claim, based on examiner's rejections, into such a narrow area or impractical scenario that it will be granted but nobody would ever likely practice the claim. Therefore, if you don't pay attention to your cases, your money for patent filing could have gone "down the drain". That's why it is important to start paying close attention early and ensure that your investment in patents eventually pays off for your company.

One of the solutions suggested by some operating companies is building a long-term relationship with an outside law firm. If the firm's main client is your company, then you will definitely get their attention. In addition, you should have at least two law firms to serve your company, one with a bigger share of volume than the other so they compete on service level.

However, companies with capabilities to draft patent applications internally probably are better off in the long run to train a staff of internal patent drafters. These drafters have more incentives to write high quality patents because they know they'll be facing the consequences if the outcome is poor.

In other words on one hand, it appears that currently most companies, large or small, outsource their patent application drafting work to outside law firms. This model helps company to deal with the ups and downs in the number of patent applications so to avoid having to lay off in-house attorneys during slow times. On the other hand, most companies seem to be extremely dissatisfied with outside law firms' drafting work because many law firms tend to use real cases as training ground for their new associates. These new associates are not part of the company Patent Review Committee, and often don't even get a chance to talk to in-house counsels ("IC"s) because in-house attorneys are too thinly staffed and don't have time to talk to outside counsels ("OC"s) before the patent drafting is started. As a result, the only person OC has some opportunities to interact with is the inventor. Inventors are more technically oriented and often are not able to articulate their true novelty point, so the OC needs to spend hours of time on areas he didn't plan initially. This causes frustrations on both the OC side as well the inventor side. ICs who review OC's claims later are equally frustrated.

The consequence is a frustrated team yielding poor quality patents that the company may not be able to use eventually. Therefore, if a company can afford some high caliber internal patent drafters, they can be tasked to draft the most important patent application cases. However, you don't want to lose sight of the other cases not deemed as important at the time of filing. They may become an important patent later on and you need to ensure they can be utilized and "polished" into a powerful "diamond" when needed. Therefore, even for patent applications drafted by OCs, there are steps you should take to improve the quality. Figure 4-2 illustrates commonly seen process issues and recommended improvements.

The schematic on the left-hand side in Figure 4-2 depicts a typical process being practiced by many companies today which is not ideal. The bullet points list sources causing the non-ideal operation, such as the outside counsel ("OC") not getting a chance to sit in the patent review meetings and thus missing the opportunity to hear questions and rebuttals between the committee and the inventor. The in-house attorney ("IC") at most only reviews important patent filings and doesn't have time to review regular cases due to limited bandwidth. Meanwhile, inventors don't have time to explain to the OC all the embodiments brought up during the patent review meeting so the OC has to start completely from scratch.

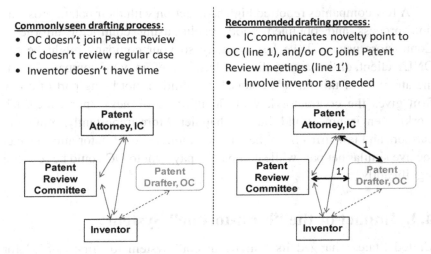

Figure 4-2   Recommend process when using outside law firms for patent drafting.

In comparison, the schematic on the right-hand side in Figure 4-2 represents a recommended better process where a company uses outside law firms for patent drafting. As shown in Figure 4-2 as line 1', either the outside counsel should be invited to the patent review committee meeting so he can hear the questions to the initial idea and objections at the meeting. In parallel, or at least alternatively, in-house counsel ("IC") should understand the novelty point clearly for regular cases as well as important filings, and communicate them to the OC as shown in line 1.

Another approach is to utilize contractors. To prevent having to lay off regular in-house attorneys (when there are too many) during down times, companies can leverage contractor lawyers. In addition, it is recommended to hire OCs with litigation experience so that he can critique the final claims with a litigator's perspective which will help the patent quality.

Some companies recommend that when you need to pick out law firms to hire, you should be cognizant to look at the quality of the associates who will be actually drafting the patent applications, not the partners. You may even want to search around social media tools to find out the associate's work ethics and quality reputation.

A few companies reported high satisfaction with their patent prosecution process and obtained good results using contractor attorneys. Contractors usually have less capacity so your company might be the ONLY client, or the largest client he has. Therefore, your company has all the attention of this outside counsel. In addition, not being part of a law firm gives the contractor lawyer flexibility. Attorneys appreciate such working environment and thus are happier. More importantly, removing partners and law firms from the cost equation, the contractor attorney can receive similar net pay, while company's payment to OC could be reduced significantly.

4.4. Impact of the "First-to-File" System

United States changed its "first-to-invent" system to "first-to-file" for applications filed on or post March 16, 2013 after the enactment of the America Invents Act (AIA). As a result, inventors in US can no longer rely on their lab notes to lock in priority dates of their inventions. Since many companies work on similar technical issues, they may eventually come up with the same technical solution as your company does (some may have already filed before your company). Therefore, you need to file your inventions timely before your competitors block you. That's why patent drafters need to work closely with their inventors to understand the invention well, and quickly file a high quality patent application in order to not lose patenting opportunity to other companies. China has always been a "first-to-file" country and thus has similar needs and requirements.

4.4.1. *Leveraging provisional patent application for US inventions*

In US, provisional patent application is a useful tool to quickly submit your invention to USPTO and lock in an early priority date. It is especially important since AIA changed the original "first to invent" to "first inventor to file". This does not mean that one can copy an inventor's idea and then file before the true inventor files his patent application. You must be a legitimate original inventor in order for the patent to be valid. However, among several original inventors who independently came up with the same invention, the one who rushes to the Patent Office first to file ("First Inventor") wins the race and is entitled to a patent (provided the idea is patentable). All the other original inventors will not be able to obtain a patent since the First Inventor's patent application is a prior art to their similar inventions. This is precisely the reason why US' provisional application could be highly effective, due to its simplicity and "faster to a priority date" process.

However, one must be cognizant that the specifications for a provisional application must be well written with sufficient support for future claims. Otherwise, you may not be able to enjoy the priority date of the provisional application after converting it to a regular patent.

To further illustrate and support our emphasis on drafting good provisional patent applications, the following Table 4-1 is an exemplary template that the authors developed. Inventors who draft their own Provisional patent applications may copy the following paragraphs and fill in relevant information in the bracket ([ ]).

Patent drafters should think of all possible workarounds of the inventor's proposed technical solution and try to disclose those in the Provisional specification. There is a saying "picture is worth a thousand words". Therefore, it is recommended that you try to **include all relevant graphs in the application without disclosing trade secrets that you don't wish the public to access**. Please be advised that these are not legal advices and you should always consult your own lawyer for a final legal opinion.

4.4.2. *How to obtain an early priority date in China*

In China, Provisional patent application is not available. To obtain an early priority date, for shape and structure-related inventions, one can use Utility Model patent to increase the speed of getting the patent filed. For other types of inventions, inventors need to work with patent drafters who know their technology areas well so that they can quickly put together an invention patent application. However, since your objective is to eventually obtain a negotiation grade or litigation grade high quality patent, the patent drafter should spend diligent effort to ensure that the claims have definitive and clear supports in the specifications.

Table 4-1   Provisional patent application template language and instruction guidelines.

Title: [What is the title of your invention? — Be as broad as possible]

Provisional Application, [What is name of the first inventor? — e.g. John Smith]. [What is name of the second inventor? — e.g. John Smith Sr.], [What is the year of filing? — e.g. 2011]

BACKGROUND OF THE INVENTIONS

(1) Field of Invention

This invention relates generally to [What is the general technology area your patent cover?], and more specifically, [Describe the uniqueness of your solution in a little more detail.].

(2) Background

[Describe what your unique solution is helpful for.]. [Describe the benefit of your unique solution.]. [Elaborate further what can your unique solution do for target users.].

[At the highest level, describe what is the technology used for.]. [Describe the status of the industry.]. [Provide a few examples of existing solutions.].

The problem with known [Insert name of your invention.] is that [list problems with the existing known solutions.].

Therefore, what is needed is a [Insert the name of your invention.] that [List all the advantage of your invention.].

BRIEF SUMMARY OF THE INVENTION

The present invention advantageously fills the aforementioned deficiencies by providing a [Put there the name of your invention including the advantages]. This invention [List the main advantage of your invention.]. In addition, the present invention [List all other advantages of your invention.].

The present invention relates to [Summarize the benefit of your invention.].

[Describe the mechanism of your invention, what made it work, how, etc.].

In one particular embodiment of the present invention, [Describe each element of the best example you have for your invention, step by step, connected together and how to make them work.].

In still another embodiment of the present invention, [Describe another example of your invention, element by element, step by step, to show how it works, and how to connect them all together.].

In still another embodiment of the present invention, [Give another example of your invention in specific details.].

In still another embodiment of the present invention, [Give another example in specific details.].

In still another embodiment of the present invention, [Give another example.].

In still another embodiment of the present invention, [Give another example.].

It is therefore an object of the present invention to [List the most important purpose of your invention. Describe why is meet your purpose.].

It is another object of the present invention to [Describe the second purpose of your invention.].

The present invention now will be described more fully hereinafter with reference to the accompanying drawings, which are intended to be read in conjunction with both this summary, the detailed description and any preferred and/or particular embodiments specifically discussed or otherwise disclosed. This invention may, however, be embodied in many different forms and should not be construed as limited to the embodiments set forth herein; rather, these embodiments are provided by way of illustration only and so that this disclosure will be thorough, complete and will fully convey the full scope of the invention to those skilled in the art.

BRIEF DESCRIPTION OF THE DRAWINGS

The invention may take physical form in certain parts and arrangement of parts, a preferred embodiment of which will be described in detail in this specification and illustrated in the accompanying drawings which form a part hereof and wherein:

FIG. **1** is a view in perspective of a [Describe Figure 1 in one or two sentences.].

FIG. **2** is a view in perspective of a [Describe Figure 2 in one or two sentences.].

DETAILED DESCRIPTION OF THE INVENTION

The present invention is directed to an [Put down name of your invention].

Referring now to the drawings wherein the showings are for purposes of illustrating a preferred embodiment of the invention only and not for purposes of limiting the same, FIG. **1** shows [Describe Figure 1 briefly.].

(Continued)

Table 4-1   (*Continued*)

[Describe Figure 1 in great detail, referencing the elements in Figure 1.].

FIG. 2 shows [Describe Figure 2 in great detail.].

While the present invention has been described above in terms of specific embodiments, it is to be understood that the invention is not limited to these disclosed embodiments. Many modifications and other embodiments of the invention will come to mind of those skilled in the art to which this invention pertains, and which are intended to be and are covered by both this disclosure and the appended claims. It is indeed intended that the scope of the invention should be determined by proper interpretation and construction of the appended claims and their legal equivalents, as understood by those of skill in the art relying upon the disclosure in this specification and the attached drawings.

Claims:

Claim 1. We claim a [Describe your invention in a general term as a device/system]. comprising of [Describe each of the key elements of your invention in a more general term].

Claim 2. The [Describe your invention in a general term as a device/system] as in Claim 1, where [Choose one of the elements described in Claim 1] is [make the chosen element more specific.].

Claim 3. We claim a [Describe your invention in a general term as a process] comprising of [Describe each of the key steps of your invention].

Abstract:

This invention relates [Describe the uniqueness of your solution in a little detail.]. [At the highest level, describe what the technology is used for.] [Describe what your unique solution is helpful for.]. [Describe the benefit of your unique solution.]. [Elaborate further what your unique solution can do for target users.]. This invention [List the main advantage of your invention.]. In addition, the present invention [List all other advantages of your invention.].

Table 4-2   Comparison of priority dates in China versus US.

Issues to Consider	US Typical Approach	China Approach: (Similar) or Different
Patent Filing System	• First-to-file on or after March 16, 2013 (first-to-invent before March 16, 2013).	• First-to-file
Ways to lock in an early priority date.	• File a well-written Provisional application.	• File a well-written Utility Model patent for shape/ structure ideas. • Use experienced patent drafters.

4.4.3. *Checklist in obtaining an early priority date*

To make readers' lives easier, the following Table 4-2 is a summary on how to effectively obtain early priority dates in US and China.

4.5. Impact of US Supreme Court's *Alice v. CLS Bank* Decision

In Section 2.7, we concluded that US patent eligibility scope has moved closer to that of China for software patents after US Supreme Court's decision on *Alice v. CLS Bank*. Patent attorneys and drafters should be keenly aware of such IP trends and take them into consideration while writing or reviewing patent applications.

4.5.1. *Observation from patent sales/purchase transaction perspective*

With the new AIA law and US Supreme Court's ruling for *Alice v. CLS Bank*, instead of clarifying what's patentable, it caused a lot of confusion. As discussed previously, there were comments such as "software patent is dead". After examining the software patent trend[1] in the patent buying and

---

[1] Based on an extracted subset of data in "Patent Value Quotient Report for Third Quarter of 2015 Shows Strong Demand and Pricing for Issued U.S. Patents!", IP Offerings. The original complete data can be found at http://www.ipofferings.com/patent-value-quotient.html.

selling market (referred to by lawyers and economists as the "secondary markets"), as shown in Figure 4-3, it appears that software patent sales continue to transact frequently, with reasonable average pricing.

Figure 4-3 is a plot of average selling price for granted US patents on the secondary markets from 2012 to mid-2015. Authors solely relied on the IP Offering source (see Footnote 1 of Chapter 4) and did not verify any data points because many are private transactions.

US Supreme Court ("USSC") decided on *Alice v. CLS Bank* at the end of June 2014, which is represented by a vertical dashed line in Figure 4-3. The horizontal axis represents the software patent sales transaction date, while the vertical axis is the average patent pricing for each deal. Open columns represent deals occurred prior to the *Alice* ruling, while solid columns represent deals after the *Alice* ruling. As can be seen, there appears to be a slowing down in software patent transactions from late 2013 to early 2014, perhaps due to the fact that IP market was anticipating the *Alice* outcome and thus stayed in a holding pattern. However, starting in late 2014, the pace of software patent sale transactions resumed. One of the software patent transactions secured a high average sale pricing, at over $1M per patent, for natural language related technology.

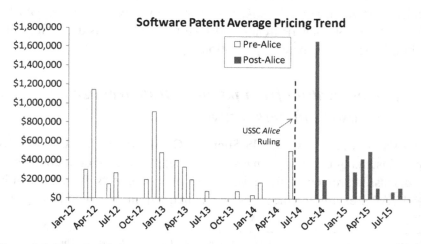

Figure 4-3 Trend of Software Patent Average Selling Price pre- and post-Alice ruling (a subset of Patent Value Quotient Report from IP Offerings).

An interesting fact, upon close examination, is that prior to *Alice*, most software patent sale portfolios were related to software applications such as e-commerce, internet, cloud, social media/networking, email, 2d-3d conversion, digital imaging, data transaction/management, document management, fleet management, and online services. In comparison, transactions post-*Alice* included technologies such as internet, natural language, video analytics, software algorithm, mobile advertizing, and file encryption. Patent portfolios related to areas more closely associated with business methods, such as fleet management, e-commerce, online services, and social media, no longer transacted after *Alice*. Instead, software subject matters that were deemed by USSC and Federal Circuit to be eligible subject matter continued to sell, e.g. internet related technologies. In addition, we observed that the patent portfolios post-*Alice* seemed to be more related to big data and artificial intelligence. In other words, the natural transition of software market from actual application implementation toward large scale data analysis is also reflected in the shift of transacted technologies on the secondary market.

Therefore, we conclude that USSC's *Alice* decision has impacted the patent secondary markets not by volume or pricing, but more profoundly by the technology type. Buyers are no longer interested in acquiring business methods related patent portfolios, probably due to the high invalidity rate for the covered business methods ("CBM") category which was nearly 100% by July 2015.[2] However, *Alice* ruling did not cause blanket reduction in software patent valuation. Instead, those software patents that are required by current and future commercial markets that can survive *Alice* test are continuously fetching reasonably high valuations.

Authors would like to point out that the above data points are a small sample set and difficult for authors to perform detailed analysis due to the proprietary nature of pricing for patent transactions and the lack of transacted patent lists. It would be better if a larger set of transparent data becomes available in the future for further evaluation of software patent portfolio trend on the secondary market.

---

[2]"Patent Invalidity Rates: The Summertime Blues Continue", Robert Saches, Law360. Can be found at http://www.law360.com/articles/697396/patent-invalidity-rates-the-summertime-blues-continue.

4.5.2. *Observation from patent filing perspective*

Patent sale/acquisition deals are typically transacted for buyer's offensive/ defensive purposes and usually involve granted patents. Therefore, they provide helpful insights to whether patent purchasers altered their behavior due to the *Alice* effect. However, their patent qualities depend on IP policies and practices at the time of patent filing many years ago, and thus are not reflective of recent events.

To assess whether *Alice* has had an impact on current patent filing quality, we take a look at an exemplary software category "search engine algorithm" in Figure 4-4. The horizontal axis is patent filing date from January 1, 2013 to December 31, 2015. At the time of this book being prepared for publication in May 2016, some patent applications filed after mid-November 2015 may have not been published yet. As a result, data points for the fourth quarter of 2015 may not be complete.

The vertical axis represents patent strength scores using Innography[3] tool. The solid line represents average patent strength (on quarterly basis) for all US granted patents and pending applications between 1/1/2013-12/31/2015. These cases were identified by typing in key words "search

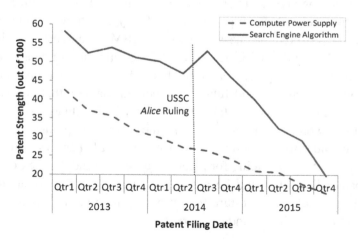

Figure 4-4   Software patent strength as a function of filing date.

---

[3] Innography data analytics tool information can be found at https://www.innography.com/.

engine algorithm" into Innography query (which searches title, abstract, and claims). As a control case, the dashed line represents average patent strength for an exemplary hardware technology "computer power supply". The vertical dotted line represents the date US Supreme Court decided on the *Alice v. CLS Bank* case. As can be seen from Figure 4-4, the dashed line (the control case) indicates that patent strength typically is lower, using Innography calculation formula, when the patent application is younger. This explains why the dashed line trends downward from left to right, nearly in linear fashion.

Similarly, for the search engine algorithm related patents, we expect the patent strength line to trend downward relatively smoothly from left to right. However, Figure 4-4 indicates that immediately after the USSC *Alice* ruling, there was an upward spike in the patent quality, at around 3rd Quarter ("Qtr3") of 2015. Is it a result of patent drafters being more careful and thorough in writing their patent applications post-*Alice*? Another explanation is that patent applicants became more timid post-*Alice* and were filing less but higher quality patents while dropping some potentially patentable software inventions. The reality could be a combination of multiple factors, but requires further observation of the trend as more patents filed post-*Alice* are published and become publicly available.

4.6. Strategy for Claim Drafting and Deployment

Authors recommend readers to pay abundant attention to your software inventions. As the contemporary world economy evolves, higher value-add jobs likely will reside in software related industries. Therefore, it is critical to establish a good process in drafting high quality software patents so that your company can protect its technology leadership. In Chapter 5, we will dive deep into various methodologies for drafting and deploying software patents. However, in this section, we'll instead focus on the overall strategy and approach.

To ensure drafters deliver a high quality patent application, applicants (companies who file patent applications on behalf of their inventor employees, or individual inventors filing on their own) should use all available tools to help the patent drafter write better specifications/claims. Patent drafters should track and monitor most recent IP law changes, case laws, new directions, potential change in policies, and write their application with all these data in mind to optimize the final outcome.

4.6.1. *Overcoming subject matter patentability §101 issue in post "Alice" world*

When drafting patents to submit to USPTO, it is helpful to understand how the PTO examiners are trained and how they will examine your case. You can then draft your applications accordingly.

Therefore, in today's post-*Alice* world, instead of abandoning software patents, you need to continue augmenting your portfolio via internal patent development and external patent acquisition, perhaps paying even greater attention to software than before to ensure high quality. However, there were no clear guidelines on how to manage software inventions so that the filed applications will more likely be granted by USPTO post-*Alice* and not easily invalidated. Advices and opinions ranged from "USPTO examiners reject cases in alignment with each supervisor's opinion" to "you need to write means-plus-function claims in order to get granted". Even law firms were not providing clear guidance, either because they didn't know the answer, or they didn't want to share their answers in case such answers hurt their business. As a result, operating companies must get as much information as possible from USPTO and guide your own internal patent drafters as well as external law firms when they draft patents for your company. The following are analysis done by the authors based on USPTO's interim guidance for its own examiners (1/2015 version) to help such efforts.

As part of the interim guidance to illustrate its Patent Eligibility test process, USPTO released a flowchart in late 2014,[4] and subsequently a revision in early 2015. However, we believe our flowchart more accurately reflects the process because the streamlined Step 2.0 (diamond shaded box, in grey) should be present in USPTO's flowchart, but was missing and merely briefly described in the text. The description

---

[4]"2014 Interim Eligibility Guidance Quick Reference Sheet", USPTO, December 2014, also available at http://www.uspto.gov/patents/law/exam/2014_eligibility_qrs.pdf .

states that <u>regardless *of* whether the claim recites a judicial exception (JE) or not, if the claim clearly does not seek to tie up any *JE* such that others cannot practice it, use streamlined eligibility analysis and a full eligibility analysis is not needed</u>. We name this step as Step 2.0 and insert it into the flow chart below to assist drafter in visualizing the overall process. In the following Figure 4-5, we highlight the added Step 2.0 box in grey color. Step 2.0 appears to be relatively more subjective due to the lack of available cases. Therefore, drafters should try to write their specifications and claims such that the examiners will more likely lean toward arriving at a conclusion of "NO" for Step 2.0.

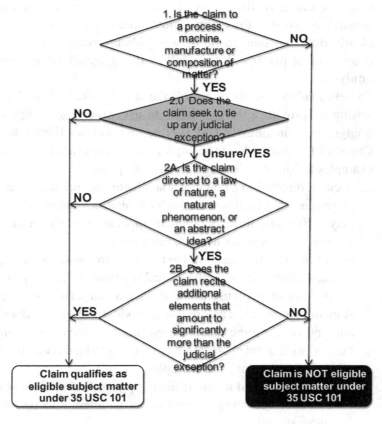

Figure 4-5   Author's modification of USPTO interim guideline for patent eligibility test.

To properly use the flowchart in Figure 4-5, you must first establish the **broadest reasonable** interpretation of the claim; analyze the claim **as a whole**. Then, you follow the following steps:

(i)   In Step 1, you determine whether a claim is directed to a process, machine, manufacture or composition of matter (PMMC).
   a. If the answer is NO, you are directed to the black box of "Claim not eligible for patents under 35 USC Section §101".
   b. If the answer is YES, you move on to Step 2.0 and ask yourself whether the claim seeks to tie up any judicial exception.

(ii) In order to answer the question in Step 2.0, you need to determine what the claim is directed to. If the claim, viewed as a whole (regardless whether the claim recites a judicial exception or not), clearly does not seek to tie up any judicial exception such that others cannot practice it, then follow the **streamlined eligibility analysis**.

(iii) To help readers effectively utilize the above guideline, in the following we provide a few **scenarios to use streamlined eligibility analysis** cited in the 2014 USPTO Interim Guidance (Footnote 4 of Chapter 4). Readers should be cognizant that these are non-limiting examples to illustrate how to carry out Step 2.0.
   a. A claim directed to a complex manufacturing industrial product or process that recites meaningful limitations along with a JE may sufficiently limit its practical application so that a full eligibility analysis is not needed. For example:
      — a robotic arm assembly having a control system that operates using certain mathematical relationship (clearly not an attempt to tie up use of the mathematical relationships);
   b. A claim that recites a nature-based product, but clearly does not attempt to tie up the nature-based product, does not require a markedly different characteristics analysis to identify a "product of nature" exception. For example:
      — a claim directed to an artificial hip prosthesis coated with a naturally occurring mineral is not an attempt to tie up the mineral; and

    c. Claimed products that merely include ancillary nature-based components do not require "product of nature" exception analysis. For example:
      — a cell phone with an electrical contact made of gold; or
      — a plastic chair with wood trim.

(iv) If the answer to question in Step 2.0 is Unsure or Yes, go to Step 2A, shown as Box 2A in Figure 4-5.

(v) Then, determine whether the claim is directed to a law of nature, a natural phenomenon, or an abstract idea (LNA). If the answer is NO, you can move on to the square white box "Claim qualifies as eligible subject matter under 35 USC Section §101" in Figure 4-5.

(vi) In the above step, it is unclear sometimes whether a nature-based product is considered a "product of nature", i.e. Law of Nature or Natural Phenomenon. The test in determining whether a nature-based product being "a product of nature" is **whether the nature based product exhibits markedly different characteristics from its naturally occurring counterpart**.

    a. If the answer to the above question is YES, then it is not a "product of nature" and thus, similar to the above step v), one can move on to the square white box "Claim qualifies as eligible subject matter under 35 USC Section §101" in Figure 4-5.

    b. On the other hand, if a natural-based (or man-made) product is essentially no different from a naturally occurring product in its natural state (**does not exhibit markedly different characteristics**), the nature-based product is "a product of nature" and falls under laws of nature and/or natural phenomena exception(s).

    c. We want to reiterate the previous Step 2.0 where (claims that clearly do not seek to tie up any JE may use the **streamlined eligibility analysis** and do not need a "markedly different characteristics" analysis.

    d. It is also noteworthy that (a claim citing a single nature-based product satisfying marketed differently characteristics analysis is eligible subject matter and does not need a "significantly more" analysis in Step 2B (which we'll cover later).

(vii)   To assist readers in proper assessment of Product of Nature, we'll provide a few examples for various tests cited in 2014 USPTO Interim Guidance.

     a. **Market differently characteristics analysis**: Compare the resultant nature-based combination to its naturally occurring (or closest) counterpart in its natural state and express as the **product's structure, function, and/or other properties**. For example:

        — A product that is purified or isolated will be eligible if a resultant characteristics is sufficient to show a marked difference from its naturally occurring counterpart.

        — A process claim is not subject to the markedly different analysis for nature-based products used in the process except where there is no difference in substance from a product claim (e.g. "a method of providing an apple").

     b. **Non-limiting examples of Characteristics**:

        — biological or pharmacological functions or activities;

        — chemical and physical properties;

        — phenotype, including functional and structural characteristics;

        — structure and form, whether chemical, generic or physical.

(viii)   To assist readers to properly follow Step 2A, we'll provide a few examples by courts. Please be cognizant that these are non-limiting examples and are not meant to be exhaustive:

     a. Laws of nature and nature phenomena means naturally occurring principles/substances, substances that do not have **markedly different characteristics** compared to what occurs in nature (product of nature). Some examples of product of nature (i.e. laws of nature or natural phenomena) are:

        — an isolated NDA;

        — a correlation that is the consequence of how a certain compound is metabolized by the body;

        — electromagnetism to transmit signals;

        — the chemical principle underlying the union between fatty elements and water.

b. <u>Abstract ideas</u> mean fundamental economic practices, certain methods of organizing human activities, ideas 'of themselves', mathematical relationships/formulas. Some examples are:
— mitigating settlement risk;
— hedging;
— creating a contractual relationship;
— using advertizing as an exchange or currency;
— processing information through a clearinghouse;
— comparing new and stored information and using rules to identify options;
— using categories to organize, store and transmit information;
— organizing information through mathematical correlations;
— managing a game of bingo;
— the Arrhenius equation for calculating the cure time of rubber;
— a formula for updating alarm limits;
— a mathematical formula relating to standing wave phenomena;
— a mathematical procedure for converting one form of numerical representation to another.

(ix) To assist readers properly follow Step 2B, we provide a few examples of consideration by US Supreme Court. Please be cognizant that these are non-limiting examples and are not meant to be exhaustive:

a. <u>Significantly more than the *JE* "inventive concept"</u>: one must include additional features to ensure the claim describes a process or product in a meaningful way, more than a drafting effort designed to monopolize the judicial exception. Consider the claim as a whole, not individual element. Every claim must be examined individually. Some examples of "Significantly More" are:
— improvements to another technology or technical field;
— improvements to the functioning of the computer itself;
— applying the JE with, or by use of, a particular machine;

— effecting a transformation or reduction of a particular article to a different state or thing;

— adding a specific limitation other than what is well-understood, routine, and conventional in the field, or adding unconventional steps that confine the claim to a particular useful application; or

— other meaningful limitations beyond generally linking the use of the judicial exception to a particular technological environment.

b. Examples of <u>NOT significantly more</u>, i.e. failing the "Significantly More" test:

— adding the words "apply it" or equivalent with the JE, or mere instructions to implement an abstract idea on a computer;

— simply appending well-understood, routine and conventional activities previously known to the industry, specified at a high level of generality, to the JE (e.g. a claim to an abstract idea requiring no more than a generic computer to perform generic computer functions that are well-understood, routine and conventional activities previously known to the industry);

— adding insignificant extra solution activity to the judicial exception (e.g. mere data gathering in conjunction with a law of nature or abstract idea);

— generally linking the use of the judicial exception to a particular technological environment or field of use.

(x) **Process for a claim reciting a plurality of exceptions:**

a. If the claim fails for any one exception under 2B, then the claim is **ineligible and no further analysis is needed**.

b. However, if the claim satisfies 2B for one exception, continue analyzing whether it satisfies all other covered exceptions.

In addition, we modified Step 2B exit path when the answer is "YES" to better guide patent drafters when they walk through each relevant flowchart steps throughout patent drafting. Figure 4-6 depicts this process. Basically, if the subject matter falls under more than one JE, when the answer for 2B is YES for the first JE, you can't simply conclude that the

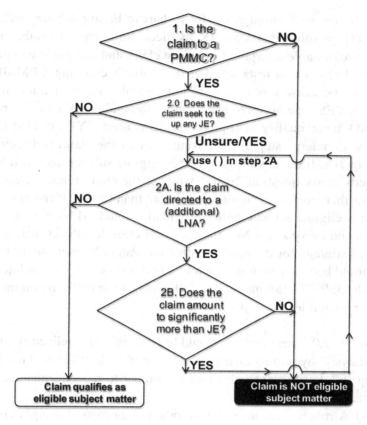

Figure 4-6   Author's interpretation of USPTO's interim guideline and proposed strategy for patent drafter and patent review committee.

claim is eligible subject matter yet. Instead, you need to go through the same process for each JE by asking, as shown in Box 2A, whether the claim is directed to additional LNA (here you are directed to use the phrase in the parenthesis instead of the preceding 'a') until every JE is exhausted and you've gotten a "YES" answer to each single JE. Then, you draw a conclusion that the claim is eligible subject matter.

This approach is important to patent drafters and attorneys when they interact with USPTO examiner. You need to diligently ask additional relevant questions at each step, anticipate potential issues which may be raised by the examiner, and prepare ahead of time to address them all.

We'll now walk through the flow chart in Figure 4-6 step by step. First, keep in mind that USPTO instructs examiners to establish the broadest reasonable interpretation of the claim and analyze the claim as a whole. In Step 1, it tests whether the claim is claiming a PMMC of matter, if the answer is NO, it is not eligible subject matter. If the answer is YES, one needs to ask whether the claim seeks to tie up any JE, if NO, it can qualify as eligible subject matter; if YES or UNSURE, then it will undergo step 2A assessing whether the claim is directed to a LNA or JEs. If the answer is NO, it is eligible subject matter; if YES, one needs to ask question 2B, i.e. whether the claim recites additional elements that amount to significantly more than the JE. If the answer is YES, it is eligible subject matter provided 2A and 2B have been asked for each and every JE; if NO, than it is not eligible subject matter. Our proposed strategy for the patent drafter and Patent Review Board is that they should be ready to argue each box in the flow chart when interacting with USPTO examiners. The following are specific recommendations for each relevant step:

(i) In Box 2.0, patent drafters should leverage the "streamlined eligibility analysis" by writing claims in conformity with "NOT seeking to tie up JE". Positive examples include, similar to recommendations discussed above:

   (a) A robotic arm assembly (product or process) having a control system that operates using certain mathematical relationship (clearly not an attempt to tie up use of the mathematical relationship).

   (b) A claim directed to an artificial hip prosthesis coated with a naturally occurring mineral (not an attempt to tie up the mineral).

   (c) Claimed products merely include ancillary nature-based components, e.g. (1) a cell phone with an electrical contact made of gold; (2) a plastic chair with wood trim; etc.

   (d) In addition, patent drafters should monitor changes in policy by USPTO, decisions from US Supreme Court, Federal Circuit and gather additional successful examples.

(ii) For Box 2A, patent drafters should try to avoid the appearance that a claim is directed to any of the 3 JEs: law of nature, natural phenomenon, or abstract idea. Some Abstract Idea examples to avoid include:

— Mitigating settlement risk;

— Processing information through a clearinghouse;

— Managing a game of Bingo;

— The Arrhenius equation for calculating the cure time of rubber;

— A formula for updating alarm limits; and

— A mathematical formula relating to a standing wave phenomena.

(iii) Additional suggestions for Box 2A: argue that software doesn't necessarily equate to Abstract Idea. For example, "A computer-implemented method comprising executing the following steps: receiving an electronic communication containing malicious code in a computer with a memory having a boot section, a quarantine sector and a non-quarantine section; storing the communication in the quarantine sector …; extracting, via file parsing, the malicious code from the electronic communication to create a sanitized electronic communication …; transferring the sanitized electronic communication to the non-quarantined sector of the memory; and deleting all data remaining in the quarantine sector." The Federal Circuit ruled that it is eligible subject matter under 35 USC §101 because the claimed invention relates to software technology for isolation and extraction of malicious code contained in an electronic communication, i.e. physically isolating a received communication on a memory sector and extracting malicious code from that communication to create a sanitized communication in a new data file. Such action does not describe an abstract concept. Another example is retaining website visitors from being diverted from a host's website to an advertiser's website for which the claimed solution is necessarily rooted in computer technology in order to overcome a problem of retaining website visitors specifically arising in the realm of computer networks, i.e. internet, and thus is eligible subject matter.

(iv) For Box 2B, demonstrate that for each directed JE, the claim includes additional elements that amount to significantly more than the JE, for example:

(1) Improves another technology or technical field (e.g. presents functional and palpable applications in the field of computer technology with specific applications or improvements to technologies in the market place);

An example is "a method for the halftoning of gray scale images by utilizing a pixel-by-pixel comparison of the image against a blue noise mask in which the blue noise mask is comprised of a random non-deterministic, non-white noise single valued function which is designed to produce visually pleasing dot profile when threshold at any level of said gray scale images."

(2) Improves the functioning of the computer itself (e.g. retaining website visitors from being diverted from a host's website to an advertiser's website for which the claimed solution is necessarily rooted in computer technology in order to overcome a problem specifically arising in the realm of computer networks);

An example is "A system ... comprising: (a) a computer store containing data ...with visually perceptible elements correspond to the plurality of first web pages ...; (b) a computer server at the outsource provider ... coupled to the computer store and programmed to: (i) receive from the web browser of a computer user a signal indicating activation of one of the links by one of the first web pages; (ii) automatically identify as the source page the one of the first web pages ..., (iii) ... retrieve the stored data...; and (iv) using the data retrieved, automatically generate and transmit to the web browser a second web page that display: (A) information associated with the commerce object associated with the link that has been activated, and (B) the plurality of visually perceptible elements visually corresponding to the source page."

(3) Applying the JE with, or by use of, a particular machine (e.g. in *O'Reilly v. Morse* Claim 6 recites of signs in combination

with the machinery for recording, with "A system of signs by closing a galvanic circuit rapidly for telegraphing, combined with machinery to record the signs" as an example; or in *SiRF Technology v. ITC* Claim 1 calculating the absolute position could not be performed without a GPS receiver);

An example is "A method for calculating an absolute position of a GPS receiver and an absolute time of reception of satellite signals comprising: providing pseudo ranges that estimates the range of the GPS receiver to a plurality of GPS satellites; providing an estimate of an absolute time of reception of a plurality of satellite signals; providing an estimate of a position of the GPS receiver; providing satellite ephemeris data; computing absolute position and absolute time using said pseudo ranges by updating said estimate of an absolute time and the estimate of positions of the GPS receiver."

(4) Effecting a transformation or reduction of a particular article to a different state or thing (e.g. repetitive recalculation and update is "Significantly More". In addition, steps in concert to transform raw rubber into cured molded rubber to improve an existing technology process);

An example is "A method of operating a rubber-molding press for precision molded compounds with the aid of a digital computer, comprising: providing said computer with a database for said press...repetitively calculating in the computer, at frequently intervals during each cure, the Arrhenius equation..., and opening the press automatically when a said comparison indicates equivalence."

(5) Adding a specific limitation other than what is well-understood, routine and conventional in the field, or adding unconventional steps that confine the claim to a particular useful application;

(6) Other meaningful limitations beyond generally linking the use of the JE to a particular technological environment;

(7) Establishes meaningful limitations on the JE;

(8) Is more than a drafting effort designed to monopolize an exception.

As shown in Figure 4-7, we also developed a special flowchart to illustrate how to determine whether a nature-based product is "a product of nature" through markedly different characteristics test and thus determine whether it is eligible subject matter.

In Figure 4-7, if the answer to Step 2.0 is Unsure or Yes, there is a Path (x) from Step 2.0 to Step 2.11. Path (x) leads to the process steps to determine whether a nature-based product is "a product of nature". Note that a process claim is not subject to the markedly different analysis for nature-based products except where it is not different in substance from a product claim. In Step 2.11, you will determine whether the claim is a non-process claim reciting a nature-based product. If the answer is NO, then you move to Step 2.21 (whether the claim is directed to additional LNA). On the other hand, if the answer to Step 2.11 is YES, you move to Step 2.12 and determine whether the product exhibits markedly different characteristics.

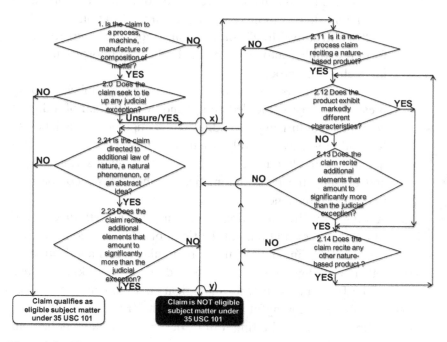

Figure 4-7   Flowchart to illustrate how to determine a nature-based product is not a product of nature and thus not directed to a JE, and therefore is eligible subject matter.

If the answer is YES, you skip Step 2.13 and move on to Step 2.14. If the answer if NO, you move on to Step 2.13 and determine whether the claim recites additional elements that amount to significantly more than the JE. If the answer to Step 2.13 is NO, it is NOT eligible Subject Matter under 35 USC Section §101. If the answer YES, you also arrive at Step 2.14 where you determine whether the claim recites any other nature-based product. If the answer is YES, you circulate back to Step 2.12. If the answer is NO, you move to Step 2.21.

From Steps 2.21 to 2.23, it is similar to previous Steps 2.1 to Step 2.2. Therefore, similar principals apply. Note that if the answer to Step 2.23 is YES, you need to move on to Step 2.21 again, following Path y), to make sure each Judicial Exception is reviewed separately.

Some examples of successfully demonstrating "Significantly More" for Box 2B are listed in the following:

— Claimed solution is necessarily rooted in computer technology in order to overcome a problem specifically arising in the realm of computer networks such as website and improves the functioning of the computer itself *(retaining customer on internet page)*.
— Present functional solution with specific improvements to certain technology *(blue noise mask for gray halftoning)*.
— Include constant measurement, recalculation *(curing rubber)*.
— Calculation could not be performed without the machinery *(GPS receiver)*.
— The claimed steps transform a material from one state to another *(rubber curing using a mathematical formula)*.

Some examples of unsuccessful demonstration of "Significantly More" for Box 2B are listed in the following, and thus should be **avoided**:

— Practically applying mathematical formula to configure a particular hardware configuration.
— Claim the mathematical procedures which can be carried out in existing computers long in use or can be performed without a computer.
— Simply limiting an abstract idea to one field of use of adding token post-solution components.

— Simply adding a "computer-aided" limitation to a claim.
— Claiming familiar mental steps routinely done.
— Claiming the well-known concept of categorical data storage, e.g. the idea of collecting information in classified form, then separating and transmitting that information according to its classification.
— Claiming generic computer functionality, transaction being performed online, at best, limits the use to a particular technological environment.
— Claiming consulting and updating an activity log representing insignificant "data-gathering steps" restricting public access and only representing insignificant post-solution activity.

Patent drafters should develop their claims based on these strategies in order to enable smooth sailing through USPTO substantive examination.

Table 4-3 summarizes how to demonstrate "significantly more". The recommendations are grouped into four categories (a, b, c, d). Category (a) examples are positive actions that have yielded previous

Table 4-3 Various examples to demonstrate that the additional elements amount to "Significantly more".

How to Demonstrate "Significantly More"?	
(a1)	Show the claimed solution is necessarily rooted in computer technology in order to overcome a problem specifically arising in the realm of computer networks such as website.
(a2)	Present functional and palpable applications in the field of computer technology with specific improvements to certain technology in the market place.
(a3)	Consider showing the calculation improves the functioning of the computer itself, or any other technology or technical field.
(a4)	Consider including improving the functioning of the computer itself, or any other technology or technical field.
(b1)	Include constant measurement, repetitive computer recalculation using the constantly updated measurement.
(b2)	Recite the system of natural phenomenon in combination with the machinery for using the natural phenomenon.

(Continued)

Table 4-3 (*Continued*)

How to Demonstrate "Significantly More"?

(b3)	Show calculating the absolute position could not be performed without a GPS receiver.
(b4)	Consider for generic computer implementation of the abstract idea, include elements which make the invention impossible to carry out manually.
(b5)	Consider disclosing chemical process at work, the monitoring of process conditions, the determination of variables in the formula from process conditions, or the means of achieving desired result or adjusting the trigger for the desired result.
(b6)	May consider to have computer calculate, then display on screen, then automatically adjust the amount of substance.
(b7)	Consider a process of combining two data sets into the device profile, tied to a specific structure/machine or claim the processor's' use of that profile in the capturing, transforming, or rendering of a digital image.
(b8)	Avoid claiming the mathematical procedures which can be carried out in existing computers long in use or can be performed without a computer and a patent on the algorithm itself.
(c1)	The claimed steps act in concert to transform material from one state to another to improve an existing technology process.
(c2)	Claim a particular mode of bringing about a known result by treating material so that it does not transform from one state to another.
(d1)	Avoid practically applying the mathematical formula to configure a particular antenna with an angle.
(d2)	Avoid simply limiting an abstract idea to one field of use or adding token post-solution components.
(d3)	Avoid simply adding a "computer-aided" limitation to a claim covering an abstract concept, without more.
(d4)	Avoid claiming familiar mental steps routinely done by doctors.
(d5)	Avoid claiming the well-known concept of categorical data storage, i.e. the idea of collecting information in classified form, then separating and transmitting that information according to its classification.
(d6)	Avoid claiming generic computer functionality, the transactions being performed online, at best, limits the use to a particular technological environment.
(d7)	Avoid claiming consulting and updating an activity log representing insignificant "data-gathering steps" restricting public access and only represents insignificant "pre-solution activity".

success so applicant should utilize them to show the examiner that they demonstrate Significantly More. Categories (b) and (c) are recommendations made to the failed cases. Category (d) comprises negative examples that are classified as non-patentable subject matter and thus should be avoided.

4.6.2. *Try to follow USPTO provided case claims — use "Nature-Based Products" as an example*

The examples provided by USPTO, including the respective court decisions are very helpful. Table 4-4 is a summary of these cases. The underlined portion means positive confirmation that it is **eligible subject matter**, while the italic case means *that it is not eligible subject matter*. Case #2 is not eligible subject matter, however, authors wonder if it would be **Significantly More** if the DNA is isolated in a way such that it encodes the same protein differently from the natural gene. Such questions will become clearer as more decisions become available from PTAB for similar cases.

You should instruct your patent drafter and/or inventors to adopt the following patent drafting and deployment strategies:

— Invention should be directed to nature-based product that has markedly different characteristics than its naturally occurring counterparts, e.g. different function and/or structure in example #1.
— Need to show enough difference in structure to avoid the impression of trying to tie up the naturally occurring counterpart. It could be a good strategy to protect invention with increasing amount of differences, e.g. examples #2, #3.

4.6.3. *Try to follow USPTO provided case claims — abstract idea/software examples*

Table 4-5 is a summary of abstract idea and software-related cases. You should instruct your patent drafter and/or inventors to study them and write claims with these cases and court decisions in mind. Note that

Table 4-4   Examples of "nature-based product".

Case Name	Representative Claim	2.11 Nature-Based Product?	2.12 Markedly Different Characteristics?	2.13 Significantly More?
#1. Diamond v. Chakrabrty	A bacterium from the genus Pseudomonas containing therein at least two stable energy-generating plasmids, each of said plasmids providing a separate gydrocarbon degradative pathway.	Bacterium	**YES** (**function** — degrade more hydrocarbons / **structure** — include more plasmids)	
#2. Association for Molecular Pathology v. Myriad	Claim 1. An isolated DNA coding for a BRCA1 polypeptide having the amino acid sequence set forth in SEQ ID NO:2.	DNA	No (structure — isolated gene is different but not markedly, encodes the same protein as the natural gene)	*No* (Myraid: isolated but otherwise unchanged enough from what exists in nature to avoid improperly tying up the future use and study of the naturally occurring gene.).
#3. Association for Molecular Pathology v. Myriad	Claim 2. The isolated DNA of claim 1, wherein said DNA has the nucleotide sequence set forth in SEQ ID NO:1.	DNA	**YES** (**structure** — has different nucleotide sequence with only exons ranther than both exons and introns)	

Table 4-5   Recommendations on how to draft abstract idea and software-related cases.

Type	Case Name	2A. Any JEs?	2B. Significantly More?
Example on how to use flow chart	Diamon v. Diehr	Law of nature/abstract idea (mathematical formula or algorithm)	**YES** (constant measurement of temperature at a mold cavity, repetitive computer recalculation of the appropriate cure time using the constantly updated measurement are "significantly more" than mere computer implementation of calculation of the Arrhenius equation. In addition, <u>the claimed steps act in concert to transform raw, uncured rubber to cured molded rubber to improve an existing technology process</u>).
	Parker v. Flook	Law of nature (mathematical formula)	**NO** (purely conventional computerized implementation of applicant's formula). *Should disclose chemical process at work, the monitoring of process conditions, the determination of variables in the formula from process conditions, or the means of setting off an alarm or adjusting an alarm system.*
	Mayo v. Prometheus	Law of nature (known relationship)	**NO** (inform about certain laws of nature, with additional steps consist of well-understood, routine, and conventional activity). *It may help to have computer calculate, then display on screen, then automatically adjust dosage.*
	Alice Corp. v. CLS Bank	Abstract idea (fundamental economic practice of intermediated settlement)	**NO** (generic computer to perform generic computer functions). *Consider including improving the functioning of the computer itself, or any other technology or technical field.*

Supreme Court decisions	O'Reilly v. Morse	Nature phenomenon	**YES** (recites the system of <u>signs in combination with the machinery for recording</u>).
	O'Reilly v. Morse	Natural phenomenon	**NO** (recites use of electromagnetism without limits on the machinery for recording). *Consider <u>including machinery for recording</u>.*
	Tilghman v. Proctor	Natural phenomenon	**YES** (the claim is directed to a particular mode of bringing about the desired chemical union, i.e. <u>by heating the water under such pressure that the water does not become steam</u>).
	Mackay Radiov. Radio Corps of America	Law of nature (mathematical formula)	**NO** (practically applies the mathematical formula to configure a particular antenna with an angle equal to twice $50.9(l/y)^\wedge(-0.513)$ degrees).
	Gottschalk v. Benson	Law of nature (mathematical formula)	**NO** (the mathematical procedures of shifting binary code can be carried out in existing computers long in use or can be performed without a computer and a patent on the algorithm itself).
	Bilski v. Kappos	Abstract idea (fundamental economic practice of hedging risks)	**NO** (limiting an abstract idea to one field of use or adding token post-solution components do not make the concept patentable).

(Continued)

Table 4-5   (*Continued*)

Type	Case Name	2A. Any JEs?	2B. Significantly More?
FC Abstract Idea decisions prior to Alice	SiRF Technology v. ITC	Law of nature/abstract idea (mathematical formula)	**YES** (calculating the <u>absolute position could not be performed</u> <u>without a GPS receiver</u>.).
	Research Corp. Tech. v. Microsoft	Law of nature/abstract idea (mathematical formula)	**YES** (the invention presents <u>functional and palpable applications</u> of halftoning of gray scale image in the field of computer technology with specific applications or improvements to imaging technology in the market place).
	Dealertrack Inc. v. Huber	Abstract idea (processing credit information through a clearinghouse)	**NO** (simply adding a "computer-aided" limitation to a claim covering an abstract concept, without more, does not sufficiently limit the claim).
	SmartGene v. Advanced Biological Laboratories	Abstract idea (provided ranked therapeutic treatment regiments)	**NO** (familiar mental steps routinely done by doctors).
	Cyberfone System v. CNN Interactive	Abstract idea (sending exploded data to different destination)	**NO** (the well-known concept of categorical data storage, i.e. the idea of collecting information in classified form, then separating and transmitting that information according to its classification, is an abstract idea).

Abstract idea decision from FC since Alice Corp.	Abstract idea (organizing information through mathematical correlations)	**NO** (generally recites a process of combining two data sets into the device profile). *Should tie to a specific structure/machine or claim the processor's use of that profile in the capturing, transforming, or rendering of a digital image.*
Digitech Image v. Electronics for Imaging	Abstract idea (organizing information through mathematical correlations)	**NO** (generally recites a process of combining two data sets into the device profile). *Should tie to a specific structure/machine or claim the processor's use of that profile in the capturing, transforming, or rendering of a digital image.*
Planet Bingo v. VKGS	Abstract idea (solving a tampering problem and minimizing other security risks during Bingo ticket purchases)	**NO** (generic computer implementation of the abstract idea and a program that is used for the generic functions of storing, retrieving, and verifying a chosen set of Bingo number against a winning set of bingo number). *Should include elements which make the invention impossible to carry out manually.*
buySAFE v. Google, Inc	Abstract idea (certain arrangements involving contractual relations)	**NO** (computer functionality is generic, the transactions being performed online, at best, limits the use to a particular technological environment and still does not make the idea non-abstract).
Ultramercial v. Hulu and WildTangent	Abstract idea (having no particular concrete or tangible from, showing an advertisement before delivering content)	**NO** (consulting and updating an activity log representing insignificant "data-gathering steps" restricting public access and only represents insignificant "pre-solution activity." Narrow idea to Internet is an attempt to limit the use of the abstract idea a particular technological environment).
DDR Holdings v. Hotels.com	Abstract idea (identifying the precise nature of the abstract idea is not as straightforward, "making two web pages look the same" ...)	<u>**YES**</u> (retaining website visitors from being diverted from a host's website to an advertiser's website for which the claimed solution is necessarily rooted in computer technology in order to overcome a problem specifically arising in the realm of computer networks. The claim recites <u>a specific way to automate the creating of a composite web page by an outsource provider that incorporates elements from multiple sources in order to solve a problem faced by websites on the Internet.</u>

Underline — Eligible.

Shaded Text — NOT eligible.

Italic — Personal opinion.

underlined portion means that these elements helped the case to be eligible, shaded texts indicate elements that made these cases ineligible and thus should be avoided. Italic texts are author's personal opinions for reader's consideration.

4.7. Drafting Strategy for Chinese Invention Patent

Drafting Chinese Invention patent is largely covered in Chapter 5. Please refer to Chapter 5 for a detailed discussion.

4.8. Train Drafters to Draft with Final Objectives in Mind

Patent drafters should keep in mind what is the purpose of the patent, what is the final goal for the corresponding IP action. Is it intended for offensive IP actions or defensive IP actions? Is it mainly a legal action or a technology play?

4.8.1. *Offensive IP actions typically include the following goals and benefits*

(1) Provides competitive advantage, prevents competitors from using your technology, protects product differentiation, revenue and profit;
(2) Can be a weapon and arsenal to assert, sue, or file injunctions against third parties. Enables IP owner to counterassert or countersue upon being asserted or sued. Optimizes financial ROI by delivering IP royalty and other benefits to IP owners, business units through outbound licensing, technology transfer and patent sales.

4.8.2. *Defensive IP actions typically include the following goals and benefits*

(1) Allows IP owner to obtain access to third party technology through cross-licensing to expand IP owner's design freedom and right to use, or leverage to reduce existing royalty payment;

(2) Is a shield and chills third parties from asserting against IP owner due to fear of reprisal. May also serve to invalidate other's IP.

4.8.3. *Typical IP actions taken by various IP Owners*

Each company, depending on its role ("IP Owner") and objective at any specific time point, will take different IP actions ("IP Action"). The same company may take a different Action at a different time point, or take a specific Action for a technology sector and a different Action for another technology sector.

Figure 4-8 depicts these various IP Actions based on patent owner's specific objectives. The vertical axis represents a focus on technology versus legal. The horizontal axis represents propensity toward offensive versus defensive approach in IP strategy. Depending on the specific product, patent owner may deploy different strategy and therefore fall within one or more of the four quadrants.

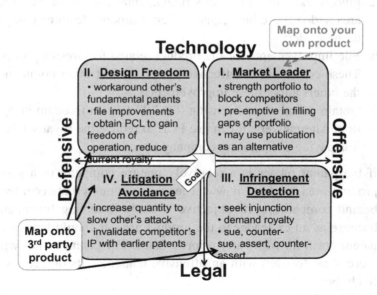

Figure 4-8   IP action chart.

(i) If the objective of the patent owner is Market Leader for a specific product, it will be more technology focused, and likely leaning toward IP offensive action. Its corresponding IP Actions taken for the specific product mainly involve:

    a. Strength patent portfolio to block competitors from copying its technology in order to maintain product leadership;

    b. Pre-emptive in filling gaps in portfolio so that it can effectively courter-sue/assert competitor's suit/assertion and block others from filing patents in those areas;

    c. May use publication as a low cost alternative versus patenting as a valid prior art in preventing others from filing a patent.

(ii) If the patent owner is a new entrance company into a product area or a close follower to the sector leader, its objective more likely will be obtaining Design Freedom. Therefore, it will be focused on technology, trying to catch up to the leader. However, its IP Actions will lean toward more defensive than offensive. Its main IP Actions are:

    a. Find workaround to other's fundamental patents in the product area and still produce equal or better product features compared to the leader;

    b. File improvements for the product related features or processes. These could still be effectively used against other companies if the others adopt these improvements;

    c. Obtain patent cross licensing ("PCL") to gain freedom of operation. Alternatively, it can use PCL to reduce the royalty rate that it is paying to operating company licensors.

(iii) If the patent owner is a relatively mature company in a specific product area, perhaps it was a leader previously but recently fell behind competitors. Its objective is likely Detecting Infringement because as an ex-leader in the product area, it should have a good patent portfolio with early priority dates. The patent owner will be more legal focused with an offensive tendency. Its objectives will likely be:

    a. Using its mature patent portfolio and seek injunctions to deter competitors or at least slow them down;

    b. Demand competitors for royalties based on its strong patent portfolio and use the licensing fee to help company bottom line;

    c. Sue or assert competitors to cause confusion and distract their business. Patent owner can also counter-sue and counter-assert.

(iv) If the patent owner is a new entrance to the specific product area, but hasn't grown into a tangible size, it likely will try avoiding Litigation. Thus its objectives will likely be:

    a. Increase patent filing quantity to slow competitor's attack;

    b. Invalid competitor's IP with earlier patents.

In other words, the patent drafter should always have specific target in mind when drafting patents. If your company falls within the upper-right quadrant (I), then your company is a market leader in the specific area. Therefore, it is likely that others will follow the lead by your company and thus adopt technology direction set by your company. In this case, patent drafter can focus on products by your own employees and try to draft claims reading onto your own products. Since your technology and products are likely to be adopted by followers, the patent likely will read onto other's products in the future.

In all other cases, such as the upper-left quadrant (II), the lower-right quadrant (III) and the low-left quadrant (IV), patent drafter must keep third party's future product directions in mind and try to write claims such that they map onto third party's products instead of your own company's products.

4.8.4. *Drafting future blocking patents*

However, it is very difficult to write claims that map onto third party products. Products that are currently available on the market are prior arts to your patent claims; while products in the future are uncertain in specific features. To assist patent drafters, the following is a table listing the objectives drafter must keep in mind, the corresponding requirements for his drafted patent applications, and the specific suggestions when he is drafting the application. Table 4-6 summarizes objectives for each type of IP market player, lays out invention criteria, points out potential issues and

Table 4-6   Drafting high quality patents — focus on objectives.

Objective	Invention Criteria	(Issues) Suggestions
I. Market Leader — to prevent competitors from infringing your inventions **A**	1. Fence off technology area **thoroughly** with regular quality patents; 2. Patents need to apply to your current or future core product	(Future technology unsure) **1. Reference R&D roadmap for your core products**
II. Design Freedom to work around 3rd party's key patents/ negotiate PCL	1. File regular quality and **negotiation grade** patents to assist PCL; 2. Patents need to read onto Competitor future product*	(Future products hard to predict) **1. Look for Standards**** **2. Study industry trend and Competitor patent filings**
III. Infringement Detection — to file countersuit / injunction against Competitors **B**	1. Only file **high quality (litigation grade or negotiation grade)** patents; 2. Patents need to read onto Competitor future core product*	(Future product hard to predict) **1. Look for Standard related patents**** **2. Study competitor roadmap, filing trend**
IV. Litigation Avoidance — to deter potential assertion or suit, to invalidate Competitor patents	1 File many regular quality patents; 2. Patents need to apply to Competitor's future core product* or in similar technology areas as Competitor's patent filings	(Future product hard to predict) **1. Study competitor roadmap 2. Study competitor patent filing trend**

makes corresponding recommendations. "*" means that the claims need to read onto competitors' future products and have an earlier priority date than the corresponding product features. "**" means accomplishing the objective is possible but the patent drafter needs to look for future standards while being cognizant that Standard Essential patent is hard to obtain injunctions for. Category A means the invention idea should target to read onto self's products. Category B means the inventive ideas should read onto third party's products.

(i) If you are a market leader in a particular technology area, your goal would be to prevent competition from infringing your inventions. The criterion for a well-drafted patent application is that it is able to fence off your technology area thoroughly so others can't easily work around your invention. In this case where you are a market leader, your patent can simply map onto your own current and future products. The advantage is that, your inventors working on future products should have some idea about what your own future product might look like. However, your patent drafter needs to be extra diligent covering all possible scenarios that future market might adopt and including the corresponding potential embodiments in the specification unless your company plans to keep them trade secrets. Even though future technology direction is not 100% certain, you can reference your own R&D roadmap for your core products to get some insights. The patent quality can be at a normal level, i.e. you can use your regular process in terms of prior art search.

(ii) If your objective is to obtain design freedom via your patent portfolio, either by working around third party's key patent or use your own patents to negotiate patent cross-licenses, you need to file negotiation grade patent, i.e. those that map well onto third party future products and can survive some diligent prior art challenges. The issue is that it is hard to predict third party future products. Possible solutions could be (a) look for standards; (b) study industry trend and third party patent filing trend to gain some insights.

(iii) If your objective is to detect infringement and file suits, assertions, injunctions, or being able to go to court to enforce these actions, then your patents must have very high quality, i.e. litigation grade. Therefore, you need to conduct thorough and skilled prior art searches to make sure your patent can survive invalidity challenges. These patents must read onto third party's future core products. Similar to the above, the issue one often encounters is that future products are unknown or uncertain. The recommended solution is to look for standard related inventions and ideas; study competitor roadmap and patent filing trend to understand their technology and product directions.

(iv) If your objective is to avoid litigation by deterring potential assertion or suit with your patent portfolio or file first to invalidate third party's patents, then you need to file enough normal quality patents (i.e. regular prior art search process) to reach a critical mass in terms of your portfolio size. The patents must read onto third party's future core products. The issue is the same as the above that future products are hard to predict. The recommended solution is to study competitor's roadmap, and study competitor's patent filing trend to get some sense on their future technology and product directions.

4.8.5. *Drafting high quality claims*

Keeping your company's IP Strategy in mind and trying to create litigation grade patents should be your typical daily mind-set if you are a patent drafter. There are some helpful methodologies which might assist delivering precise, water-proof claims, such as the Patent Deconstruction approach.[5] We'll use a pencil eraser combination idea as an exemplary example to illustrate how to use such approaches. Some interesting background on the pencil eraser patent is that on March 30, 1858, a lead pencil eraser combination patent US19783 was granted to Hymen Lipman. Four years later in 1862, Lipman sold his patent to Joseph Reckendorfer for $100K, who went on to sue a pencil eraser manufacture, Faber. It is interesting to discover that a patent, back in the nineteenth century, was valued so high and "patent troll" already existed. However in 1875, US Supreme Court declared the patent invalid. In addition, USSC ruled that Faber did not infringe because it was using a ferrule instead of Lipman's wood casting holding both the lead pencil core and the eraser stick.

---

[5]"Improving Patents and Designing Around Blocking Patents Using Patent Deconstruction Method", Vladmire Proseanic & Svetlana Visnepolschi, vproseanic@ideationtriz.com (October, 2010).

As early as 1853, an eraser attached to a pencil was already in use.[6] Charles Goodyear published an article[7] in 1853 stating "Pencil-Heads. These are made of the artist's India rubber…, they are set into metal sockets…or are formed into rings or heads which are intended to slip over the ends of a wooden pencil…". Our example will focus on this original ferrule approach, assuming no prior arts exist at the time of patent filing and the combination is not obvious.

As shown in Figure 4-9, pencil A and eraser B are combined together by a ferrule C. Your initial broadest independent claim based on Goodyear's description may look like the following:

Claim 1. A pencil eraser combination, comprising: a pencil; an eraser; and a ferrule connecting the pencil and the eraser.

Using the Patent Deconstruction (see Footnote 5 of Chapter 4) approach, the above claim can be represented by the following flowchart, as shown in Figure 4-10. Each element after "comprising" is represented by a thick-rim box with a thick arrow pointing to it. The connectors are

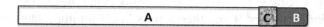

Figure 4-9   Exemplary pencil and eraser combination idea.

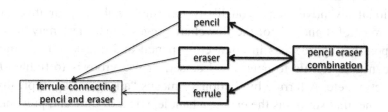

Figure 4-10   Using patent deconstruction approach to assist high quality claim drafting.

---

[6]"History of Lead Pencil", Early Office Museum, http://www.officemuseum.com/pencil_history.htm.

[7]"The Applications and Uses of Vulcanized Gum-Elastic", Vol. II, New Haven, 1852, Page 39.

represented by elements associated with it and thin arrows pointing to it. You want to make sure that there are no boxes dangling without connecting with other boxes (dangling element defect). You should also remove unnecessary elements (extra unnecessary element defect). You also want to express each box as broadly as you can (with possible practical use and without overlapping with prior arts). The following are author's own interpretation of how to utilize such flow charts to improve a claim. They may differ from that of the Patent Deconstruction methodology described in the footnote reference. Readers may want to study other approaches and choose the one that fits your needs the best for future daily use.

As can be seen, in Figure 4-10, each box is close looped with other boxes with no boxes dangling. Therefore, your initial broad claim has no obvious definition problems which may make the claim "infinite".

We can also leverage such flow chart to check whether your claim is fully enabled. As diligent observers may discover that a box typically represents an object and arrows representing directions. A box with two or more arrows pointing toward it typically represents an action or a process step. In Figure 4-10, "ferrule connecting pencil and eraser" has three arrows pointing toward it and therefore is likely an important step which often represents your key novelty point. If a person having ordinary skill in the pencil making industry at the time of this invention is not able to make the pencil-eraser combination based on the above claim without additional inventive steps, you likely have not enabled your invention. A more careful analysis of the flowchart suggests that there may be several possible approaches in connecting pencil and eraser. For example, you can glue ferrule to pencil and eraser, or use grooves to tighten the connection, etc. A ferrule by dictionary means "a ring or cap, typically a metal one, that strengths the end of a handle, stick, or tube and prevents it from splitting or wearing", or "a metal band strengthening or forming a joint". To enable the claim, patent drafter probably will include detailed description in the patent application specification. Thus, such a claim might be interpreted as a "means-plus-function" claim (which will be addressed in detail in Chapter 5) and be limited to the specific embodiments described in the specification.

However, a good drafter should start with a detailed description of main steps so that one can easily follow the steps to arrive at the intended results. Then, the drafter can gradually take away unnecessary elements to make the claim broader, harder to work around while keeping in mind to avoid overlapping with prior arts.

Based on these principles, one possible claim is as follows:

Claim 1. A pencil eraser combination, comprising:

a wooden pencil;

an India rubber with the outside shape made the same as said pencil; and a metal ring with the inside shaped the same as the outside of said pencil, said ring attached securely to the top portion of said pencil and clamping tightly onto the bottom portion of said rubber.

Again, using the flow chart approach, the above claim can be represented by Figure 4-11.

First step is to check that there are no obvious mistakes in the claim, i.e. no dangling boxes. Then, the next step is to eliminate unnecessary limitations, while being keenly aware of prior arts, to make the claim as broad as possible and difficult to work-around. This can be done by

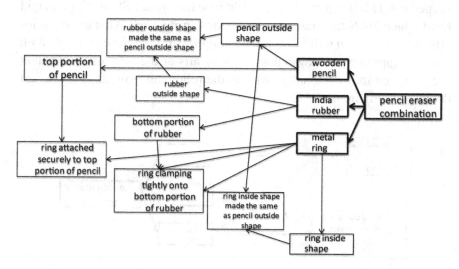

Figure 4-11   Flowchart representation of a pencil–eraser combination claim.

removing thin rimed boxes that only act as a transient element. For example, a "wood pencil" usually has an "outside shape", and the outside shape box is merely serving as a transitory obvious element, then we can remove it from the flow chart (while still describing each element clearly in all the embodiments in the specification). Similarly we can remove "ring inside shape", "bottom portion of rubber", and "top portion of pencil".

You should also look at the action boxes, or process steps boxes where two or more arrows point to, and decide whether they can also be removed in order to broaden your claim, while at the same time enabling your claims. For example, perhaps rubber doesn't have to be made the same shape as the pencil outside shape. As long as the metal ring can tightly clamping onto the bottom portion of the rubber, it may be sufficient.

You should also look at each box to see if all the words are necessary. For example, is "wood pencil" a good description, what would happen if we simply use the word "pencil"? Is "Indian rubber" a good description, will the word "eraser" better serve your needs provided you capture in detail possible erasers include artist's Indian rubber, etc. Does the ring have to be metal, what if it is plastic or some other material? Is the word "ring" clear, what if it is not a ring but instead a hexagon or octagon shaped band? If it is just a band, would it be too broad? Should it be a rigid band which holds the eraser in place better during use? What are the prior arts out there which will prevent your simplification of the elements? With such an approach and awareness of prior arts at the time of your patent drafting, you may eventually arrive at the following simplified flow chart depicted in Figure 4-12.

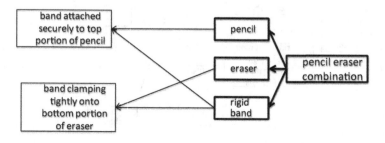

Figure 4-12   Simplified flow chart of pencil–eraser combination invention.

This description in Figure 4-12 compared with that in Figure 4-10 has more clarity. However, if one wants to avoid claims being treated as means plus function, you may want to further clarify the utility which enables "secure attachment" and "tightly clamping". We'll leave it to the reader's entertainment for such a task.

The last step is to modify your claim in correspondence with the simplified flowchart. As a result, you may eventually arrive at a claim substantially similar to the following:

Claim 1. A pencil eraser combination, comprising:
    a pencil;
    an eraser; and
    a rigid band attached securely to the top portion of said pencil
    and clamping tightly onto the bottom portion of said rubber.

4.9. How to Improve an Existing Portfolio Through Strategic Patent Prosecution

The above are detailed processes and methodologies to build a patent portfolio from scratch. As explained in Chapter 3, in addition to organically building a strong patent portfolio from scratch through your company's own inventions, one should also consider strategically acquiring high quality patents from external sources. The combination of both enables a company to build a strong patent portfolio quickly and cost effectively with powerful results.

In addition, one should monitor pending applications diligently and strategically improve them. Regardless whether you are improving internally filed pending applications, or improving the pending applications in the acquired patent portfolios, it is important to have a consistent strategy. By modifying pending cases via continuations, in combination with accelerating certain patent prosecution cases, one should be able to obtain a superbly strong patent portfolio. Figure 4-13 depicts a detailed flowchart to carry out this process.

Whether an existing patent portfolio is already strong or in a relatively weak position, to properly manage a patent portfolio, portfolio manager must continuously monitor market situation, future technology roadmaps,

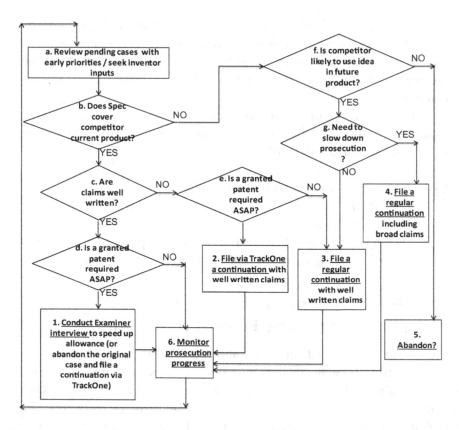

Figure 4-13   Flow chart on improving an existing pending application through patent family branching and optimization of the patent family.

and competitive landscape. In response to these changes, the portfolio manager needs to dynamically tweak core patent families so that the portfolio overall is in tune with the current market status. We'll walk through the entire process in details step by step in the following sections.

4.9.1. *Step (a): Review pending applications with early priority dates*

Step (a) recommends reviewing pending cases that have early priority dates. If the inventor or domain experts believe the idea has little prior art issue and is a relatively good idea that others likely will use either in the future or are already using today, then proceed to the next Step(b).

4.9.2. *Step (b): Determine whether specification covers target products*

Step (b) is where to ask the question whether the written description is sufficient to support the claims, especially if the specification cover competitor's current product. Proceed to Step (c) (to inspect the claim quality) if the answer is YES, and proceed to Step (f) (to look for other possible coverage) if the answer is NO.

4.9.3. *Step (c): Assess whether claims are well written*

Even if the claims potentially map onto competitor's existing product, this step addresses whether claims are well written. Sometimes claims are poorly written either choosing the wrong word, or too narrow or unclear such that it is subject to interpretation. This is the step to examine whether the existing claims written (or with minor modifications through supplemental amendment) will map well onto target competitor's product. A YES answer leads to Step (d) (to understand the urgency) and a NO answer leads to Step (e) (to evaluate timing requirement).

4.9.4. *Step (d): Determine whether desire patent issuance soon*

Step (d) inquires about whether you need a granted patent immediately. If you anticipate a near-future encounter with the target competitor, for example, via licensing or even litigation, you may need a granted patent as soon as possible. If the answer is YES, it leads to Action (1) (to try various paths speeding up prosecution process); while a NO answer leads to Action (6) (to proceed as a normal case).

4.9.5. *Step (e): Determine whether expedited patent issuance is required for non-optimized claims*

Step (e) also examines whether a granted patent is required ASAP when the claim is not well written. A YES answer leads to Action (2) (to expedite continuation case); while a NO answer leads to Action (3) (proceed with regular continuation cases).

4.9.6. *Step (f): Assess whether spec will likely map onto future target product*

Step (f) inquires about whether the pending application likely will read onto competitor's future product even though it doesn't read onto current competitor product. A YES answer leads to Step (g) (need to slow-down or not), while a NO answer leads to Action (5) (abandonment).

4.9.7. *Step (g): Decide whether need to slow-down patent prosecution*

Step (g) examines whether there is a need to actually slow-down the patent prosecution process. For example, if competitor's product is not out yet, or the targeted standard specification that patent is trying to read onto takes additional time to finalize, then you may want to slow-down the patent prosecution process to give yourself time to tweak the claim further to map better onto the competitor's product or the final standard specification. A YES answer leads to Action (4) (file continuation case with broad claims); while a NO answer leads to Action (3) (file a regular continuation case).

4.9.8. *Action (1): Speed up patent prosecution via all possible paths*

Action (1) requires you to try everything appropriate to speed up the prosecution process so that a granted patent can be obtained as soon as possible. Typical, tactics include conducting interviews with the examiner to understand his/her issues and convince him/her with well-prepared facts. This step is represented by underlined text to highlight the final objective which is to promptly obtain the desired patent claims. If the pending application is still early in the prosecution phase and an OA is 6 months or longer away, then you may want to abandon the current application and file the same application again as a continuation via USPTO's prioritized examination program TrackOne. TrackOne usually provides an OA in 6 months and a final determination whether to grant or not in a year. TrackOne requires an additional $4000~$4800 upfront fee to USPTO, but applicants often save money during the entire prosecution process because its faster prosecution process significantly reduces associated number of office actions ("OA"s) and needed answers to these OAs.

4.9.9. *Action (2): Accelerate prosecution via TrackOne*

Action (2) requires you to file a new continuation with well written claims via TrackOne. It is also represented by underlined text to illustrate the urgency of this action. Although a continuation itself is often speedy with an OA coming back as soon as in 3 to 6 months, TrackOne is a surer path to fast process.

4.9.10. *Action (3): Re-write claims to optimize*

Action (3) recommends re-write the claims to ensure they read onto current, if any, and future target products, and then file a regular continuation case.

4.9.11. *Action (4): Add broad claims*

Action (4) recommends writing good claims that potentially read onto future products. Meanwhile, add one or more broad claims to extend the prosecution length and delay possible near-future grant in order to gain some additional time to map better onto future products.

4.9.12. *Action (5): Decide whether to abandon the case*

Action (5) requires you to examine the case carefully and determine whether it is time to abandon the case. If the case does not read onto competitor's current products and is unlikely to read unto competitor's future products, then you may want to drop the case as soon as possible to prevent incurring additional cost on a case that will not contribute toward your portfolio quality.

4.9.13. *Action (6): Monitor prosecution progress carefully*

Action (6) is a required step for all active cases, i.e., continuously monitor your prosecution progress carefully and take appropriate actions in a timely manner.

4.10. Protect Your Company's Trade Secrets and Resist the Habit of Drafting Overly Broad Claims

To sum up, we recommend patent drafters keep in mind your company's objectives throughout the entire application drafting/prosecution process, and deliver the highest quality patent portfolio to your company that enables your company to successfully execute its business strategy. Specifically, this requires the patent drafter to have a good understanding about potential relevant prior arts, and not draft overly broad claims to protect your company's trade secrets.

Although we strongly advocate including all embodiments in the specification to block your competitor's potential workaround, one should be cognizant to avoid including trade secrets that are unlikely to be granted as a claim. This could inadvertently leak out your company's trade secrets that you don't want competitors to know.

We use Figure 4-14 to illustrate this point. The large elliptical area represents all the embodiments included in the specification. Patent

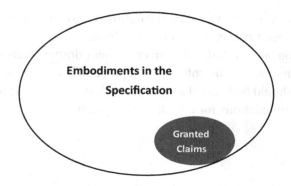

Figure 4-14   Over broad claims may inadvertently leak out trade secrets.

drafter should design the writing such that most of the disclosed embodiments have a reasonable chance of being covered in the final granted claims or the patent applicant doesn't mind donating the unclaimed portions to the public. Therefore, you do need to strategize whether examiners will likely reject your claims, for example, as being anticipated by other prior arts, or being too obvious in view of two of more combinations of prior arts. Typically applicants narrow their claims in order to overcome the prior arts to get some claims granted. As a result, the granted claims will cover a smaller subset of the original embodiments. We use a dark elliptical area to represent the final claimed protection. As can be seen, it is much smaller than the original elliptical area. It is important that the original elliptical area outside the dark elliptical area does not include information falling within the upper left quadrant in Figure 3-6. This quadrant corresponds to inventions that are unlikely to be granted by USPTO or SIPO but are likely be used significantly by others in 2~20 years. These, according to recommendations in Chapter 3, should be treated as "Restrictive Trade Secrets", i.e. only be accessed by limited number of employees on "need to know" basis.

One might argue that if there are prior arts, someone has already thought of it or patented it previously. However, if one or more of the combined prior arts are published articles or conference proceedings, it is possible that your competitors haven't yet figured out the optimum solution as you did. Therefore, unless you are likely to obtain USPTO/SIPO's allowance for the claim, you should carefully consider whether to include in the initial specification or the original claim.

In addition, we strongly recommend patent drafter to also follow the suggestions laid out for Inventors in Chapter 3. Then, your drafted patent applications should be in good alignment with the business strategy which is one of the foundations for a high quality patent.

Chapter 5

For Anyone Interested
in a Detailed Discussion
of Software Patents

This book is not intended to cover all the patent basics. Instead, it is intended to share best practices and lessons learned to help you avoid or minimize potential pitfalls. As a result, we want to dedicate a chapter to key software patent-related issues due to the recent US court rulings and the overwhelming interest in this subject. This is a global issue which all main economic entities face.

The most crucial software patent issues in all jurisdictions may be boiled down to two topics: (1) subject matter eligibility; and (2) scope determination. We'll focus, in this Chapter 5, on these two software patent issues in US and China, and their differences.

As discussed in Chapter 2, software patents are subject to increased scrutiny in United States after the US Supreme Court (USSC) issued its opinion on *Alice v. CLS Bank* in June 2014. China has always been skeptical of software patents and continues to enforce strict requirements regarding software patents. For example, several other jurisdictions, such as US and Europe, provide patent protections for computer readable media-related software inventions. China, on the other hand, has much greater restrictions on patentable software inventions and does not allow computer media related software patents. However, such increased challenge to software patents in US and China doesn't mean you should not file software patents. In fact, the best approach is to thoroughly understand potential issues when filing software patents and establish a strategy to overcome these issues prior to filing.

For high tech companies, such strategy is particularly important because many hardware patents are narrow and specific which often renders them easy to work around and thus hard to enforce. On the other hand, software patents can be broader and thus may provide more value to the patent owners. In addition, as software plays ever greater roles in today's modern technology world, many breakthrough innovations rely on software invention and implementation, or solutions that are software in nature without substantial hardware variations. In fact if one examines the patent claims carefully, many inventions could be considered software patents. As a result, there is a real need to understand how to write software patents properly both for China State Intellectual Property Office (SIPO) and US Patent and Trademark Office (USPTO.)

5.1. Software Patents Prior to *"Alice"*

5.1.1. *Definition of software patents*

First of all, what is a software patent? There isn't a universally accepted definition for software patents. The following are a few definitions by various sources:

— Foundation for a Free Information Infrastructure (FFII): Software patent means "patent on any performance of a computer realized by means of a computer program".
— Dictionary.com/Legal: Soft patent means "a patent intended to prevent others from using some programming technique".
— IPWatchdog.com: Software patent is "any patent that covers a computer implemented process".

Even before US Supreme Court's ruling on *Alice* v. *CLS Bank*, due to the fact that software patents are inherently conceptual, there were great uncertainties associated with them. On September 3, 2013, Washington Post published an article stating that "the patent troll crisis is really a software patent crisis". It was deemed four times more likely to be in litigations than chemical patents. The common opinion of software patents was that they have unclear property rights, with prevalence of low quality and overly broad claims. Several Federal Court judges disliked software patents strongly, some individuals started calling for doing away with software patents or limit the term to 5 years.

It is our sincere believe that regardless of how software inventions are defined, many truly involve creative and innovative ideas. In fact, some without doubt are even more innovative than inventions from other technical fields. The issue is how to provide legal protection commensurate with the specific characteristics of software inventions. In other words, the question should be how to protect software inventions via appropriate mechanisms adopted by patent law, rather than simply rejecting or excluding software ideas from patenting. Some of these potential mechanisms include US congress changing its current patent law or creating new IP laws to address software patent issue at its source, such as:

(i)   setting a higher standard for obviousness in the easily predicable technology fields;

(ii) providing avenue to ascertain and assure a commensurate scope of the so-called functional limitation claims for software inventions through modifying the current 35 U.S.C. Section §112(f); or

(iii) creating a new provision specific for software patents by redefining current dichotomy of structure/functionality feature.

It is our opinion that putting too much resources and emphasis on regulating already granted software patents in an attempt to resolve current patent system problem may not yield the hoped for results. This type of *ex post* regulation is typically not helpful towards resolving the root cause of the issues.

5.1.2. *How was software patent drafted just prior to "Alice"*

It is noteworthy to observe that China and US are not alone in treating software patents with a critical view. On February 19, 2016, India's Patent Office issued a revised guideline on patenting software inventions.

Compared to the liberal approaches taken by the previous guideline in India, the new guideline greatly limits the scope of software patents.

However, China, India, and US IP laws are not unique in their critical treatment of software patents; other jurisdictions also attempted to address this critical issue. For example:

— New Zealand in May of 2013 announced that software patents are not patentable and recommend protection under copyright which has a long period of protection of author's life time plus 70 years. The issue is that although this approach is more economical, it only protects the expression not the idea itself. Therefore, people can easily work around the copyright by rewriting the code.

Table 5-1 is a summary of the pros and cons of copyright versus patent.

Table 5-1   Comparing pros and cons of copyright versus patent.

	Copyright	**Patent**
Protection	Expression	Idea
Protection starts	Immediate	After Filing
Protection period	Author Life +50 Yr	Filing Date +20 Yr
Cover range	WW	Applied Country
Cost	Minimal	US $10K–30K+

— European Patent Convention (EPC)'s policy is that: computer program, methods of doing business *per se* is not patentable and must have a technical character in order to be patentable. To establish such technical character, EPC adopts the following test:
   (a) Inventions that use computer programs to provide a business process, e.g. an internet auction system — does not cause a "further technical effect" which goes beyond the inherent technical interactions between hardware and software, then it is not patentable.
   (b) However, if the invention improves signal strengths between mobile phone, even if by modifications to the phone software, is a technical program and thus is patentable.

The development of US software invention protection has undergone many twists and turns in the past half century. A couple of tests have been used and discarded in the US software invention protection history. For example, US typical practice prior to *Alice* had been: software patents are patentable provided it passes the *Bilski* Machine-or-transformation (MOT) test:[1]

(a) Requires a process to be tied to a particular machine or apparatus; or

(b) Transforms a particular article into a different state of thing.

For clarity, the US Supreme Court held that the MOT test is not the sole test for determining the patent eligibility of a process, but rather "a useful and important clue, an investigative tool, for determining whether some claimed inventions are processes under §101."[2]

IPWatchdog.com founder Gene Quinn recommended[3] comprehensive patent application drafting methodologies to meet *Bilski* test, such as adding "computer-implemented" to the preamble, "using/by/on a processor" and "on/within/in a memory" and other machine limitations in the body of the claim. Meanwhile, ensure the following:

(a) Describe the overall computer system architecture;

(b) Prepare a single flowchart that depicts the overall software functionality;

(c) Prepare a series of flowcharts that show with painstaking detail the various routines and subroutines that together connect to create and deliver the complete functionality of the computer system as enabled by the software.

China's typical practice for software patent drafting relies heavily on functional limitation, which will be addressed in the following sections.

---

[1] In re Bilski, 545 F.3d 943, 88 U.S.P.Q2d 1385 (Fed. Cir. 2008).

[2] Bilski v. Kappos, 561 (6/28/2010) by US Supreme Court.

[3] "A Guide to Patenting Software: Getting Started", Gene Quinn, available at http://www.ipwatchdog.com/2013/02/16/a-guide-to-patenting-software-getting-started/id=35629/.

5.2. Software Patent's "Post *Alice*" Fate — Subject Matter Patent Eligibility Issue

Chapter 4 and Section 5.1 discussed the significant impact US Supreme Court's ruling of "*Alice v. CLS Bank*" had on subsequent PTO and Court decisions. Some think software patents are no longer worth pursuing due to their beliefs that most software patents will either be rejected by USPTO, or invalidated later by USPTO's PTAB or in court based on subject matter ineligible for patenting under 35 U.S.C. Section §101 (the "§101 Issue"). However, a detailed analysis of USPTO's final rejection statistics indicates that certain types of software patents continue to receive low rejection rate post-*Alice*.

Table 5-2 is a summary of the final §101 Rejection percentage before and after *Alice*. For business method-related art units, such as 3600,

Table 5-2   Statistics of USPTO §101 rejection rates before and after Alice[4]

USPTO Art Unit Number Technology Category	§101 Rejection Rate Before Alice (%)	§101 Rejection Rate After Alice (%)
1600 Biotechnology and Organic Chemistry	8.1	16.7
2100 Computer Architecture and Software	21.8	16.2
2400 Networking and Security	15.3	11.3
2600 Communications	10.0	7.7
3600 Trans., Constr. Biz. Methods:		
— Business Crypto	38.0	56.7
— Business Processing & Modeling	44.0	96.4
— Cost/Price, Reservations	37.6	72.8
— E Shopping	37.9	97.2
— Health Care, Insurance	34.0	83.5

(*Continued*)

---

[4]Robert R. Sachs, "#Alicestorm in June: a Deeper Dive into Court Trends, and New Data on Alice Inside the USPTO", August 10, 2015, available at http://cpip.gmu.edu/2015/08/10/alicestorm-in-june-a-deeper-dive-into-court-trends-and-new-data-on-alice-inside-the-uspto/.

Table 5-2   (*Continued*)

USPTO Art Unit Number Technology Category	§101 Rejection Rate Before Alice (%)	§101 Rejection Rate After Alice (%)
— Incentive Programs	36.2	87.4
— Incentive, Oper., Eshopping-, Insur., Retail	44.4	95.0
— Operations Research	46.4	95.6
— POS, Inventory, Accounting	23.2	77.7
3700 Mechanical Eng. & Manuf.		
— Amusement & Education	16.5	30.1

the final rejection rates have indeed dramatically increased post *Alice*. Unexpectedly, rejection rates for some hardware-related art units such as 3700 Mechanical Engineering & Manufacturing have increased as well. Therefore, subject matter eligibility issue applies to both software and hardware patents you should follow the patent drafting strategy proposed in Chapter 4 and address the §101 patent eligibility issue early on in your patent strategy and application drafting.

Evidently, USPTO §101 rejection rate post *Alice* for Art Unit 3600 (Transportation, Construction, Business Methods) has indeed skyrocketed, some to as high as 95+%. However, not all software patents face such "penalties". Art Units 2100 (Computer Architecture and Software), 2400 (Networking and Security) have both seen a stable a reduced §101 rejection rate after *Alice*, at below 20%. Therefore, you should obtain a better ROI for applications falling in Art Units 2100 and 2400 compared to those in Art Unit 3600. In addition, you should draft your patent applications in accordance with the strategies laid out in Chapter 4 and prepare well ahead before filing at USPTO in order to overcome §101 rejection issues.

However, overcoming §101 rejection is only one of the first steps toward obtaining a useful software patents. It is important to have a holistic strategy in your software patent drafting, filing, prosecution, and global portfolio augmentation. Therefore, it is critical to have a detail look at and gain a solid understanding of typical software patent structures.

5.3. Functional Limitations Widely Used for Software Patents

Software inventions are inherently difficult to describe and more abstract than hardware ideas. As a result, patent drafters frequently need to resort to describing in the claim what the software does (i.e. its function) which is considered functional limitation rather than what it is (i.e. its structure). This kind of limitation is usually viewed as functional limitation.

In 1946, in the *Halliburton* case, the Supreme Court held that "[t]he language of the claim thus describes this most crucial element in the 'new' combination in terms of what it will do rather than in terms of its own physical characteristics or its arrangement in the new combination apparatus. We have held that a claim with such a description of a product is invalid as a violation of [the indefiniteness requirement]" *Halliburton v. Walker*, 329 U.S. 1 (1946). After *Halliburton*, congress enacted section §112 Paragraph (f), originally paragraph three to allow functional limitation but narrowed the scope of the functional limitation to the corresponding structure described in the specification.

Although functional limitation is permitted by the US statute, its limited scope discourages prevailing adoption. Applicants have been reluctant to use the means-plus-function (MPF) language in claims. Instead, they tend to use functional language not strictly conforming to the MPF format in order to circumvent the application of 35 U.S.C. §112(f). Their rationale is that the use of general functional limitation is permitted by case law as long as the claim is not regarded as pure functional limitation. This is particularly relevant in the software patent area because software inventions are difficult to establish the so-called structural limitation.[5]

---

[5]Although the US Court of Appeals for Federal Circuit (CAFC)'s case law acknowledged that algorithms can be viewed as structure in software implemented patent as those physical structures in traditional mechanical and electronic technology fields, a generalized algorithm is readily deemed as function. This treatment is very different from that for the traditional mechanical and electronic technology field in which the generic term is usually still deemed as structure term. Therefore, applicants are recommended to put specific algorithms into independent claim. Even when they are doing so, the claim still faces the risk of being interpreted as functional limitation since whether an algorithm is a function

The *Manual of Patent Examining Procedure (MPEP)* also states that "[f]unctional language may also be employed to limit the claims without using the means-plus-function format. Unlike means-plus-function claim language that applies only to purely functional limitations, functional claiming often involves the recitation of some structure followed by its function". For example, in *In re Schreiber*, the claims were directed to conical spouts (the structure) that "allow[ed] several kernels of popped popcorn to pass through at the same time" (the function). As noted by the court in *Schreiber*, "[a] patent applicant is free to recite features of an apparatus either structurally or functionally" (quoting *MPEP 2173.05(g) Functional Limitations* [R-07.2015], internal citation omitted). In addition, the Federal Circuit, in *Microprocessor Enhancement Corp. v. Texas Instruments Inc.*, explained, "[a]s this court recently stated, apparatus claims are not necessarily indefinite for using functional language . . . Functional language may also be employed to limit the claims without using the means-plus-function format."(Internal citation omitted). Such tendency of using non-means functional limitation claim is also bolstered by some empirical investigations. A statistical observation by professor Dennis Crouch indicated that the use of traditional MPF language in patent claims has dropped dramatically since early 1990's and continues to drop. At the same time, usage of functional limitation by using phrases such as "configured to/for" language or other verbiage other than "means", such as "circuit for" or "instructions for" exhibited a rise since 1990s which matched the decline in MPF usage.[6]

Over the past two decades, US Federal Circuits, and Court of Appeals for the Federal Circuit relaxed their restrictions on the functional claim construction. If one doesn't use MPF language in the claim, it is typically interpreted broader than the claim recited structure. For example,

---

or structure in the MPF sense strongly depend on the comparison of the abstraction degree between two algorithms which comparison does not exist since the claim usually only includes a general algorithm. To some extent one can consider the structure/function dichotomy as a concept of relativity and they can be transferred to each other based on the degree of specificity versus abstraction. As a result, an algorithm put into an independent claim is usually deemed as function limitation even though it is pretty detailed.

[6]Dennis Crouch, "Functional Claim Language in Issued Patents", http://patentlyo.com/patent/2014/01/functional-language-patents.html.

in *re Schreiber, 128 F.3d 1473, 1478 (Fed. Cir. 1997)*, the court noted "a patent applicant is free to recite features of an apparatus either structurally or functionally"; in *Watts v. XL Sys, Inc. 232 F3d. 877, 880-881 (Fed. Cir. 2000)*, the Court stated "means-plus-function claiming applies only to purely functional limitations that do not provide the structure that performs the recited function". Therefore, there has been a sharp increase in functional claims for software patents. In fact, many patent drafters use template structures and corresponding languages which adopt such functional approach.

°5.3.1. *Caution about functional limitations — Williamson v. Citrix*

As discussed above, applicants search for and gravitate toward an approach which enables them to avoid invoking §112(f) so that they can enjoy both the advantages of functional limitations and yet not be restricted to the scope limitation imposed by §112(f). However, such tactic has been struck down in several CAFC's cases. For example, in the court decision for *LG Electronics*, it utilized "a claim term that does not use 'means' will trigger the rebuttable presumption that §112 ¶ 6 does not apply."*Lighting World, Inc. v. Birchwood Lighting, Inc.,* 382 F.3d 1354, 1358 (Fed. Cir. 2004) (quoting *CCS Fitness, Inc. v. Brunswick Corp.,* 288 F.3d 1359, 1369 (Fed. Cir. 2002)). Such presumption can be rebutted "by showing that the claim element recite[s] a function without reciting sufficient structure for performing that function" *Watts v. XL Sys.,* 232 F.3d 877, 880 (Fed. Cir. 2000) (citing *Rodime PLC v. Seagate Tech., Inc.,* 174 F.3d 1294, 1302 (Fed. Cir. 1999)). However, the presumption "is a strong one that is not readily overcome." *Lighting World, Inc.,* 382 F.3d at 1358 (quoting *LG Electronics, Inc. v. Bizcom Electronics, Inc.,* 453 F.3d 1364, 1372 (Fed. Cir. 2006)). Notwithstanding the above, an applicant can still enjoy the advantage of the presumption that §112(f) does not apply and the presumption is a strong one that is not readily overcome. The great difficulty in overcoming such presumption is patently evident in *Flo Healthcare Solutions, LLC v. Kappos,* 697 F.3d 1367, 1374 (Fed. Cir. 2012), in which the court stated "[w]hen the claim drafter has not signaled his intent to invoke §112(f) by using the term 'means,' we are unwilling to apply that provision without a showing that the limitation essentially is devoid of anything that can be construed as structure".

However, in the recent *Williamson v. Citrix Online, LLC,* 792 F.3d 1339 (2015), CAFC (*en banc*) overruled the strong presumption declared in a series of past cases, such as *Lighting World* and *Flo Healthcare Solutions,* and restored the test to prior-*Lighting World* standard *which is* whether the words of a patent's claim are understood by persons of ordinary skill in the art ("POS") to have a sufficiently definite meaning as the name for a structure. *Greenberg,* 91 F.3d at 1583.

For software patent drafters who have been relying on claims that generally recite a term which can be understood by persons of ordinary skill in the art to have a sufficiently definite meaning as the name for structure, such as "processor", "circuit", "circuitry" or "computer" that performs a function, yet not being viewed as MPF at the CAFC level,[7] will have to change their patent drafting strategy. In addition, even if MPF is not applied to a claim which they drafted using functional limitation approach, there still exist other challenges that they must be prepared to deal with, such as general indefiniteness issue,[8] *Halliburton* challenge,[9]

---

[7]PTAB in a few previous cases such as, Ex parte Erol (Appeal 2011-001143, US app. s/n 11/461,109), Ex parte Lakkala (Appeal 2011-001526, US app. s/n 10/949,568), and Ex parte Smith (Appeal 2012-007631, US app. s/n 12/579,383), has interpreted the "processor" as "means" and accordingly invoked §112(f), but in a later decided case, Ex Parte Cutlip (Appeal 2011-0011658, US app. s/n 11/345,010), PTAB panel reversed the Examiner's rejection saying that "the claimed processor and memory very clearly refer to structural elements".

[8]The general indefiniteness issue is used here to differentiate it from the cases where indefiniteness stems from invoking §112(f) to interpret the claim with no structure or inadequate structure being disclosed in the description.

[9]In the two exemplary cases, Ex Parte Miyazaki, 89 USPQ2d 1207 (BPAI 2008) (Precedential) and *Ex parte Rodriguez, 08-0693* (BPAI 2009) (Precedential), BPAI rejected some of the applicant's claims under 35 U.S.C. §112, first paragraph, for lack of an enabling disclosure commensurate with the scope of the claim according to the Halliburton rule. It is uncertain whether CAFC would affirm this rejection ground if the two cases were appealed in front of CAFC, but at least before USPTO the rejection ground is still available if §112(f) is not invoked (e.g., in the situation of not using "means" format) and the claim limitation at issue is viewed as pure functional limitation. Although the

general enablement or written description issue,[10] and §102/§103. Therefore, we recommend a structured approach to combat these issues systematically.

5.3.2. *Recommended approach*

Ever since *"Alice"*, there is a lack of direct guidance on exactly how to write software patents to increase its grant probability by USPTO. Although PTO promulgated a series of guidelines after *"Alice"*, it seems that the situation and standard has not become clearer.

More voices have been heard about adopting MPF perhaps due to their beliefs that MPF is more likely to overcome §101 rejections based on *In re Alappat*, 33 F.3d 1526 (Fed. Cir. 1994). However, the problem is that MPF is often too narrow which may render a patent useless during litigation.

In absence of a consensus on the most optimum recommendations for software patents, we recommend the following approach.

— If your claim is for a product which has some kind of structure, we recommend drafters develop your claims around these structures regardless of whether the product is hardware or software;

— However, if it is impossible to find a feature or structure for the product, then you should use functional limitations in the claim, but diligently avoid the claim being interpreted as MPF claim;

— When all others fail, you may write your claim as MPF;

---

functional limitation followed by "processor for" or "processor configured to" is usually not viewed as pure functional limitation (otherwise §112(f) will be invoked), and thus does not meet the *Halliburton* requirement, PTO may still apply the Halliburton rule to some other terms which are in dispute of whether it has a sufficiently definite meaning as the name for a structure.

[10]The general enablement or written description issue is used here to mean adopting general enablement or written description test and analysis to determine whether the claims at issue meet the enablement or written description requirements, which is different from applying the "Halliburton rule" to directly conclude the violation of enablement requirement of §112(a) without performing detailed analysis.

— In all above scenarios, make sure to include at least one set of MPF as a "safe guard"; and
— In all above scenarios, make sure that the specification is written for the worst case scenario of MPF claim interpretation.

To assist patent drafters strategize whether to use MPF type of functional limitation, and when to use non-MPF type of functional limitation, the following is a "deep dive" into functional limitation laws specified by Chinese law versus US law, with practical recommendation at each step. By utilizing MPF claims, you may encourage the examiner to lean toward choosing the Step 2.0 "streamlined eligibility process" and bypass Step 2A and 2B. Even if the examiner gets to Step 2A and 2B, by including detailed technical embodiments into the claim through MPF interpretation, the claim might be viewed to provide "significantly more" and thus pass Step 2B.

5.4. Differences Between China and US in Functional Limitations for Patent Prosecution and Litigation

Regardless of whether it is in China or US, functional limitation is a difficult and complicated problem, especially for software or computer implemented inventions.

5.4.1. *Status of functional limitations in US and China*

In US, MPF only represents a very small portion of functional limitation because most functional limitations are not appropriate for MPF and in fact are not interpreted as MPF either before USPTO or in courts.

Compared with MPF which has relatively more mature analysis framework and more complete and systematic development and therefore can provide relatively clear predictive outcome, the outcomes of non-MPF types of functional limitations are largely uncertain. This is due to the ambiguity of what standards or tests should be applied to these types of functional limitations, and how to apply various standards or tests to these types of functional limitations. This is especially true for software implemented inventions. Even though one can apply the traditional i) Enablement, ii) Written Description, and iii) Indefiniteness tests to these non-MPF types of functional limitations, some of the principals are very abstract when dealing with new technological development. For example for software implemented invention, there is no available consistent, predictable guidance or analysis model to help patent drafters.

In China, for patent substantive examination process there is a separate chapter of guideline (GPE) (Chapter 9, Part II of GPE) for patent examination by China's State Intellectual Property Office ("SIPO") with a special focus on computer or software implemented inventions. It appears to have solved the functional limitation issue for computer or software implemented inventions. However, the simplistic, inflexible requirements deployed by the guideline could not cover or balance various scenarios encountered by most patent drafters. More importantly, these types of guidance and requirements to the claims and description for the software implemented invention during prosecution have not obtained the support of the Chinese court. The Chinese court has its own independent interpretation principle for functional limitation which is different from that of SIPO.[11] The court's interpretation principle for functional limitation is incomplete and non-systematic. Although the newly promulgated Article 8 of the *"Interpretation (II) of the Supreme People's' Court ("SPC") on Several Issues concerning the Application of Law in the Trial of Patent Infringement Dispute Cases"* (*Interpretation (II) of the SPC*) provides more detailed guidance and supplement on how to apply Article 4 of "Interpretation (I) of the Supreme People's Court on Several Issues concerning the Application of Law in the Trial of Patent Infringement Dispute Cases" (hereafter referred as to *Interpretation (I) of SPC*, promulgated

---

[11] According to §3.2.1 of chapter 2, Part II of GPE, the functional limitation in a claim should be interpreted as to cover all the implementations which are capable of implementing the claimed function. However, according to the "Interpretation (I) of the SPC" and "Interpretation (II) of the SPC", the functional limitation in a claim should be interpreted as to only cover the specific embodiments implemented the functional limitation described in the specification and the equivalents thereof.

December 28, 2009 and went into effect on January 1, 2010), it still lacks systematic approach and has no corresponding detailed matching rules. These have created great uncertainty, and thus are not enabling to patent drafters/applicants in predicting the corresponding outcomes.

5.5. What is Functional Limitation?

5.5.1. *Overview of US law and Chinese law*

According to US case law, a claim term is functional when it recites a feature "by what it does rather than by what it is" (e.g. as advanced by its specific structure or specific ingredients). In 1946, in the *Halliburton* case, the US Supreme Court viewed certain limitation as functional limitation by holding that "[t]he language of the claim thus describes this most crucial element in the 'new' combination in terms of what it will do rather than in terms of its own physical characteristics or its arrangement in the new combination apparatus."[12]

5.5.2. *Chinese law*

In China, according to Article 4 of the *Interpretation (I) of Supreme People's Court*, for technical features expressed by function or effect in the claims, the people's court should combine specific embodiments of the functions or effects and their equivalent embodiments described in the specification and accompanying drawings to determine the content of the technical features.

Chinese Patent Examination Guidelines state: product claims typically should avoid the usage of functions or effects of features to define the invention. Only when structural features cannot be defined in a technical feature, or the technical characteristics defined by structural feature is not as appropriate as using functional or effect as limitation and such function or effect can be validated directly and affirmatively using the experiment or operations described in the specification or those commonly used by the ordinary skilled in the art, then using functional

---

[12]Halliburton v. Walker, 329 U.S. 1 (1946).

characteristics or effect characteristics as limitation for the invention is permissible.[13]

Patent Examination Guidelines Part II, Chapter II, Section 3.2.1 further states: the functional limitation in a claim should be interpreted as to cover all the implementations which are capable of implementing the claimed function. Article 8 of the "Interpretation (II) of the SPC" states that "functional features mean the technical feature which is defined not by using the structures, components, procedures, conditions or the mutual relationship thereof, among others; but is defined by using their functions or effects in the invention, with the exception of when the ordinary skilled in the art can directly and explicitly recognize the specific implementation for achieving the aforesaid functions or effects only by reading the claims. Where, in comparison with the indispensable technical features for achieving the functions or effects as mentioned in the preceding paragraph as described in the specifications and the attached drawings, the corresponding technical features of the accused infringing technical solution perform the same functions in substantially same way to achieve the same results as the indispensable technical features, with which an ordinary skilled in the art is able to associate without any creative activity when the accused infringing act occurs, the people's' court shall determine the corresponding technical features are identical with or equivalent to the functional features."

5.5.3. The Differences

Chinese *Interpretation (I) of the SPC* differs from United States' MPF-approach as mainly defined by the 35 U.S.C. §112(f) as well as case law cited in the following discussions. We'll compare them and point out the differences.

(1) The *Interpretation (I) of the SPC* is similar to the second half phrase of §112(f), but without the condition of means/step plus function structure (i.e. requirements of means plus on functions) set forth in the first half phrase of §112(f).

---

[13] See §3.2.1 of Part II, Chapter II of GFPE.

(2) The *Interpretation (I) of the SPC* is viewed to apply to all types of functional limitations, because it does not clearly specify that this Article 4 is only applicable to combination elements. According to the general expression of this provision itself, it should also be applicable to single means claims, part of the structure plus function claims, and even pure functional limitation claims.

(3) So far for Chinese Patent Guideline, there isn't anything similar to §112(f) with supplementary and matching institutional support, such as USPTO's applicable guideline for §112(f) and a wealth of case law. Therefore, China interpretation likely will cause greater dispute when applied.

(4) The *Interpretation (I) of the SPC* covers both functional limitation and effect limitation, i.e. it does not differentiate the functional limitation from effect limitation. This does not address cases where function and effect is different.

(5) The interpretation approach of the functional limitation is different in the course of the prosecution examination including the post-grant examination proceeding and in the course of the litigation in court for both China and US.

(6) §112(f) clearly states that the claims only cover structures described in the specification and their equivalents, while China interpretation simply states that the contents of the technical feature is determined by using the specific embodiments described in the description and the drawings and their equivalents instead of clearly stating that the scope of the functional limitation only covers the structures described in the specification and their equivalents.

Although Article 8 of the *Interpretation (II) of the SPC* provides some detailed direction of the application and interpretation of the functional limitation, it nevertheless differs from USPTO's §112(f) in the following aspects:

(1) Similar to above, it also lacks the first half phrase condition set forth in §112(f), i.e. the specific structural requirement on whether to invoke the means/step plus function style. Instead, it is applicable to

all types of functional limitation, e.g. single means, part of the structure plus function, and even the pure functional limitation.

(2) Only the claim itself can be used to interpret whether the limitation at issue is a functional limitation as required by the *Interpretation (II) of the SPC*, which is completely different from §112(f). In §112(f), similar to the conventional claim construction, all the resources including claims, specification, file wrapper, and even the external evidences could be used to interpret the terms in the claim and then to determine whether the term amounts to "means" and whether the limitation following the "means" can be viewed as functional instead of structural limitation.

(3) It is unclear whether the exception of functional limitation claim which states "except when the ordinary skilled in the art can directly and explicitly determine the specific implementation for achieving the aforesaid functions or effects only by reading the claims" is directed only to the particular term before the modified functional limitation or only to the functional limitation following the term, or either one of them. If it is directed to the functional limitation portion that means the claim should not be viewed as functional limitation claim as long as the functional limitation is prior art feature which can be implemented by the ordinary skilled in the art.

5.6. Case Studies

There are several recent seminal cases in China addressing the functional limitation issue, e.g. *Hu Beier v. Communication Device Corp. of Changzhou* (Suzhimin Zhongzi 0139/2011) by Jiangsu High people's Court, and *Nokia v. Huaqin* (Hugaominsan (Zhi) Zhongzi 96/2013) by Shanghai High People's Court. They illustrate all the differences outlined above. It should be noted that although these cases have no binding effect or legal force even in the same jurisdiction district due to Chinese's civil law system, they still have significant reference value to other courts in the same or other jurisdictions since these cases are final judgment of high people's court from relatively more influential regions.

5.6.1. *Rulings for the seminal case:*
HuBeier v. Communication Device Corp.
of Changzhou (Suzhimin Zhongzi #0139/2011)

This case provided the test on how to determine whether a claim limitation is a structural limitation or functional limitation. The court ruled that:

(1) if a claim limitation does not use the structural limitation to limit the product or apparatus, such as the specific structure, shape and other mechanical composition as well as the associated connection relationship, position relation, coordination relationship among the components, etc;

(2) if the claim uses technical terms which are uncommon or unknown to the skilled in the art in the related technical field, and only describes to the skilled in the art the function or final achieved result of the feature; and

(3) does not expressly or impliedly limit in an exhaustive manner such feature to one or more specific structures in the specification,

Then, the claim limitation is considered as functional limitation or functional feature.

As can be seen from the above test, it creates ambiguity in interpretation. For example, it is unclear whether step S(3) is directed to the technical term itself corresponding to the "means" part of the US MPF style claim or to the functional limitation modifying the means corresponding to the "function" part of the US MPF style claim. Furthermore, it is unclear how to meet the requirement of "limiting *in an exhaustive manner* such feature to one or more specific structures" in the specification for step S(3). In practice, it is usually impossible to exhaustively list all the specific structures.

According to the test in the *Hu Beier* case, if a technical term is a common or well-known term to the skilled in the art, regardless of whether the well-known aspect is software, hardware, non-structure or structure, the technical term should **not** be viewed as functional limitation, which is less strict than the counterpart test of MPF application in US.

As for US MPF, according to the *Williamson v. Citrix* (Fed. Cir. 2015, *en banc*), only if the terms are understood by persons of ordinary skill in the art to have a sufficiently definite meaning as the name for the structure, then the claim might not be viewed as functional limitation. Meanwhile, as discussed above, if step S(3) is directed to the function part, and if the specification limits the functional or result feature to one or more specific structure in an exhaustive manner, then the claim is still not viewed as functional limitation claim even if the technical term is not well known. This interpretation seems to yield a strange outcome because it causes conflicts between the determination of whether a claimed feature is a functional limitation claim and the determination of the scope of the functional limitation.

In addition, the case provided how to determine the scope of the functional limitation when the claimed feature is deemed as functional limitation or feature. The case ruled that the scope of the claimed functional limitation only covers the essential technical features as a whole that perform the functional limitation in each of the embodiments. More specifically, those features that have no direct and necessary connection with the performance of the functional limitation should be excluded. The essential technical features that performed the claimed functional limitation from each of the multiples embodiments should be considered as the alternative content or structure for the claimed functional limitation. This general approach of ascertaining the scope of the functional limitation is similar to that in US. However, it is not clear from this case whether there is a difference between a disclosure without structure limitation and a disclosure with inadequate structure, and whether the corresponding results differ between these two scenarios. Furthermore, the case didn't address the equivalent issue in the literal interpretation phase, but instead considered the equivalent issue in the infringement determination phase. Therefore, it seems that the case adopted a different analysis framework by taking a distinct position on the structure equivalent from US MPF law which differentiates statutory structure equivalent from the judicial equivalent doctrine. In other words, this case treated the structure equivalent under the general equivalent doctrine and didn't differentiate between lacking structure disclosure versus inadequate structure disclosure. Such treatment of the two equivalent issues is usually governed by Article 4 of the *Interpretation (I) of SPC* which differentiates the two equivalent issues.

Moreover, the case established a three-step test for determining whether the accused product maps to a functional limitation:

(1) determining whether the accused product has performed the claimed functional limitation or result;
(2) determining the specific implementations of the accused product that performed the same functional limitation or result; and
(3) comparing the implementations of the accused product which performed the identified claimed functional limitation with the implementations, including the essential technical features, that performed the claimed functional limitation in the patent to see if they are the same or equivalent. If the answer is a "yes", then the infringement is established.

In addition, the case explained that multiple essential technical features of each embodiment that performs the claimed functional limitation should be treated as a whole when performing the equivalent analysis instead of comparing essential feature individually. This is the same approach as the structure equivalency analysis of US MPF law. In *Odetics*, the US Federal Circuit stated that "[t]he individual components, if any, of an overall structure that corresponds to the claimed function are not claim limitations. Rather, the claim limitation is the overall structure corresponding to the claimed function."[14]

In addition, the equivalency analysis of the *Hu Beier* case only takes the function and approach into account without looking at the results of implementations between the claimed functional limitation and the accused product. This is slightly different from the structure equivalency analysis of US MPF law which adopts a function-way-result test. The US test usually takes the position that once identity of function is established,

---

[14]Odetics, Inc. v. Stroage Technology Corporation, 185 F.3d 1259, 51 USPQ2d 1225 (Fed. Cir. 1999).

the test for infringement is whether the structure of the accused device performs in substantially the same way/approach to achieve substantially the same result as the structure disclosed in the patent at issue.[15]

5.6.2. *Nokia v. Huaqin (Hugaominsan (Zhi)* *Zhongzi 96/2013)*

In 2011, *Nokia* brought a lawsuit against *Huaqin* alleging Huaqin's products infringed its 8 telecom patents and demanding 90 million RMB Yuan for damages. *Huaqin* then initiated invalidation proceedings twice before China Patent Reexamination Board (PRB) against the subject Chinese patent 200480001590.4 titled "Selecting a data transfer method", which accounted for 20 million RMB Yuan among the total damage amount. The said patent was partially invalidated by the PRB in the first invalidation proceeding, which was affirmed by Beijing High People's Court. The said patent was invalided in its entirety by the PRB in the 2nd invalidation proceeding. Despite the invalidation of said patent, Shanghai High People's Court proceeded to hear the infringement case without dismissing the case due to the invalidation of the claims.

This case provided the test on how to determine whether a claim limitation is a structural limitation or functional limitation. The court ruled that:

> "Functional features mean technical features which define the structures, components, procedures, conditions or the mutual relationship thereof, among others, through their functions or effects in the invention, except when the ordinary skilled in the art can directly and explicitly determine the specific implementation for achieving the aforesaid functions or effects only by reading the claims."

In this case, the court ruled that functional technical feature refers to the technical feature defined not by using the structure, part, component of a product, or the mutual relationship thereof, or the steps and conditions

---

[15]Minks v. Polaris Industries, Inc., 546 F.3d 1364, 1378-79 (Fed. Cir. 2008).

of a method, or the mutual relationship thereof, but is defined by using their functions, effects, or result in the invention, with the exception of when the ordinary skilled in the art can directly and explicitly determine the technical content of the technical feature upon reading the claims, description, and the drawing.

This test is very similar to Article 8 of the "Interpretation (II) of the SPC" which is promulgated after the court's ruling. The only difference rests on the exception part of the two tests, particularly, in *Nokia* case, the combination of the claims, description, and the drawing being the reference to determine whether an ordinary skilled in the art can directly and explicitly recognize the technical content of the technical feature. In contrast, according to Article 8, only claims are the reference to determine whether an ordinary skilled in the art can directly and explicitly recognize the technical content of the technical feature. '

Similar to *Hu Beier* case, the *Nokia* test is also unclear whether "the recognized technical content of the technical feature" in the exception part is directed to the technical term itself corresponding to the "means" part of the US MPF style claim, or to the functional limitation modifying the means corresponding to the "function" part of the US MPF style claim. Following the logic of US MPF law, it should be directed to the technical term itself corresponding to the "means" part of the US MPF style claim, rather than to the function limitation. Furthermore, according to the ruling, it requires that "technical content" instead of using "structure for performing the claimed function" needs to be recognized as required by the US MPF law. In addition, the references could be used to interpret the corresponding "means" part as only including the claims, description and drawings. The external sources, such as the knowledge of the skilled in the art outside of the specification are excluded from use as the interpreted reference.

The court further ruled that the use of "configured to" is usually interpreted as functional or effect limitation, which ignores to some extent the weight of "term" (i.e. "means" part) before the "configured to" (corresponding to "for" of the "means for" format) on the determination of whether a technical feature is a functional limitation. This approach is different from the presumption principle of US MPF, which looks to the combination of the "means" part with the "for" part.

As for how to determine the scope of a claim when the claim is determined as functional claim by using "configured to" in the context of computer implemented software invention, the court concluded that the specification and the drawings do not describe how to apply the described implementation in the specification to the terminal device and message editor. In other words, although the description describes the detailed algorithm or steps to perform the function, as long as the description does not disclose how to apply the described implementation in the specification to the terminal device, the specification and the drawings are nevertheless considered to not provide the specific embodiments implementing the corresponding function which the terminal device and the message editor is configured to perform. And accordingly, the scope of claim cannot be ascertained and thus the court dismissed the action.

The representative claim of Patent ZL200480001590.4 at issue is claim 7 which reads:

7. A terminal device of claim 6, the terminal device <u>is further configured to: apply the data transfer method selection to a message editor used for entering messages;</u>

   the terminal device is configured to: transmit the message, based on the selection of the data transfer method carried out in the message editor, to a data transfer application supporting the selected data transfer method;

   the terminal device is configured to: transmit the message, according to a data transfer protocol used by the data transfer application, to a telecommunications network.

Some issues arise from the ruling of this case:

i. It should distinguish from "MPF" Software implementation specific embodiment itself including specific procedures, algorithms, etc., similar to the US software invention algorithm structure differing from how to apply the software implementation specific embodiment to general purpose hardware, i.e., how to use the common hardware, to perform the specific software implementation embodiment itself. Usually, the former should be disclosed in the description, and the later is common knowledge for the skilled in the art and thus need not be disclosed in detail.

ii. It should distinguish how to use specific hardware structure to perform the claimed function from how to use the software structure to perform the claimed function.

The former is a specific hardware implementation, in which the specific hardware structure performed the claimed function is required to be disclosed; while the later is a specific software implementation. In the later case, as long as the disclosure of the software process, steps or algorithms to implement the claimed functions is adequate, how the software process, step or algorithms are executed by general purpose hardware belong to the prior art and need not to describe in detail. In contrast, it needs to be disclosed in detail for the hardware components and the interconnection relationship thereof, so that the skilled in the art know how to perform the claimed function.

iii. Merely the use of "configured to" followed by functional limitation in a claim does not necessary limit to use hardware implementations to perform the claimed function or hardware implementations to perform the claimed function. The description may either include software implementations performed the claimed function, or may also include hardware implementations performed the claimed function or both of them; therefore, even if there is no disclosure of a specific hardware implementation embodiment, it is still possible to determine the technical content corresponding to the function.

iv. Disclosure requirement is different between the invention novelty point and the common knowledge to the skilled in the art. Whether software or hardware specific implementation embodiments to perform the claimed function, both require to disclose the novelty point part of the claimed subject matter, but need not to disclose the content which is deemed as prior art or common knowledge to the skilled in the art.

5.7. Categories of Functional Limitations and the Corresponding Issues

There are several types of functional limitation in US including means-plus-function ("MPF"), step plus function ("SPF"), single means, general functional limitation (e.g. mixture of functional limitation with structural limitation, e.g., processor configured to ...), pure functional limitation (at apparatus level instead of element level, e.g. an apparatus configured to ..., the later is covered by MPF).

The following describes each of these types one by one.

5.7.1. *MPF — Watch out for §112(f), §112(a)*

The statute of 35 U.S.C. §112(f) states:

> (f) ELEMENT IN CLAIM FOR A COMBINATION.—An element in a claim for a combination may be expressed as a means or step for performing a specified function without the recital of structure, material, or acts in support thereof, and such claim shall be construed to cover the corresponding structure, material, or acts described in the specification and equivalents thereof.

The classic MPF style claim usually refers to an apparatus claim[16] having at least two elements forming the combination of the apparatus, and the element itself is only a placeholder, nonsense word or nonce word without any structural meaning and is modified by function language. In other words, MPF claim applies only to purely functional limitations that do not provide the structure either in the element (means) part or in the function part.[17] The following is a typical example of the MPF style claim:

---

[16]For simply purpose, the apparatus claim refers to two of the four categories statutory subject matter, i.e. machine and manufacture. As for the composition of matter claim, it has the same situation as the apparatus.

[17]Phillips v. AWH Corp., 415 F3d. At 1311 (Fed. Cir. 2005).

An apparatus comprising:

> means for (or other non-structural terms like "mechanism for", "module for", "device for", "unit for", "component for", "element for", "member for", "apparatus for", "machine for", or "system for")[18] ...;
>> means for ...;
>> means for ....

Although MPF claim usually applies to apparatus claims, MPF analysis (not the SPF) may also extend to method claims in some cases, such as in *Media Right*[19] and *Inventio AG*.[20]

The illustrative claim of *Media Right* is:
A method of preventing unauthorized recording of electronic media comprising:

> activating a *compliance mechanism* in response to receiving media content by a client system, said compliance mechanism coupled to said client system, said client system having a media content presentation application operable thereon and coupled to said compliance mechanism;
>> *controlling a data output pathway of said client system with said compliance mechanism by diverting a commonly used data pathway of said media player application to a controlled data pathway monitored by said compliance mechanism*; and
>> directing said media content to a custom media device coupled to said compliance mechanism via said data output path, for selectively restricting output of said media content.

---

[18]USPTO, "Supplementary Examination Guidelines for Determining Compliance With 35 U.S.C. §112 and for Treatment of Related Issues in Patent Applications" (2011).
[19]Media Rights Technologies, Inc. v. Capital One Financial Corp. (Fed. Cir. 2015).
[20]Inventio AG v. ThyssenKrupp Elevator Americas Corporation (Fed. Cir. 2011).

The illustrative claim of *Inventio AG* is:

A method of modernizing an elevator installation having at least one elevator controlled by at least one elevator control by way of at least one call report, comprising:

a. installing at least one floor terminal at each floor served by an elevator controlled by an elevator control for at least one of the input of destination call reports and for recognition of identification codes of users;

b. installing at least one *computing unit* and connecting the at least one computing unit to said floor terminals for at least one of evaluating the destination call reports and association of destination floors with recognized ones of the identification codes, and for the output of at least one destination signal; and

c. installing at least one *modernizing device* and connecting the at least one modernizing device to said floor terminals and said at least one computing unit for reading the destination signal, for converting the destination signal into at least one call report and for controlling the elevator control by way of the call report.

The limitation *"controlling a data output pathway of said client system with said compliance mechanism by diverting a commonly used data pathway of said media player application to a controlled data pathway"* recited in claim 1 of U.S. Patent No. 7,316,033 (the'033 Patent) (denoted as *Media Right* style claim) in *Media Rights Technologies, Inc. v. Capital One Financial Corp* is not different from the general method claim language, such as "controlling, by a control module, a state of …". If this kind of expression is subject to MPF treatment, then a large amount of method claims for computer implemented software invention would be under the shadow of the restricted and uncertain scope due to the application of MPF because many computer implemented software inventions adopt the *Media Right* style in the method claims.

The following is a hypothetical method claim:

A method for performing a terminal device, comprising:

receiving, by a receiver, a message… ;

extracting, by an processing module, an indicator from the message;

> comparing, by the processing module, the indicator with a mapping
> of ... ;
>   switching, by the processing module, the state of the terminal device
> from a first work state to a second work state.

According to the analysis framework of *Media Right*, the "extract-ing", "comparing" and "switching" steps in the above hypothetical method claim should invoke MPF. In addition, as *Williamson v Citrix* (Fed. Cir. 2015) (*en banc*) case overruled the strong presumption of not invoking MPF in the absence of "means" in a claim, *Media Right* style method claim becomes much more vulnerable to be governed by the MPF law. Another factor which may trigger applications of MPF to *Media Right* style method claims is that step plus function (SPF) is hardly applied to method claims due to the strict requirement and vague criteria of invoking SPF. In this situation, applying MPF to method claim appears to be more justified in view of current trend in constraining software pat-ent with broad applications of functional limitation.

Patent practitioners should pay attention to MPF's application to method claim and draft their specification with detailed and various embodiments as if all of the limitations in the method would be governed by MPF.

"Single means" is another type of functional claim. The following is a typical example of the MPF style claim:

> An apparatus for authenticating an end user, comprising: an <u>authentica-</u>
> <u>tion means/module</u>, configured to/for ....

Although the standard of determining whether a term is a "means" in the sense of "single means" and whether the limitation modified the "means" is function rather than structure are the same as MPF analysis framework, the outcome and principle is different between the two kinds of "means". For "single means", as long as the first step of determination is done, e.g., the answer is yes, then claim is deemed to be invalid straightway on the ground of not meeting the enablement requirement under 35 U.S.C. §112(a) without going into determining the scope of the function limitation as the MPF law does in step two. As for the MPF, after the first step determination is done, e.g., the answer is yes, the second step is performed to determine the structure corresponding to functional limitation or the scope of the functional limitation. Only when there is no or inadequate corresponding structure performing the claimed function in the description, the claim should be deemed invalid on the ground of not meeting the definiteness requirement under 35 U.S.C. §112(b).

"Single means" is a judicial created doctrine to negate the use of pure functional limitation at the entire apparatus level. The theory behind it seems to be similar to the *Halliburton* case for which the Supreme Court held that using pure functional limitation (even at the element level) is not permitted and the claim should be invalided on the ground of not meeting the definiteness requirement under 35 U.S.C. §112(b). Although 1952's Act permits applicants to use pure functional limitation at the element level, it must be interpreted under the so called "MPF" regime to limit the scope of the claim using function limitation. According to the statutory language, 35 U.S.C. §112(f) (originally the third paragraph, and then the sixth paragraph pre-AIA) only addressed the pure functional limitation to an individual element of the combination with at least two elements rather than to the entire apparatus or method. Therefore, in the case of using pure functional limitation to modify the entire apparatus or method instead of individual element thereof, 35 U.S.C. §112(f) is inapplicable and the *Halliburton* rule prior to 1952 Act should still be applicable to this situation. The seminal case *In re Hyatt* addressed this problem and invalided claim 35 at issue on the ground of not meeting the enablement requirement under 35 U.S.C. §112(a).

In other words, the issue with "single means" is that as long as the limitation is determined as "single means plus function", the claim is straightway invalided regardless whether the generalized level of the function is high or low (i.e. the scope of the function is excessive broad or only covers a relative narrow scenario), whether the function limitation is prior art or not, and whether the description provides enough variety of embodiments to support the function.

Accordingly, the simple recommended practice for a patent practitioner is to divide single means into two means or using "non-means", such as processor and circuit, to replace the "means" to avoid immediate invalidation.

Another problem is whether the "single means" doctrine is applicable to *Media Right* style method claim. The following are two hypothetical method claims:

> *Claim 1, A method for performing a terminal device, comprising:*
>
> *obtaining, by the device, the route information from a received message;*
> *comparing, by the device, the route information with a mapping of ... ;*
> *forwarding, by the device, the message according the mapping result.*
>
> *Claim 2, An apparatus configured to implement a method performing the following steps:*
> *obtaining the route information from a received message;*
> *comparing the route information with a mapping of ... ;*
> *forwarding the received message according the mapping result.*

In the hypothetical method claims, there is only a single "device" in claim 1 and a single "apparatus" in claim 2 which would denote non-structure and therefore should amount to "means", and the function should be the "obtaining", "comparing" and "forwarding" processes. Although there is no precedential CAFC case addressing this issue, the patent practitioner should take precaution against the application of "single means" to this kind of claim by replacing "*the device*" or "apparatus" with "router" or "switch" which denote structural meaning or have a definition of physical device in the description.

5.7.2. *Partial functional claiming — might be interpreted as non-MPF*

The third category functional claim is partial functional limitation[21] which has some structure limitations without complete structure to perform the

---

[21]Although MPEP named this kind of limitation as "function limitation", we called it partial functional limitation here to differentiate from the "function limitation" which we use to refer to a more generic conception covering the three types of MPF/SPF, single means and partial function limitation.

function as compared to purely functional limitation without any structure limitation. As set forth in the MPEP:

> Unlike means-plus-function claim language that applies only to purely functional limitations, *Phillips v. AWH Corp,* 415 F.3d 1303, 1311 (Fed. Cir. 2005) (en banc) ("Means-plus-function claiming applies only to purely functional limitations that do not provide the structure that performs the recited function."), functional claiming often involves the recitation of some structure followed by its function. For example, in In re Schreiber, the claims were directed to a conical spout (the structure) that "allow[ed] several kernels of popped popcorn to pass through at the same time" (the function). In re Schreiber, 128 F.3d 1473, 1478 (Fed. Cir. 1997).

MPEP 2173.05(G) Functional Limitations [R-07. 2015]. In the context of computer implemented software invention, the following typical formats might be considered as the partial functional limitation claims in certain circumstances:

> Claim 1, An apparatus for forwarding a data packet, comprising:
>
> A receiver, configured to ...;
> A processor, configured to ...;
> A transmitter, configured to ...
>
> Claim 2, An apparatus for forwarding a data packet, comprising:
>
> A application server, configured to ...;
> A switch, configured to ....

In the above hypothetical method claims, the "processor" in claim 1 and the "switch" or "application server" in claim 2 denote structure and thus MPF is inapplicable, and meanwhile, the limitation followed the "processor" or the "switch" might be deemed as functional limitation in some cases. Therefore, they are deemed as partial functional claims. Although MPF or "single means" is not applicable to the partial functional limitation, the general section 112(a) and (b) requirement (i.e. written description, enablement and definiteness requirements) would be the key tests for the function limitation besides section §101, §102 and §103 tests.

From a practical point of view, patent practitioners must not treat this kind of claim lightly and should provide enough detailed and varied embodiments in the description, as if the partial functional limitations would be governed by MPF, so as to avoid written description, enablement and indefiniteness issues. See *Halliburton Energy Services, Inc., v. M-I LLC,* 514 F.3d 1244, 85 USPQ2d 1654 (Fed. Cir. 2008), and *United Carbon Co. v. Binney & Smith Co.,* 317 U.S. 228, 55 USPQ 381 (1942).

5.7.3. *Step plus function*

Step plus function (SPF) is parallel to MPF as established by the statute, and SPF is applicable in the context of method claim.

> (f) ELEMENT IN CLAIM FOR A COMBINATION—An element in a claim for a combination may be expressed as a means or step for performing a specified function without the recital of structure, material, or acts in support thereof, and such claim shall be construed to cover the corresponding structure, material, or acts described in the specification and equivalents thereof.

We now analyze the Step Plus Function: "step for" + doing (structure and material go with means, acts go with steps).

As discussed above, MPF usually applies in the context of apparatus claims and SPF applies to process claims. As ruled in *Tekmar,* combination process or method claims are subject to step-plus function treatment "only when steps plus function <u>without acts</u> are present. (*O.I. Corp. v. Tekmar Co., 115 F.3d 1576 (Fed. Cir. 1997).*)

Compared with the relatively broad application of MPF, the application of SPF's is more limited. After doing a simple search, to date a total of 10 cases involve SPF and only two of them are considered suitable SPF ultimately.

The mere fact that a method claim is drafted with language parallel to an apparatus claim with means-plus-function language does not mean that the method claim should be subject to an analysis under §112, paragraph 6. Rather, each limitation of each claim must be independently reviewed to determine if it is subject to the requirements of

§112, paragraph 6 (*Generation II Orthoti s,* 263 F.3d at 1368 (citations omitted).)

The court of *Tekmar* case also cautioned against construing every method limitation as a step plus function limitation or treating every "ing" as a step-plus-function limitation: we note that the Halliburton case concerned an apparatus claim, not a process claim, and we must be careful not to extend the language of this provision to situations not contemplated by Congress. If we were to construe every process claim containing steps described by an "ing" verb, such as passing, heating, reacting, transferring, etc. into a step-plus function limitation, we would be limiting process claims in a manner never intended by Congress. *O.I. Corp. v. Tekmar Co.,* 115 F.3d 1576 (Fed. Cir. 1997).

Similar to MPF, if there is no use of "step for" language, the presumption is that the method claim does not apply SPF. However, the *Williamson* ruled that the "strong presumption" is overruled and the en banc *Williamson v. Citrix* (Fed Cir 2015) should also apply to SPF context. Therefore, according to the new presumption standard, even if the claim does not use "step for" language, SPF can be invoked. How to coordinate *Williamson* rule with the caution of *Generation II Orthotics Inc.* and *O.I. Corp.* is worth observing in future cases.

In view of the ambiguity boundary between the act and function, and there is no clear bright line criteria for determining which limitation is deemed as act and which limitation goes for function, the overall tendency is not easily to apply SPF to the method claim.

5.7.4. *Practical recommendations*

In general, we recommend splitting the limitation in each step of a method claim into at least two levels, one is at general level and another is at specific level. In this case, even if the limitation at general level is interpreted as function, the specific portion might be interpreted as act to implement the general function limitation, and thus avoid the application of SPF.

Do not use the "step for" in the preamble or before each step, such as "comprising the steps for:", "comprising the steps of:", or "step of ...". Use, instead, "comprising the acts of:" or "comprising the following:", or "comprising:". In addition, divide the limitation in each step of a method claim into two levels of generalization, one is directed to general limitation, the other is directed to specific limitation. Thus the limitation as a whole is more likely to be interpreted to cover both the function and acts of performing the function, instead of only covering functional limitation, so as to avoid invoking SPF.

5.8. Claim Construction of Functional Limitations — Structure

What to consult in determining whether a feature is a structure feature or non-structure feature? The following are some sources to consider.

5.8.1. *PTO/MPEP*

To determine whether a word, term, or phrase coupled with a function denotes structure, examiners are instructed by MPEP to check whether (i) the specification provides a description sufficient to inform one of ordinary skill in the art that the term denotes structure; (ii) general and subject matter specific dictionaries provide evidence that the term has achieved recognition as a noun denoting structure; and (iii) the prior art provides evidence that the term has an art-recognized structure to perform the claimed function.

5.8.2. *US Case Law*

Readers can also reference the following few cases as examples on how to determine whether a feature is a structure.

— Invention AG v. ThyssenKrupp Televator Americas Corp. (Fed. Cir. 2011)
— Healthcare Solutions v. David J. Kappos (Fed. Cir. 2012)
— Richard A. Williamson v. Citrix Online, LLC (Fed. Cir. 2015)

5.8.3. *Chinese Cases: Hu Beier v. Communication Device Corp. of Changzhou (Suzhimin Zhongzi 0139/2011)*

If the claim uses technical terms which are uncommon or unknown to the skilled in the art in the related technical field, and only describes to the skilled in the art the function or final achieved result of the feature, and does not expressly or impliedly limit in an exhaustive manner such a feature to one or more specific structures in the specification, then the technical term is deemed as non-structural limitation and thus belongs to functional limitation.

5.8.4. *Nokia v. Huaqin (Hugaominsan (Zhi) Zhongzi 96/2013)*

Functional features mean technical features which define the structures, components, procedures, conditions or the mutual relationship thereof, among others, through their functions or effects in the invention, except when the ordinary skilled in the art can directly and explicitly determine the specific implementation for achieving the aforesaid functions or effects only by reading the claims.

For technical feature which is defined by functional language, if the technical feature is understood by the skilled in the art upon reading the claims, description and the accompanying drawings are consistent with the common understanding by the skilled in the art, and the skilled in the art know how to implement the function or effect associated with the technical feature, in this case, the technical content of the technical feature is determined just in accordance with the common understanding, and the technical feature is not deemed as functional limitation. Otherwise, the technical feature is functional limitation.

5.8.5. *The Interpretation (I) of the SPC (2016)*

Article 8 states that "functional features mean the technical feature which is defined by not using the structures, components, procedures, conditions or the mutual relationship thereof, among others, but is defined by using their functions or effects in the invention, with the exception of when the ordinary skilled in the art can directly and explicitly recognize the specific implementation for achieving the aforesaid functions or effects only by reading the claims. Where, in comparison with the indispensable technical features for achieving the functions or effects as mentioned in the preceding paragraph as described in the specifications and the attached drawings, the corresponding technical features of the accused infringing technical solution perform the same functions in substantially same way to achieve same results as the indispensable technical features, with which an ordinary skilled in the art is able to associate without any creative activity when the accused infringing act occurs, the people's court shall determine the corresponding technical features are identical with or equivalent to the functional features.".

5.9. Claim Construction of Functional Limitations

What can be consulted to determine the function? The following are references and suggestions:

5.9.1. *Claim construction*

The language describing the function is constructed according to the general rules of claim construction, e.g. based on specification, prosecution history, dictionary, etc. [*Carroll Touch, Inc. v. Electro Mechanical System, Inc, 15 F.3d 1573, 1577-78 (Fed. Cir 1993)*].

5.9.2. *Caution*

Caution should be used by importing the structures to the claim recited function limitation when interpreting the function limitation according to the specification. The following cases address this issue and can provide some hints and guidelines to determine the function limitation in step one of the MPF interpretation as compared with step two in determining the structure corresponding to the determined function in step one.

- *Applied Medical Resources Corporation v. United States Surgical Corporation, 448 F.3d 1324, 1334 (Fed. Cir. 2006).*
- *BBA Nonwovens Simpsonville, Inc. v. Superior Nonwovens, LLC 303 F.3d 1332 1343-44 (Fed. Cir. 2002).*
- *JVW Enterprises, Inc. v. Interact Accessories, Inc., 424 F.3d 1324 1330 (Fed. Cir. 2005).*

5.9.3. *Practical recommendation*

Once it is determined that §112(f) is applicable, next comes the two-step interpretation process: i.e. 1) Determine the claimed function; 2) Determine the functional corresponding structure in the specification. Special attention should be paid in Step 1 to distinguish: (i) interpret functional limitation in accordance with the specification; and (ii) import the unessential structure limitation in the specification into the functional limitation. It is suggested to clearly describe the function limitation and the corresponding structure, and make them clearly identifiable and distinguishable from each other instead of blending them together.

5.10. Claim Construction of Functional Limitations — Claimed Function

What is the claimed function? The following are references and suggestions:

5.10.1. *Gregory Baran v. Medical Device Technologies (Fed. Cir. 2010)*

Be careful about the adjective or modifier language in front of "means/ means-less (e.g., unit, module, etc.)":

> For example: the "release means for retaining" in the claimed language "[a] *biopsy instrument comprising . . . a manually operable charging member for moving the guide to the charged position against the urging of the coil spring, and a release means for retaining the guide in the charged position.*

In this case, *MDTech* argued that the claimed "release means for retaining" required a structure that exhibited both a releasing function and a retaining function. *Dr. Baran* argued that the claimed function was only that of retaining. On appeal, the Federal Circuit agreed with the lower court that the means-preamble "release" added a functional limitation to the claim element. Therefore, in this case, the function includes both before releasing and retaining" and accordingly the description needs to disclose structure implementation for performing both of functions respectively.

5.10.2. *Signtech USA ltd. v. Vutek Inc.* *174 F.3d 1352 (Fed. Cir. 2009)*

> For example, the "ink delivery" in the claimed language "[a]n apparatus for reproducing an image on a first side of a substrate and a mirror image on a second side of said substrate, comprising:… ink delivery means positioned on opposite sides of said substrate… "

In this case, the claim element "ink delivery means" uses the term "means" with the preamble modified "ink delivery" which is deemed as a function. Although it does not use the phrase "means for", the phrase "ink delivery means" is equivalent to the phrase "means for ink delivery," because "ink delivery" is purely functional language without any structure denotation. The magistrate therefore correctly applied §112, p 6 to the claim element and treated "delivering ink" as the function limitation in associate with the "means".

5.10.3. *Practical recommendation*

(a) According to the above cases, the functional language before "means" can also be treated as function limitation, therefore, when naming the term, do not attempt to use non-structural modifier before the term, so as to avoid the pre-term modifiers being constructed as an independent functional limitation in addition to the normal functional limitation after the term.

(b) The following provides an exemplary claim. A terminal device, comprises: receiver, configured to receive a request message to forward a data packet from the ingress node to egress node; mapping module, *configured to obtain the addresses and corresponding port number of the ingress node, and determine the port according to the port number; forwarding module, configured to forward the data packet to the egress node through the determined port.* In this exemplary claim, the "mapping" may be interpreted as the module's independent function in addition to the functional limitation following the "module", i.e., "obtain the addresses and corresponding port number of the ingress node, and determine the port according to the port number".

5.10.4. *Practical recommendation — pay special attention to the following*

Not all of the limitation behind the "means" are deemed as functional limitation needing to have specific structure in the description. Only those limitations that are actual function, determination of the structure embodiment from the description is necessary. If the limitation behind the "means" is not real function limitation according to the interpretation, you do not need to find the structure in the specification, instead, one may interpret it according to the usual interpretation rules. The following are some cases relating to this issue:

a. *Ims Technology, Inc. v. Haas 206 F.3d 1422* (Fed. Cir. 2000) (the relevant term is "Data block")
b. *O.I. Corporation v. Tekmar Company Incorporation*, 115 F. 3d 1576 (Fed. Cir. 1997) (the relevant term is "passage")
c. *BBA Nonwovens Simpsonville, Inc. v. The position of Superior Nonwovens, LLC*, 303 F.3d 1332 1343-44 (Fed. Cir. 2002) (the relevant term is "corona means ..." and "positioned" behind the "corona means ...")
d. *ICON Health &. Fitness, Inc. v. Octane Fitness, LLC*, (Fed. Cir. 2012) (non-precedential) (the relevant term is "connecting" all the limitation behind the "connecting" is the functional limitation).

As for the claim drafter, you should reflect the multiple levels of functional parts, which will make it interpreted as both including general level function and relative specific level implementation, which could avoid to some extent being interpreted as functional limitation. In addition, clearly distinguish between functional limitation and structure limitation, placing only functional limitation behind "means" without blending with structure limitation to avoid triggering §112(f).

5.11. Claim Construction of Functional Limitations — Claimed Structure

What is the recited Structure? How much structure recited in the claim for performing the recited function is required to overcome §112(f) application when using "means"? Recitation of some structures may not be sufficient to overcome §112(f) application, but how much would be enough is not very clear. The following are various interpretations:

5.11.1. *The structure must be sufficient to entirely perform the function*

Some cases require that the structure must be sufficient to entirely perform the function.

  i. Positive cases include:
- *lighting World, Inc. v. Birchwood Lighting, Inc., 382 F.3d 1354* **(Fed. Cir. 2004)**
- *Sage Pods., Inc. V. Devon Indus., Inc. 126 F.3d 1420* **(Fed. Cir. 1997)**

 ii. Opposite cases include:
- *Altiris, Inc. v. Symantec Corp., 318 F.3d 1363* **(Fed. Cir. 2003)**

5.11.2. *The claim recites sufficiently definite structure to perform the function*

Some cases require that the claim should recite sufficiently definite structure for performing the function.

  i. Positive cases include:
- *Wenger Mfg. Inc. v. Coating Mach. Aycs. Inc. 239 F.3d 1679, 1687-88* **(Fed. Cir. 2001)**

- *Rodime PLC. V. Seagate Tech., Inc. 174 F.3d 1429, 1434* (Fed. Cir. 1999)
- *Phillips v. AWH Corp.*, 415 F.3d 1324-25 (Fed. Cir. 2005) (En Banc)
- *Trimed, Inc. v. Stryker Corp.*, 514 F.3d 1788-90 (Fed. Cir. 2008)

The standard in Trimed case reads: "sufficient structure exists when the claim language specifies the exact structure that performs the function in question without need to resort to other portions of the specification or extrinsic evidence for an adequate understanding of the structure." *Trimed, Inc. v. Stryker Corp.*, 514 F3d. 1788-90 (Fed. Cir. 2008).

5.11.3. *Practical suggestions*

It should be noted that under US current law, the requirement for the detailed level of structure disclosed in the description for performing the claimed functional limitation following the "means" is different from the requirement for the detailed level of structure for the "mean-less" term (e.g., unit, module, etc.) in the claim to constitute structural term so as to not invoke §112(f). The former requirement for the detailed level of structure seems higher than the later, the former requires the description providing sufficient or adequate structure performing the claimed functional limitation. However, the latter requires the non-means term being understood by persons of ordinary skill in the art to have a sufficiently definite meaning as the name for structure according to the Williamson case.[22] When considering whether a claim term recites sufficient structure to avoid application of §112(f), we have not required the claim term to denote a specific structure. Instead, we have recommended that it is sufficient if the claim term is used in common parlance or by person of skill in the pertinent art to designate structure, even if the term covers a broad class of structures and even if the term identifies the structure by their function.

---

[22]Williamson v. Citrix Online LLC, 792 F.3d 1339 (Fed. Cir. 2015).

5.12. Claim Construction of Functional Limitations — Structure and Required Details

5.12.1. *What is the structure? What degree of details is required?*

The following cases shed light on how detailed structure is required to perform the function and thus constitute the scope of the claim.

(a) *Chiumintta Concrete Concepts, Inc. v. Cardinal Industries Inc.* 145 F.3d 1303 (Fed. Cir. 1998) — broader structure v more detailed structure.

(b) *University of Pittsburgh v. Varian Medical Systems* (Fed. Cir. 2014) — Two steps algorithm versus Three step algorithm.

(c) *Noah Sys., Inc. v. Intuit Inc., 675 F.3d 1302, 1318 (Fed. Cir. 2012)* — Partial structure is not enough, amount to no structure.

(d) *Atmel Corp. v. Information Storage Devices, Inc.*, 198 F.3d 1374 (Fed. Cir. 1999) — Not allow open ended reference and note Incorporated by reference.

(e) Chinese Cases: *Hu Beier v. Communication Device Corp. of Changzhou* (Suzhimin Zhongzi 0139/2011) — The scope of the claimed functional limitation only covers the essential technical features as a whole that perform the functional limitation in each of the embodiments. More specifically, those features that have no direct and necessary connection with the performance of the functional limitation should be excluded. The essential technical features that performed the claimed functional limitation from each of the multiples embodiments should be considered as the alternative content or structure for the claimed functional limitation.

5.12.2. *Practical recommendations*

Even though only essential technical features performing the functional limitation can be read into the claim as the structure of the claimed function, it is still suggested to draft the embodiments with multiple levels of generalization, i.e., from generalized structure implementation to specific structure implementation, so as to avoid incorporating too much detailed content into the structure and then read into the claim. The interpreter (the examiner or the judge) may skip the non-essential structure with respect to the performance of the function in the course of claim interpretation, but will not help you to generalize the detailed structure embodiment to obtain a general structure implementation with a broader scope.

Under the current prosecution practice, when facing the §112(f) plus §112(b) rejection, common practice is to amend the claims to overcome the application of §112(f) and accordingly mooting the §112(b). When it is hard to make such amendment to avoid §112(f) application, another approach is to identify the corresponding necessary structure to perform the claimed function. In this case, the description having multiple level of detailed structure would be very helpful to avoid too narrow a structure being read into the claim.

5.13. Claim Construction of Functional Limitations — Two Cases with Inadequate Structure

5.13.1. *In re Aoyama, No. 10-1552 (Fed. Cir. August 29, 2011)*

The disputed claim 11 read: A system for supply chain management comprising:

> an order controller system including reverse logistics means for generating transfer data; and
> a warehouse system receiving the transfer data and generating shipping data.

The specification discloses the following flow chart depicted in Figure 5-1.

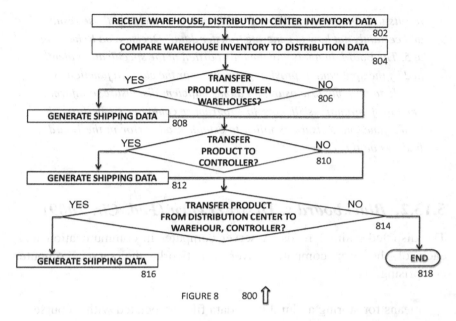

FIGURE 8   800 ⇑

Figure 5-1   An exemplary flowchart for a claim in a litigation case.

In this case, the appeal court stated:

This court agrees with the Board's conclusion that Figure 8 "fails to describe, even at a high level, how a computer could be programmed to produce the structure that provides the results described in the boxes." *Id. at 4-5. Moreover, the Board's finding is consistent with the Examiner's finding. The Examiner recited that "[t]he proper test for meeting the definiteness requirement is that the corresponding structure . . . of a [mean-plus-function] limitation must be disclosed in the specification itself in a way that one skilled in the art will understand what structure . . . will perform the recited function." Examiner's Answer of April 23, 2007, at 10-11. After analyzing Figure 8 and its accompanying description, the Examiner was unable to find any structure disclosed that performed the claimed function. Id. Figure 8 only "presents several*

*results to be obtained, without describing how to achieve those results,
and certainly not how to generate transfer data." Decision on Rehearing
at 5. The Board, in analyzing the only portion of the specification identified by the applicant as providing structure for the claimed function, was
unable to find any disclosure, let alone sufficient disclosure to inform a
person of ordinary skill how to program a computer to perform the
stated function. Mitsui has failed to establish any error in the Board's
findings on this issue.*

5.13.2. *Blackboard v. Desire2Learn (Fed. Cir. 2009)*

The disputed claim 1 reads: A server computer in communication with
each of the user computers over a network, the server computer
comprising:

> means for storing a plurality of data files associated with a course,
> means for assigning a level of access to and control of each data file
> based on a user of the system's predetermined role in a course;
> means for determining whether access to a data file associated with
> the course is authorized;
> means for allowing access to and control of the data file associated
> with the course if authorization is granted based on the access level of
> the user of the system.

The specification of the disputed patent reads in the relevant parts:

"Access control manager 151 creates an access control list (ACL)
for one or more subsystems in response to a request from a subsys-
tem to have its resources protected through adherence to an ACL.
Education support system 100 provides multiple levels of access
restrictions to enable different types of users to effectively interact
with the system (e.g. access web pages, upload or download files,
view grade information) while preserving confidentiality of
information."

In this case, the appeal court stated:

The specification contains no description of the structure or the process that the access control manager uses to perform the "assigning" function. Nor has Blackboard ever suggested that the "access control manager" represents a particular structure defined other than as any structure that performs the recited function. In fact, before the district court, counsel for Blackboard defined the term "access control manager" in precisely those terms. He stated, "We suggest that the corresponding structure for [the function of assigning a level of access to and control of each data file] is the access control manager. That's not really a revolutionary thought. The access control manager manages access control." Counsel also stated of the access control manager that "the name of it pretty much describes what it does. It assigns a level of access to and control of a user's role in a course." Blackboard's expert made clear that he did not regard the term "access control manager" as limited even to software. He stated, "Although the access manager in Figure 1 is described as software, there is nothing in the '138 patent specification that would limit the performance of the access manager's functions to software; one of ordinary skill in the art would know that hardware could be used." In other words, the access control manager, according to Blackboard, is any computer-related device or program that performs the function of access control.

...

That ordinarily skilled artisans could carry out the recited function in a variety of ways is precisely why claims written in "means-plus-function" form must disclose the particular structure that is used to perform the recited function. By failing to describe the means by which the access control manager will create an ACL, Blackboard has attempted to capture any possible means for achieving that end. Section 112, paragraph 6, is intended to prevent such pure functional claiming. Aristocrat, 521 F.3d at 1333. We thus agree with the district court that the '138 patent discloses insufficient structure to perform the function of "assigning a level of access to and control of each data file based on a user of the system's predetermined role in a course.

5.14. Claim Construction of Functional Limitations — PTO Interpretation for Patentability

5.14.1. *In Re Morris, 43 USPQ2d 1753 (Fed. Cir. 1997), revised on rehearing 127 F.3d 1048, 44 USPQ2d 1023 (Fed. Cor. 1997)*

Donaldson (Fed. Cir. 1994) did not alter the rule that the PTO may give claim language the broadest reasonable interpretation (BRI).

In addition, MPEP also states (section 2181 Identifying and Interpreting a 35 U.S.C. §112(f) or Pre-AIA 35 U.S.C. §112, Sixth Paragraph Limitation [R-07.2015]):

> The Court of Appeals for the Federal Circuit, in its en banc decision In reDonaldson Co., 16 F.3d 1189, 1194, 29 USPQ2d 1845, 1850 (Fed. Cir. 1994), held that a "means-or-step-plus-function" limitation should be interpreted as follows:
>
> > Per our holding, the "broadest reasonable interpretation" that an examiner may give means-plus-function language is that statutorily mandated in paragraph six. Accordingly, the PTO may not disregard the structure disclosed in the specification corresponding to such language when rendering a patentability determination.
>
> > Therefore, the broadest reasonable interpretation of a claim limitation that invokes 35 U.S.C. §112(f) or pre-AIA 35 U.S.C. §112, sixth paragraph, is the structure, material or act described in the specification as performing the entire claimed function and equivalents to the disclosed structure, material or act. As a result, section 112(f) or pre-AIA section 112, sixth paragraph, limitations will, in some cases, be afforded a more narrow interpretation than a limitation that is not crafted in "means plus function" format.

5.14.2. *Ishida Co. v. Taylor, 221 F.3d 1310, 1316 (Fed. Cir. 2000)*

For anticipation purpose, a prior reference that discloses any of the structures encompassed by the MPF clause anticipates that claims. A disclosure of a species anticipates a claim to a genus.

Accordingly, in infringement determination proceedings, so long as the accused product also has implemented one of the specific structures and their equivalents described in the specification, infringement can be found. The court stated in *Dealertrack, Inc. V. Huber, 674 F.3d 1315, §101 USPQ2d 1325 (Fed. Cir. 2012)*:

> The question before the Court was whether infringement requires practicing all of the algorithms that were corresponding structure or whether just one would suffice. The court ruled that infringement require an accused product to have any one of the algorithms. They are alternative structures, citing *Creo Products, Inc. v. Presstek, Inc., 305 F.3d 1337, 1345, 64 USPQ 1385* (Fed. Cir. 2002).

5.14.3. *Fresenius USA, Inc. v. Baxter International, Inc. (Fresenius II), No. 12-1334 (Fed. Cir. July 2, 2013) Citing In re Donaldson Co., 16 F.3d 1189, 1193 (Fed. Cir. 1994) (en banc) (Fed. Cir. 1994)*

The court in Fresenius stated:

> Just as a patentee who seeks to prove infringement must provide a structural analysis by demonstrating that the accused device has the identified corresponding structure or an equivalent structure, a challenger who seeks to demonstrate that a MPF limitation was present in the prior art must prove that the corresponding structure — or an equivalent — was present in the prior art. *See In re Donaldson Co.*, 16 F.3d 1189, 1193 (Fed. Cir. 1994) (en banc).

The underlying logic behind this statement is that because the statutory equivalent under §112(f) is covered in literal scope of the claims, therefore, when determining the patentability of a claim (particularly in terms of innovation review) in the course of examination proceeding or in invalidation proceeding, equivalent features also need to be taken into account.

5.14.4. *Practical suggestion*

Attention should be paid to understanding the logic of the examiner during the prosecution, as long as the prior art structure disclosed one of the embodiments of structure as described in the examined application (note that the prior art structure must be a necessary structure or its equivalent to achieve the claimed function), the structure is deemed as disclosed by the prior art structure. The BRI should still be used to interpret what is the structure when comparing with the prior art structure. In this case, you can modify functional limitation following the means , making it more specific so as to cover more specific structure or argue that the structural features corresponding the claimed functional limitation explicitly link or associate to a more specific structure.

5.15. For China

In China, the examination proceeding and the infringement litigation adopt different interpretation approach to determine the scope of the claim.

According to Patent Examination Guidelines Part II, Chapter II, Section 3.2.1, the functional limitation in a claim should be interpreted as to cover all the implementations which are capable of implementing the claimed function. However, according to Article 4 of the *Interpretation (I) of Supreme People's Court*, for technical features expressed by function or effect in the claims, the people's court should combine the specific embodimentsof the functions or effect and their equivalent embodiments described in the specification and accompanying drawings to determine the content of the technical features.

5.16. Subject Matter Eligibility Functional Limitation

The question of Subject Matter Eligibility addresses the issue of whether the claim sought is an abstract idea, law of nature, or a natural phenomenon without a specific application.

On the other hand, §112(f) deals with whether the technical term is defined or limited, whether the function is defined only by the functional language without structures or acts; and determining whether the specification discloses the corresponding structures, material, or steps performing the claimed function.

5.16.1. *Exemplary claims with the mix of §101 and §112(f) issues*

Claim 1. An device comprising:

> module a, configured to do A;
> module b, configured to do B; and
> module c, configured to do C.

The examiner may reject Claim 1 on the grounds of software per se and accordingly not meet the §101 requirement. At the same time, the examiner may also apply §112(f) to Claim 1, and reject it 1 on the grounds of §112(b) if the corresponding structure is not disclosed or deemed to have inadequate disclosure after applying §112(f);

If Claim 1 is modified to the structure of "memory + processor", software per se rejection can be overcome, and meanwhile, the problem of §112(f) may also be avoided; or

Instead of modifying Claim 1, you may identify the corresponding structure described in the specification that performed the functional limitation following the "module", which may also overcome the §112(f) and §101 if the specific structure implementation is tied to a hardware apparatus.

Claim 2. An server comprising:

> module a, configured to store a parameter; and
> module b, configured to execute an formulation according to the parameter.

The examiner may reject Claim 2 on two grounds; 1) being an abstract idea implemented in a general purpose computer, and 2) based on the ground of §112(b) if the corresponding structure is not disclosed or has inadequate disclosure after applying §112(f).

Merely modifying Claim 2 by using the "memory + processor" style can't overcome the abstract idea rejection, but the modification may avoid invoking §112(f) and accordingly overcome the §112(b) rejection under the current law practice.

Instead of modifying Claim 2, an alternative strategy is to identify the corresponding structure described in the specification that performed the functional limitation following the "module", which may also overcome the §112(f) and §101 if the specific structure implementation is tied to a hardware apparatus and constitutes a specific application of the abstract idea.

5.16.2. *A few case studies*

(a) In re Alappat, when 33 F.3d 1526, 31 USPQ2d 1545 (Fed. Cir. 1994) (en banc):.

The representative claim 15 in this case reads:

A rasterizer for converting vector list data representing sample magnitudes of an input waveform into anti-aliased pixel illumination intensity data to be displayed on a display means comprising: (a) means for determining the vertical distance between the endpoints of each of the vectors in the data list; (b) means for determining the elevation of a row of pixels that is spanned by the vector; (c) means for normalizing the vertical distance and elevation; and (d) means for outputting illumination intensity data as a predetermined function of the normalized vertical distance and elevation.

The Federal Circuit held that "[A]s recently explained in In re Donaldson,... the PTO is not exempt from following the statutory mandate of 112.6.... The board majority therefore erred as a matter of law in refusing to apply 112.6 in rendering its §101 patentable subject matter determination."

(b) *Allvoice Developments US, LLC v. Microsoft Corp.* (Fed. Cir. 2015)
The representative claim 60 reads:

A universal speech-recognition interface that enables operative coupling of a speech-recognition engine to at least any one of a plurality of different computer-related applications, the universal speech-recognition interface comprising: input means for receiving speech-recognition data including recognisedz words; output means for outputting the recognisedz words into at least any one of the plurality of different computer-related applications to allow processing of the recognisedz words as input text; and audio playback means for playing audio data associated with the recognisedz words.

The claim is interpreted as a pure software or software per se and thus does not meet the requirement of §101 (non-statutory subject matter) and accordingly is invalid, and Federal Circuit affirmed the invalidation of the claim. According to the footnote on page 17 of the slip opinion, the defendant didn't motion to require to interpret the claims under §112(f) before determining the §101 issue.[23] The Federal Circuit nevertheless addressed this missing argument and held that even if making §112(f) interpretation, the claim should still be invalided as the description didn't disclose tangible structures to save the claim from pure software.

a) *Enfish, LLC v. Microsoft Corp.* (Fed. Cir. May 12, 2016)
The representative claim 17 at issue recites:

A data storage and retrieval system for a computer memory, comprising:

means for configuring said memory according to a logical table, said logical table including:

a plurality of logical rows, each said logical row including an object identification number (OID) to identify each said logical row, each said logical row corresponding to a record of information;

a plurality of logical columns intersecting said plurality of logical rows to define a plurality of logical cells, each said logical column including an OID to identify each said logical column; and

means for indexing data stored in said table.

---

[23]The footnote stated: "[a]lthough Allvoice did not ground its opposition to Microsoft's motion for summary judgment on any benefits received from employing functional claiming under §112(6), it is also significant that the means-plus-function limitations, as construed by Allvoice, do not correspond to tangible structure, as opposed to software instructions."

The district court construed the "means for configuring" language as requiring a four-step algorithm pursuant to 35 U.S.C. §112 ¶ 6 (2006) before performing the subject matter eligibility analysis. The U.S. Court of Appeals for the Federal Circuit (Federal Circuit) didn't disturb the district court's construction approach and outcome, but reversed the district court's subject matter ineligibility conclusion based on improvement in computer functionality theory.

b)   *TLI Communications LLC v. A. V. Automotive, LLC* (Fed. Cir. May 17, 2016)
     The representative claim is claim 17 which reads:

A method for recording and administering digital images, comprising the steps of:

recording images using a digital pick up unit in a telephone unit, storing the images recorded by the digital pick up unit in a digital form as digital images,

transmitting data including at least the digital images and classification information to a server, wherein said classification information is prescribable by a user of the telephone unit for allocation to the digital images,

receiving the data by the server,

extracting classification information which characterizes the digital images from the received data, and

storing the digital images in the server, said step of storing taking into consideration the classification information.

Independent claims 1 and 25 recite substantially the same concept but direct to an apparatus or system. Claim 1 includes a "means for allocating classification information prescribed by a user of said at least one telephone unit to characterize digital images obtained by said digital pick up unit." Likewise, claim 25 recites a "means . . . to allocate information in the corresponding digital still image data."
The Federal Circuit stated:

The district court declined to give patentable weight to the claims' recitation of a telephone unit or a server, or to the "means for allocating" limitation in claims 1 and 25. As a result, the district court granted the defendants' motion to dismiss.

...

Because we agree with the district court that the patent-in-suit claims no more than the abstract idea of classifying and storing digital images in an organized manner, we affirm the district court's judgment and do not reach the §112 ¶6 issue.

As can be seen from this case, the Federal Circuit affirmed the district court's skipping the interpretation of the "means for…" limitation before performing the subject matter eligibility analysis.

c) *Apple, Inc. et al v. Mirror World Technologies, LLC* (CBM2016-00019) The PTAB concluded in this CBM case that the claim format is not the determining factor in a §101 analysis:

> In reaching this determination, we have considered the arguments pre-sented in the parties' supplemental submissions (Papers 9 and 11), addressing *Enfish* as well as the Federal Circuit's recent decision in *In re TLI Commc'ns LLC Patent Litg.*, Nos. 2015-1372 et al. (Fed. Cir. May 17, 2016). We are not persuaded by Petitioner's argument that the chal-lenged claims are "analogous" to the claims in *TLI*. Paper 11, 2. Nor do we attach significance to the fact that the claims considered in *Enfish* had means-plus-function limitations, as claim format is not the deter-mining factor in a §101 analysis. Id. at 4–5.

Based on the logic of this case, PTAB seems to not perform "means for…" limitation interpretation before doing subject matter eligibility analysis.

5.16.3. *Practical suggestions*

(a) For a software implemented invention, even if there is a correspond-ing algorithm structure representing the claimed function following the "means" in the specification, and if the algorithm structure is not combined with hardware structure executing the intangible algorithm structure (e.g., processor, computer, microprocessor programmed with the algorithm), then it not only may cause §101 problems (i.e., facing §101 rejection on the grounds of software per se), but also may result in §112(b) according to PTO's guideline for Determining Compliance With 35 U.S.C. §112[24], which requires the corresponding structure to be an algorithm and the computer or microprocessor programmed with the algorithm. Therefore, when you write software implementation embodiments for performing the claimed function, you not only need to disclose in the specification the detailed algorithms structure, such as the processes, steps, etc., corresponding to the claimed function, but also need to disclose the hardware apparatus or device executing the software algorithms.

(b) As for rejection or invalidation during prosecution or litigation, if you can overcome the rejection or invalidation through applying §112(f), then you may want to consider the triggering requirements of applying §112(f). However, this is not an omnipotent tool that can be used anywhere, the use of this approach must meet some basic conditions. A statement that use of MPF language would help overcome prior art does not magically transform language that clearly does not meet the court's legal test for §112.6 into MPF language. (See Trimed, Inc. v. Stryker Corp., 514 F3d. 1788-90 (Fed. Cir. 2008)).

5.17. Software Invention and Functional Limitation

5.17.1. *Federal Circuit's Case Law: the corresponding structure is the algorithm*

In the following sections, we'll analyze a few US cases addressing algorithms being the structure for functional limitation claims.

(a) WMS Gaming, Inc. v. International Game Technology, 184 F.3d 1339, 1349 (Fed. Cir. 1999).
(b) Harris Corp. v. Ericsson Inc., 417 F.3d 1241, 1249 (Fed. Cir. 2005).
(c) *Aristocrat Technologies Australia Pty Ltd v. International Game Technology, 521 F.3d 1328 (Fed. Cir. 2008).*

---

[24]Supplementary Examination Guidelines for Determining Compliance With 35 U.S.C. §112 and for Treatment of Related Issues in Patent Applications, Federal Register / Vol. 76, No. 27 / Wednesday, February 9, 2011 / Notices.

In Aristocrat, 521 F.3d 1328, the court set forth that for a claim to a programmed computer, a particular algorithm may be the corresponding structure under §112, *sixth paragraph:* For a patentee to claim a means for performing a particular function and then to disclose only a general purpose computer as the structure designed to perform that function amounts to *pure functional claiming*. Because general purpose computers can be programmed to perform very different tasks in very different ways, simply disclosing a computer as the structure designated to perform a particular function does not limit the scope of the claim to "the corresponding structure, material, or acts" that perform the function, as required by section §112 paragraph 6.

Thus, in a MPF claim "in which the disclosed structure is a computer, or microprocessor, programmed to carry out an algorithm, the disclosed structure is not the general purpose computer, but rather the special purpose computer programmed to perform the disclosed algorithm."[25]

The court in [Harris Corp.] characterized the rule of WMS Gaming as follows: "[The corresponding structure for a §112 ¶ 6 claim for a computer-implemented function is the algorithm disclosed in the specification."[26]

5.17.2. *Guidelines for Determining Compliance With 35 U.S.C. §112*[27]

PTO guideline is that the corresponding structure is an algorithm and the computer or microprocessor programmed with the algorithm.

The PTO seems to require the combination of the software algorithm and the hardware performing the software algorithm to constitute a complete corresponding structure performing the claimed function. The following are several statements from the guideline in relevant parts:

---

[25]WMS Gaming, Inc. v. International Game Technology, 184 F.3d 1339, 1349 (Fed. Cir. 1999).
[26]Harris Corp. v. Ericsson Inc., 417 F.3d 1241, 1249 (Fed. Cir. 2005).
[27]Supplementary Examination Guidelines for Determining Compliance With 35 U.S.C. §112 and for Treatment of Related Issues in Patent Applications, Federal Register / Vol. 76, No. 27 / Wednesday, February 9, 2011 / Notices.

Often the supporting disclosure for a computer-implemented invention discusses the implementation of the functionality of the invention through hardware, software, or a combination of both. In this situation, a question can arise as to which mode of implementation supports the means plus function limitation. The language of §112, ¶ 6 requires that the recited "means" for performing the specified function shall be construed to cover the corresponding "structure or material" described in the specification and equivalents thereof. Therefore, by choosing to use a MPF limitation and invoke §112, ¶ 6, applicant limits that claim limitation to the disclosed structure, *i.e.* implementation by hardware or the combination of hardware and software, and equivalents thereof. Therefore, the examiner should not construe the limitation as covering pure software implementation.

However, if there is no corresponding structure disclosed in the specification (*i.e. the limitation is only supported by* software and does not correspond to an algorithm and the computer or microprocessor programmed with the algorithm), the limitation should be deemed indefinite as discussed above, and the claim should be rejected under §112, ¶ 2. It is important to remember that claims must be interpreted as a whole; so, a claim that includes a means-plus-function limitation that corresponds to software *per se (and is* thus indefinite for lacking structural support in the specification) is not necessarily directed as a whole to software *per se unless the claim lacks* other structural limitations.

5.17.3. *China practice*

According to Article 4 of the *Interpretation (I) of Supreme People's Court*, for "technical features expressed by function or effect in the claims, the people's court should combine the specific embodiments of the functions or effect and their equivalent embodiments…" described in the specification and accompanying drawings; and then determine the content of the technical features. Article 4 only requires the patent application to disclose the specific embodiments of the functions or effect and their equivalent embodiments in the specification and accompanying drawings as the technical content of the functional feature, there is no special requirement for what the structure needs to be.

Chapter 6

For Portfolio Managers, Patent Sellers/Buyers, CFOs, VCs, or Investment Bankers (Relating to IP Valuation)

6.1. Intellectual Property

Patent portfolio managers need to have a good understanding of patent filing trends in the relevant industries, stay on top of competitor's patented technologies, and constantly assess how his portfolio compares with other's portfolios. In other words, he is required to have a solid grasp of the IP landscape.

The same requirement applies to patent buyers and sellers. Buyers need to know who has what kind of patents and whether they are willing to sell. Sellers need to know who likely needs what kind of patents during certain time period and what are the reasonable pricings to ask for those assets.

There are many tools available to perform such analysis, such as Innography, Thomson Reuters, Questel, Dolcera, Wisdomain, IPortfolio, AcclaimIP, etc. USPTO and SIPO provide free patent search capabilities as well. As an example, Figure 6-1 depicts the electrical car patent filing statistics for all the currently active patents (granted or pending) up to the

Mining Ideas for Diamonds

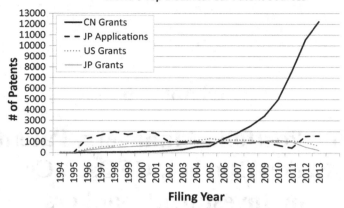

Figure 6-1   World-Wide Electrical Car Patents Filing trend.

end of 2013. This particular figure was produced using the Innography tool. For electrical car related innovations, it is evident that Japan used to dominate the world-wide patent filing activities. In Figure 6-1, it appears that there were relatively high filing rates in Japan for electrical car inventions from 1998 through 2001. However, by 2002, Japan patent filings have suddenly dipped. Since then, Japan patent filings stayed at a relatively flat lower level till 2011, and then had a resurge of activities in 2012 and 2013 to the previous level prior to 2001. In contrast, China's patent grant rate related to electrical car has taken off drastically in the past several years, suggesting both the growing importance of this technology to Chinese companies and the large number of innovations associated with such huge investment. On the other hand, US patents in the electrical car area seem to have no major breakthroughs.

In the above exemplary case, companies in electrical car industry can study these trends and compare with their own IP strategy. More importantly, by highlighting the significant "outliers" that stand out among other indicators, you might be able to spot potential upcoming changes or disruptive technologies/events which may trigger changes in your strategy. If there are differences between your portfolio and these trends, you may revisit your own patent filing strategy. If you are still confident that you are on the right track, then you can choose to continuously stay on the previous course. If you discover that your previous IP strategy neglected some important factors, then you may want to modify your IP strategy going forward.

Applying patents and getting them allowed takes time; and the final granted patent qualities are sometimes difficult to control. Therefore, companies frequently keep an open mind and look into acquiring patents either for the purpose of defending their current or future products, or for product development freedom of use. One can get a glimpse of a company's potential technology/product directions through their patent acquisition behaviors. These transaction data are public information. It was reported that some companies try to conceive such patent purchase activities using patent-holding "shell companies" or simply not record them. However, White House executive action, USPTO proposed rule, and US congress patent reform bill attempted promoting patent ownership transparency where patent owners not timely recording their assignments may, for example, lose the right to enforce these patents until the date of registration. Such initiatives, although they did not become final policy, nevertheless hopefully have prompted many companies to record patent assignments properly and swiftly.

To illustrate this point, Figure 6-2 is a graph of Google's 2014 patent acquisition data of acquired US granted patents, using publically available USPTO information combined with the Innography tool. The horizontal axis is the recorded patent purchase agreement Execution Date (i.e. patent acquisition date), the vertical axis is the number of acquired granted US patents, while the depth axis represents the names of patent owners who originally owned the patents that were eventually sold to Google in 2014. The legends above or beside the data bar represent the patent owner name, technology area these patents cover, and the number of patents. A few data bars also include the CPC code (represented by darker black fonts) of the corresponding patent clusters. As can be seen from Figure 6-2, there were 10 patent acquisition deals in 2014 and the acquired technologies include optical fiber, SMS portfolios, LED, Content Delivery Network, UI/User profile, low power transparent keypad, etc. These patent acquisition technology areas, timing, the number of acquired patents, and the amount paid can all provide some insights into a company's IP strategy.

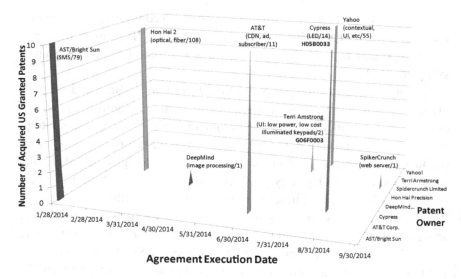

Figure 6-2   Google 2014 granted US patent acquisition information.

6.2. Spotting "Disruptive Technologies" or "Disruptive Triggers" in Specific Industries

One can use similar landscape approaches to track competitor's utility patent filing activities as well as patent purchase or patent sales activities. They can help one spot which direction competitors are paying special attention to. Compared to trend analysis using pure patent filing volume, the increase in patent filing from year-to-year is a better indication of the growth areas. High volume of patent filing might mean that there is a big team who continuously work on this technology area and thus keep generating more patents than other teams. However, the rate of increase for patents generated from one year versus the year before might be an indication of the "high investment growth area" by a particular company. If looking at the entire industry, it might uncover a "disruptive technology" or "disruptive feature" that's in the making.

Figure 6-3 is a graph of patent filing annual growth rate for different smartphone-related technologies between 2007 and 2010. To spot important trends, we only look at those patent technology categories that are growing at least 100%+ of previous year's filing rate. As can be seen from

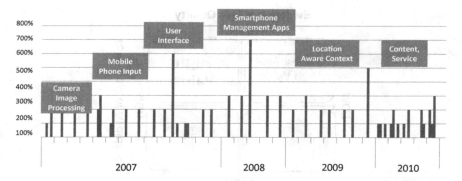

Figure 6-3   High investment areas by smartphone companies during 2007–2010.

Figure 6-3, in 2007, camera image processing, mobile phone input, and user interface are among the high investment technology areas for smartphone companies. In 2008, the investment was more focused on smartphone applications. By 2009, location aware context was the high investment area. In 2010, how to deliver content and services to smartphone users became the focal point of smartphone companies. For companies who didn't have access to similar analysis or the proper tools, they may end up investing in the wrong technology areas that are not in alignment with the industry. As a result, they may completely "miss the boat" of the next revolution in their industries. On the other hand, if you regularly monitor patent filing trends, you may spot opportunities that others miss and thus gain the "first mover" advantage in seizing the new market leadership position.

However, identifying the next great business opportunity is not limited to discovering a new "disruptive technology". A "disruptive business model" can lead to a great new market as well. Uber is a good model to illustrate this point, where a new business model quickly took business away from traditional taxi companies and became a "Billion Dollar" company overnight.

In addition, through studying patent filing trends, you may also spot a "disruptive trigger" that destroys existing businesses. For example, in Figure 4-4 of the above Chapter 4, quality for software patents spiked up after USSC's *Alice* decision. Such real change in market behavior indicates a significant impact of Supreme Court's decision. One could have

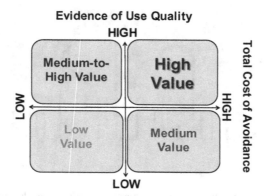

Figure 6-4   Matrix to value a patent.

thus anticipated other rippling effects such as high patent invalidity rates, reluctance of licensees' paying royalties, etc. The subsequent difficulties in non-practicing-entities ("NPE")'s licensing efforts drove many NPEs to bankruptcy. If one spotted such a "disruptive trigger" early on, he may be able to build a business model leveraging such a "disruptive trigger".

These patent filing trend analyses are useful to more than just patent Portfolio Managers. They are also helpful to Chief Financial Officers (CFOs), Venture Capitalists (VCs), and Investment Bankers. A CFO is responsible for his/her company's financial bottom lines and thus should be aware of its own patent status versus industry. For example, he/she may need to question the Portfolio Manager if there are gaps or excess of certain types of patents compared to industry trends and your company's short/long-term needs. The CFO would want to and should understand the reasons behind any imbalances as well as future plans to correct them so that he/she can plan the budget approval accordingly.

A Venture Capitalist, on the other hand, needs to understand his/her portfolio company's IP strength and weaknesses compared to competitions, in order to gain a good understanding of future financial/legal risks and whether the company is able to protect its market share.

Similarly For investment bankers, whether they are investing, purchasing, or divesting a company with IPs, they need to understand the valuation of such company's patent portfolio so they can put a market price to the IP portfolio for the transaction. However, having a good understanding about the valuation of the patent portfolio is an extremely challenging task and, we believe, there are currently no good solutions on the market and many are not using the correct matrix. We'll discuss the related issues and explore some practical approaches based on our first-hand experiences.

6.3. Gap Analysis

Company management often asks employees to do a gap analysis. This doesn't mean comparing your total number of patents with that of competitors. Your IP needs are likely different from that of your competitors. Even your own needs today are likely different from yours a year ago. Therefore, gap analysis should mean conducting an IP portfolio assessment to see if it meets your company's business needs. You need to answer whether your IP supply is meeting the requirement of your IP demand.

The purpose of performing an IP landscape analysis is to compare relative strength and weakness; discover gaps and fill them as soon as possible. This involves not simply comparing the number of patents each party owns, patent quality comes into play as well and is perhaps the most important factor. Currently, due to the lack of available analytics tools that look at whether a patent maps onto a product, most such analysis must be done manually.

Ideally one should have a desired number of high quality patents mapped onto each target company's products. If there is a gap between the current portfolio and the desired goal, portfolio managers need to have plans on how to fill that gap, within what time frame, either accomplished via internal patent filings or via external patent acquisitions. However, before we discuss how to perform such analysis, we must be on the same page regarding what is considered a high value patent.

6.4. How to Define a High Value Patent

6.4.1. *Defining a "high quality patent"*

To ensure a high quality patent portfolio, the first step ("Step 1") is to make sure the right decision is made regarding whether an invention is worth filing. The second step (Step 2) is controlling process and choke points vigorously during patent application drafting and prosecution to increase the probability of generating high quality patents. Let's look at what constitutes a high quality patent.

People often say that "beauty is in the eyes of the beholder", i.e. whether a patent is a high value or not depends on who is buying. The authors disagree. We believe that there should be a common measure regarding a patent's quality. In this chapter, we propose a more accurate model in defining a high value patent. However, it is undeniable that the price a buyer is willing to pay for a high quality patent depends on the potential buyer's particular situation. For example, a litigation defendant may be willing to pay more for a patent in order to better defend itself in the court. On the other hand, a licensing entity may not want to pay too much even for a high quality patent if there is no immediate time pressure. In this chapter, we focus largely on the intrinsic value of a patent which can be objectively measured. The final pricing of such a patent are influenced by the external factors such as buyer's special needs at the time of purchase, seller's particular situation at the time of sale, number of bidders, market perception, etc. They will only be discussed briefly.

There are a few main approaches in evaluating a patent, for example, market approach, cost approach, or income approach. All three approaches are based on gaining a substantial understanding of the quality of a patent, so as to benchmark it in the market, estimating cost to buy the patent or offensive/defensive income that could be generated from the patent. There are many objective indicators being used to value a patent, such as the number of forward citation, countries covered by counterparts, number of claims, length of independent claim, etc. These objective indicators may be useful to quickly get a sense of the value of a patent, but most of the times they are not accurate. For example, one patent may have a lot of forward citations, which may indicate that it is technically important. However, if the patent claims are poorly drafted and doesn't map onto any products, the patent's quality decreases significantly.

In the following, we propose that patent valuation shall be determined mainly by two key parameters, (1) Total Cost of Avoidance (TCA) and (2) Evidence of Use Quality (EoUQ).

6.4.2. *Total Cost of Avoidance (TCA) — technical/ business question*

(i) TCA means the amount of money and resources required as well as the financial impact experienced to avoid patent infringement. This will include how broad is the claim that will likely survive an invalidity challenge (a broader claim typically means a bigger market size, but is more likely to be invalidated due to prior arts), how many workaround there are, how difficult it is to switch from one solution to another for current users and installed base, how many industries is the invention applicable to, how angry customers might be upon switch, whether the feature is a mandatory required feature for a commonly used Standard, etc.

(ii) Nowadays, the practice of "patent fencing" or "patent surrounding" is popular in some industries. Often one may file several patents covering a single product feature. As a result, another company will have to obtain rights to all relevant patents when designing around this one feature. Therefore, it is also important to assess the TCA taking into consideration of all related patents, or what are required to avoid the entire family.

Another factor to consider is how difficult it is to invalidate the patent. In the US, Patent Trial and Review Board (PTAB) currently construes patent claims broadly and thus produces a high percentage of invalidity decision in its *inter partes review (IPR)* rulings. Although China State Intellectual Property Office (SIPO) doesn't have the exact equivalent procedures to *IPR* or *covered business method* (CBM), one can petition to invalidate a Chinese patent as well by bringing the case in front of SIPO's Patent Reexamination Board (PRB). Therefore, one should keep in mind these considerations and be cognizant that the cost of patent invalidity dependents on the particular country.

6.4.3. *Evidence of Use Quality (EoUQ) — legal/ business question*

(i) EoUQ refers to how well a patent maps onto the product, how easy it is to detect the infringement, how good is the specification and file history in supporting the claims, and how well a claim is written.

(ii) The EoUQ analysis also needs to consider different practices in different countries. For example, USPTO routinely allows claims that may not be fully described in the specification. In comparison, Chinese patent law imposes more restrictive criteria than that of the US patent law in order to support priority claims. In addition, a complainant, for example, can file a patent suit seeking injunctive relief in US ITC court provided that it meets the domestic industry requirement. On the other hand, a plaintiff in China's patent infringement litigation bears a heavy burden of producing evidence. Although legislative efforts have been made in recent years, it remains a well-recognized problem for the plaintiff to produce evidences of infringement and damage in a Chinese court. If a patent claims computer implemented methods, algorithms or software modules that are difficult to reverse engineer, chances are that plaintiff will lose a lawsuit for lack of evidence in China.

In summary, if both TCA and EoUQ are high, meaning it will be very difficult for the infringer to switch to another solution without spending a lot of money or resources, while at the same time the patent (a) maps onto third party products very well; (b) is supported and enabled by the specification; (c) there are no estoppels in the file history; and (d) patent claims are well drafted, then it is definitely a high value patent.

On the other hand, if both TCA and EoUQ are low, then it is deemed as a low value patent as shown in Figure 6-4. The cases in between are either medium or medium-to-high value patents. If EoUQ is high, even if the TCA is low, it could still be a reasonable patent and thus is deemed as a medium-to-high value patent.

6.5. Patent Portfolio Valuation Methods

6.5.1. *Existing patent valuation methodologies*

There are many different ways to value a patent portfolio. Some utilizes the innovation cycle S-curve as shown in Figure 6-5, which suggests that innovation goes through four phases, starting initially at the Infancy phase (or Incubation phase), may move onto to Growth phase, then Maturity

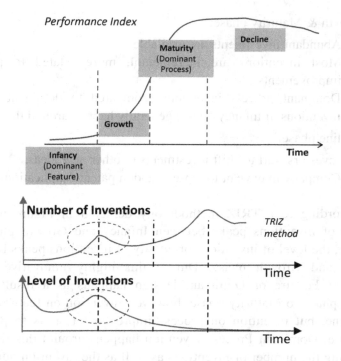

Figure 6-5   Performance index S-curve and its relationship to inventions.

phase, and finally to Decline phase. Each phase has its own following characteristics.

(a) Infancy phase:
   (1) Technology may not be fully proven.
   (2) Cautious investment by investors because the concept is market proven (even though not fully adopted by market).
   (3) More innovative patents are being invented, patent volume (indicated as number of inventions in Figure 6-5) and patent quality (represented by Level of Inventions in Figure 6-5) should peak around late stage of this phase, according to TRIZ methodology. The patent volume and patent quality peaks are highlighted with a dashed-line circle for each case.
   (4) Dominant feature or dominant design innovations happen during this phase.

(b) Growth & Maturity phase:

    (1) Abundant investments are available.

    (2) Most inventions are incremental, more related to process improvements.

    (3) Dominant process inventions (compared to dominant feature inventions in Infancy phase) generally happen around this period.

(c) Decline phase:

    (1) Investors start to shift investments to other new ideas.

    (2) Company may want to lapse/abandon patents/applications.

According to a TRIZ methodology depicted in Figure 6-5, the number of inventions peaks between Infancy and Growth phase. In addition, the level of inventions or quality of inventions peaks between Infancy and Growth phase. During this highly innovative phase, Dominant Feature or Dominant Design happens as a result. From Growth phase to Maturity phase, however, invention on features starts to decline, but invention on process improvement starts to pick up. Therefore, Dominant Process invention happens around this time. By examining the number of inventions as well as the invention quality, in conjunction with the product performance, one can identify key ideas, who are key players, high potential new entrances, key technology categories, potential new usages, global strategy and evolution, and potential partners. In addition, you might be able to uncover which phase a technology is currently in, should your company focus on design or process, how long technology may last, how much effort your company should invest in the technology, where should your company invest in, etc.

Other valuation method combines theoretical assumption with market pricing. Such theory relies on the assumption, as shown in Figure 6-6(a), that patent value ("Value") is a function of a few parameters, one of which is patent's remaining life. Initially in the Infancy phase, the patent has low value because market hasn't discovered the technology. Thereafter, as market moves into Growth phase and Maturity phase, value increases with adoption of the technology. However, as the market moves into Decline phase, value decreases.

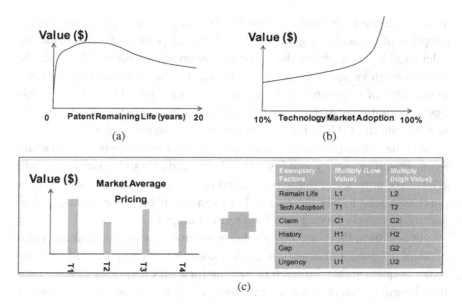

Figure 6-6   Exemplary theoretical assumptions for patent valuation.

Figure 6-6(b) depicts the relationship of Value as a function of market adoption of the specific technology. The greater adoption percentage the technology has gained by the market, the higher Value the patent has. As the market adoption approaches a critical mass, patent Value goes up faster because mass adoption becomes inevitable.

Similarly, Value depends on current market average pricing as shown by the left graph in Figure 6-6(c). The horizontal axis represents transactions occurred in the past, while the vertical axis represents average pricing per patent for each past patent sale/purchase transactions (T1, T2, T3, T4, etc). A patent's final pricing is calculated based on the average market pricing modified by the parameters listed in the table on the right-hand side of Figure 6-6(c). The table includes a few Exemplary Factors being listed (not in order of importance) for illustration purposes such as Remaining life, Technology Adoption %, Claim broadness, File History cleanliness, Gap in purchaser's patent portfolio, Urgency of purchaser's needs to fill the gap.

In summary, Figure 6-6 presents an exemplary theoretical model for the final market pricing estimation of a patent. The assumptions include

a) value depends on patent remaining life; (b) value depends on market adoption of the technology; (c) the final market pricing of a patent can be calculated by multiplying the value dependencies on various key factors. The low/high values of such top key parameters are listed and symbolized in the table of Figure 6-6 as L1/L2 for remaining life, T1/T2 for technology adoption rate by the market, C1/C2 for claim quality, H1/H2 for file history quality, G1/G2 for gap in purchaser's patent portfolio (i.e. how good is the patent purchaser's current portfolio. For example, is he starting from scratch or merely making minor improvements to his portfolio), and U1/U2 for urgency in purchaser's need (i.e. how urgently does the patent purchaser need to buy the patent. For example, is he in the middle of litigations or merely buying as a long term strategy).

In addition, there are many other valuation approaches that are independent of patent transaction market average pricing. Instead, it only looks at quantifiable parameters such as forward citation, backward citation, length of patent prosecution, whether in litigation in the past, number of corresponding CPC codes, number of claims, length of claim, etc.

6.5.2. *What's missing in current patent valuation tools?*

However, none of the current available methodology utilizes the most important factor when valuing a patent, i.e. **whether the patent reads onto a target company's product. They also don't look at other important factors such as how easily detectable is the infringement, or how big is the market adoption**. All the currently available analytics tools use various combinations of factors that are intrinsic to the patent itself, such as forward citation, backward citation, length of prosecution, length of independent claims, rather than looking at whether a patent maps onto competitor's products or available standards. Part of the reason might be the fear of putting tool users "on notice" and thus expose them to potential willful infringement risks in the future. However, there are ways to mitigate or avoid such a risk. Other reasons include that it is very difficult to scan products available on the market (or coming onto the market soon) and determine whether they infringe a particular patent. Many infringements are difficult to detect. However, patent analytics tool vendors should embrace such challenges rather than shun away from them. They should seize such opportunities and develop a solution that truly meets client's needs.

6.5.3. *Patent value may change with product cycle*

In addition, products available on the market change with time. A patent's value could drop significantly overnight if it is determined to not read onto a popular product or, even worse, to be deemed invalid by court. On the other hand, a medium value patent that maps onto a niche feature today could become a high value patent in a few years because the covered feature has been widely adopted by most products or deemed as mandatory by a Standard. Thus, portfolio managers need to re-evaluate their patent valuation periodically in order to not miss such product cycle change or other important "triggering" events.

Therefore, authors propose the following patent valuation methodology. Before we dive into details, our previous methodology continues to apply, i.e. for pending applications, you should start out with the most important two factors described in Chapter 3 as to whether to file a patent, i.e. (i) will someone use this idea significantly within the patent lifetime; and (ii) will the pending application be allowed, if not already a granted patent, with claims unlikely to be invalidated. For granted patents, you use the two factors discussed in this chapter for high quality patents, i.e. (i) EoUQ; and (ii) TCAs. One may attempt to define patent value as when a patent transaction occurs, each patent will have a commercial value attached to it, although this value could vary with time and change significantly for each potential buyer depending on their specific purpose at the time of purchase. The rationales for these extrinsic dependences have been discussed briefly in the above section.

However, we believe portfolio valuations should be performed based on an intrinsic valuation. This intrinsic value represents a fair market value to the IP industry and is independent of each particular buyer. A transaction will only occur when there is a reasonable match between the intrinsic value and a particular buyer's need at a particular time.

Initially we did not plan to look at the intrinsic valuation because we falsely believed that until a patent is to be transacted or prepared to be used for an IP purpose either defensively or offensively, there is no reason to attach a value. However, we now realize that modern portfolio management requires a thorough understanding of what you have in your portfolio; where the gaps are and how to mitigate them; what the strength are and how/when to leverage those strengths to your company's greatest advantage. Then, you have truly mastered your own IP destination and can fully seize each opportunities presented your way. A good analogy is the investment housing value, i.e. your second or third house located in a volatile part of the world as an investment rather than the primary house your family lives in. Assume you don't own the land but are merely leasing the land for 20 years. Then, your investment housing price could face similar fate as a patent and change overnight, for example due to discovery of non-conformance to building code, invalid ownership rights, newly discovered disaster or toxic zone, or an impending domestic/local war. In fact, your investment house could be foreclosed if you don't pay your property tax. The valuation of your house will be similar to those around you, with variations caused by how well your house was built initially, how well you maintained it, how good the overall market is at the time, the property tax you pay, local natural resources under your property, and how eager is a potential buyer due to his/her special situation. Having a good understanding about the potential value of your investment house will impact your making a wise decision whether/when to remodel, sell, lease, and exclusively have somebody rent the house or let multiple renters share the house, or simply do nothing.

Similarly for corporations, it is important to understand the potential value of your IP portfolio, what you can do with it if you choose to, so that you can make corresponding informed and well contemplated choices. For example, if you know your patent portfolio is sorely needed by another company, it might change your business strategy on how to deal with that company, whether it is a competitor, suppler, customer, partner, or a company with very little existing business relationship. Therefore, authors strongly recommend all business entities, regardless of big or small to conduct a thorough valuation analysis of your IP portfolio as well as an overall landscape analysis and continuously monitor the changes. We are indeed in the era of IP strategy truly assisting, or under certain circumstances driving, innovation and business strategy. In the current competitive and fast moving world, your company should leverage all the information available to you in order to stay ahead or, in some cases, simply stay alive.

6.5.4. *Our proposed methodology to evaluate patent intrinsic values*

We propose to consider internal or intrinsic valuation first and perform external valuation based on external factors. A flow-chart of how to arrive at such an intrinsic valuation is illustrated in Figure 6-7. Our intrinsic valuation methodology is based on EoUQ and TCA in the following order:

(a) Does the patent map onto any third party's products?

— This question is actually asking whether the patent maps onto any third party products that are not licensed. You need to first evaluate whether the patent maps precisely onto any current products by third parties that are not licensed. Please be aware that, as discussed in Chapter 3, only patents that read onto third party products have value. If it reads onto your own products, it has value provided third parties might use this patent in the future. To answer this question, one needs to be cognizant that you should only look at products in the geography that your patent covers. For example, for a US granted patent or patent application, you should look at products that are being used, made, have made, sold, being offered for sale, being imported into US. Similarly for a Chinese patent, you'll look at these actions in relation to China. If the answer is a "no", then ask **how likely it will read onto any future products by unlicensed third parties, in the geography covered by the patent, within patent lifetime,** if the answer is still a "no", then stop here and assign a valuation of $0 to this patent. If the answer is a "yes" or "maybe", you can proceed to the next step.

As stated previously, whether a patent maps onto a third party product could change over time, for example the previously covered product might become obsolete, or to be made in a different country where you happen to have neglected applying for patent protection. Therefore, the valuation of your portfolio, even when you don't take any actions, could change with time. Thus, it is important that you regularly revise the valuation of your portfolio and take actions that help increase your strength/valuation. More importantly, you can execute and deliver appropriate IP motions effectively/timely whenever your portfolio is called upon to action.

(b) How difficult is it to invalidate the patent?

This must take into consideration prior arts, how well the patent was drafted, whether the claim was overly broad, and if the claims are supported by the specifications. In addition, you also need to consider the local IP practices and the relevant venues. For example in US, one can invalidate a patent via *IPR*, CBM, PGR invalidation process in front of PTAB, or via a patent suit in district courts such as declaratory judgment proceedings.

However, even if all claims of a patent are likely to be invalidated, it doesn't necessarily mean the patent has low value. It may still have medium value if its other family members or foreign counterparts are not invalidated. In those cases, it still has value as a supporting patent during negotiation. Therefore, you can depreciate the patent valuation in this case because mapping onto a third party's product is the most important criteria in valuation.

(c) Is the covered product significant?

This is not simply asking for revenue of products covered by the patent, you need to take into consideration the strategic importance of the covered product to the companies making the product. For example, a high volume product with very little or negative profit may not necessarily be considered a significant coverage if the company is planning to shift out of that product already. Of course, knowing this fact, you can put the third party on notice to start accruing past damages. Then in that case, the coverage could be turned into a significant one. Similarly for small volume products, if it is highly profitable or highly strategic to the third party's business direction, it could be a very significant coverage. In addition, as discussed in the above section, you should keep in mind the geography your patent covers, and whether the significant impact could spread to other geographies. For example, an injunction in one country could impact another country so this fact should be taken into consideration.

In addition, the degree of significance may vary depending on the target companies even for the same product. It also varies with time as a target company's strategy changes. Therefore, similar to the discussion in (a), you need to re-value your portfolio regularly and make sure to look at each infringing company individually, takes into consideration of market size of each infringing company, how important

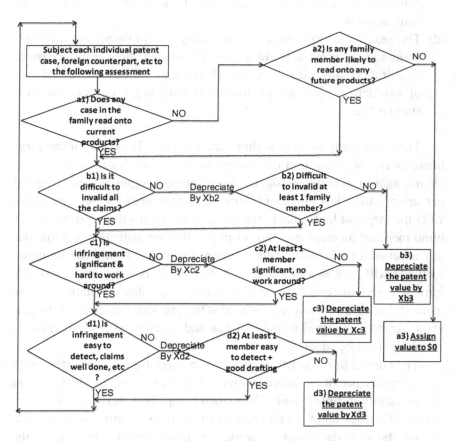

Figure 6-7   Flowchart to deduct the intrinsic value of a patent portfolio.

are these markets to such infringing company, what are the life time of each infringing product, and how much life time is left in the patent.

In addition to the covered product being significant, it is also important to understand how difficult it is to work around the infringed solution. These are related questions because if it is hard to work around an infringement and customers really need it, then it is significant.

Another important factor to consider here is the encumbrances of the patent. If a patent is licensed to a company, that company's products are no longer infringing and thus should be taken into consideration.

(d) The next factor to consider is how easy it is to detect the infringement and other evidence of use quality such as how well the patent was drafted, how clean is the file history, as well as the rest of cost of avoidance, such as whether it is mandatory or optional in a standard, etc.

There are many tools providing patent scores. They are attempts trying to assess the patent intrinsic value. Due to the fact that it is hard to map claims against specific products, these methodologies all use external perceptions to reflect the patent intrinsic value, somewhat like describing what the elephant looks like based on the blind men's descriptions in "six blind men and an elephant". For example, if many patents in a particular day all cited a particularly patent (forward citation), then these valuation methods will give this patent a higher score. It is not that the patent's intrinsic value increased due to the increased number of citations, these methodologies are merely admitting that the previous valuation of the patent's intrinsic value was mistakenly low and needs to be readjusted based on newly available data.

The correct intrinsic value using our methodology is illustrated using an exemplary patent as shown in Figure 6-8. At grant date D1, the patent attains certain intrinsic value. Then when company A & B cite this patent at date D2, since there are no changes to the relevant intrinsic factor discussed above, if the initial valuation was done correctly previously, the intrinsic value stays the same. Thereafter, when a company takes a license

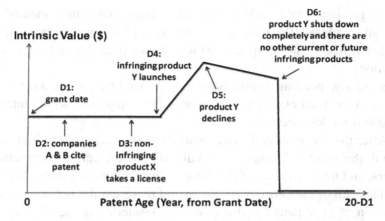

Figure 6-8   Intrinsic value should only be affected by the relevant intrinsic factors.

of the patent as part of an overall patent portfolio for company's product X, shown in Figure 6-8 as date D3 "non-infringing product X takes a license", market perception might go up even though X doesn't have any infringing features. However, this should not affect the patent's intrinsic valuation so the intrinsic value should be unchanged. On the other hand, if an infringing product Y launches on date D4, (infringing here means that the product is unlicensed), then the intrinsic value of the patent should increase as the significance of the patent to product Y increases. On the other hand, the intrinsic value decreases after market saturation date D5, and drops significantly if product Y shuts down completely (or product Y becomes licensed) and there are no other infringing products. However, the patent may retain some residual value if there is still a likelihood that other infringing products will ship within the patent lifetime.

In comparison for most existing patent valuation tools available today, if a particular patent is used in litigation and the patent is deemed valid and infringed by the defendant, then this patent's score will suddenly increase significantly. Clearly this is an indication that the previous patent score was not reflective of the intrinsic value of the patent. It's not a market pricing either which should depend on specific purchasing party. These valuation methodologies are admitting that previous score was mistakenly lower than the actual intrinsic value and needs to readjust in light of newly available information. More importantly, their methodologies fail to address the most important factors for a patent value: i.e. i) whether it reads onto a product; ii) market significance; and iii) ease of detection.

Similarly, pending applications can be analyzed while keeping in mind that the final claims are not scoped out completely so the intrinsic valuations are less accurate.

After the above analysis, one should use a typical industry high valuation dollar number for the patent multiplied by the various depreciation factors, and then arrive at a final dollar valuation for each individual patent. The sum of the entire portfolio should represent the holistic intrinsic valuation of your patent portfolio when considering the total market as a whole.

6.5.5. *Estimation of the extrinsic value (market pricing) of a patent*

However, if you are ready to sell a patent or are approached by others to buy your patent, or alternatively you need to buy other's patents to negotiate licensing/business deals, you need to combine buyer's particular situational factors with the above intrinsic valuation in order to arrive at an estimated market pricing, which is different for each buyer. As a result, it is viewed to be even more unpredictable and changes even more significantly with time than the intrinsic valuation. This is the so-called extrinsic value or the market pricing. It depends on the buyer's needs at the time of the transaction. We propose a methodology to evaluate this market pricing. If a buyer is clear-headed and objective about the pricing, he/she should be able to arrive at a relatively objective market pricing and a fair value.

Buyers should take a patent's intrinsic value, modify it up or down based on his/her specific situation. If the buyer is in the middle of a patent litigation or licensing negotiation and urgently needs to buy a relevant patent portfolio to counter sue or counter assert another company, then he/she needs to take a look at the asking price by the asserting party, probability and associated cost of winning/losing the litigation, the total budget available to him/her, supply and demand of relevant patents in the market.

Such factors might modulate the intrinsic value up and down somewhat, but should not vary too much if the patent transaction market were transparent and fair. Of course, even in a transparent market, if a buyer has a lot of money and really wants to obtain a patent, it is not unfair for him/her to pay significantly above the intrinsic value if supply is clearly less than demand.

6.6. Build a World-Class IP Strategy — Portfolio Development Considerations

Patent filing costs money and maintaining it costs money. The total fees include drafting fees to the patent application drafter, government fees charged by patent offices in filing countries, and periodic government fees to keep the patent alive. For a typical patent family, the total fee runs between $20–30K+ in US alone, and can be as high as $100K+ when filing internationally. In addition, maintaining it costs money as well. Therefore, it is critical to keep your final objective in mind when developing your patent portfolios. Even companies with a large IP budget, you need to build a solid IP strategy to avoid money being spent in the wrong areas and still not well protected after investing a significant amount of money in IP.

As discussed previously, many companies treat patent portfolio as a "natural" byproduct of their R&D efforts. Such approach is not considered an IP strategy; instead it is only a passive outcome of your company's R&D strategy. A world-class IP strategy requires figuring out what are your company's IP demands as part of its short term and long term business strategy, then designing your patent portfolio specifically to meet those demands.

6.6.1. *IP demand — cross-licensing, litigation/ assertion, monetization*

As discussed above, regardless of whether a company is in US or China, planning to develop/expand in US or China, with a size of large enterprise, medium or small business, they all must keep the final objectives in mind when they develop their patent portfolios. We'll analyze an exemplary case in Figure 6-9. To manage the Patent Portfolio 1 for Company 1 shown in Figure 6-9, the Portfolio Manager needs to first examine what are the IP Demands required for Patent Portfolio 1. As discussed in Chapter 1, Section 1.3, a world-class patent portfolio is able to effectively enable the company to carry out its IP Strategy to successfully support its business strategy. The demand #1 or D1, as depicted in Figure 6-9, could come from Cross-Licensing team/actions to serve as an IP shield for Company 1's business and to help Company 1 gain freedom of operation in certain technology spaces. For cross-licensing transactions, IP rights typically flow in both directions, represented by a dashed line with an arrow on each end. Demand #2 or D2 could come from Litigation/Assertion team/actions to serve as an IP sword or IP weapon. Company 1 may leverage Patent Portfolio 1 to defend its technology leadership or market share by asserting or suing competitors in order to slow down their businesses. Demand #3 or D3 is from Monetization team/activities which could include patent sales, licensing patent portfolios out to third parties, which typically involves transferring IP outwardly and thus is represented by an outward arrow in Figure 6-9. For patent sales, as part of D3 activities, it involves transferring patent

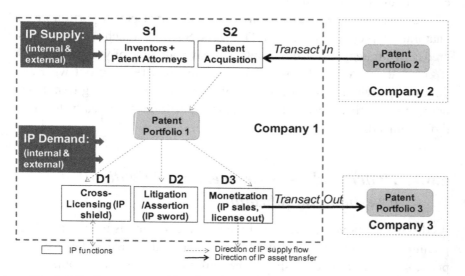

Figure 6-9   Factors to consider when developing an exemplary patent portfolio 1.

assets to another company, for example, to Company 3, and thus is represented with a sold arrow in the figure.

6.6.2. *IP supplies — internal invention, external patent acquisition*

To meet these various IP demands, the Portfolio Manager for Patent Portfolio 1 must make sure its IP Supply pipeline lives up to the requirements of these IP demands. There are two channels for IP supply. The first channel of IP supply, or S1, is from internal sources via inventors coming up with inventions and working with patent attorneys to turn the inventions into useful patents. The second channel of IP supply, or S2, is patent acquisition by buying targeted patents from other companies, for example as shown in Figure 6-9, purchasing Patent Portfolio 2 from Company 2.

Many large IP owners neglect the second IP supply channel S2 because they believe their large volume of patents are sufficient to execute its IP strategy. However, depending on the specifics of the IP demand from D1, D2, and D3, it is possible that there are gaps in the company's patent portfolio. Since internal invention takes time to obtain granted patents, then patent acquisition should be considered as one of ways to fill the gap.

6.6.3. *High patent quality — a "must" for all IP demands today*

A decade ago, when IP licensing activities were at their early prime phase in US, operating companies often negotiate patent cross-licensing agreements based on the number of patents they own and thus the so-called "comparing who has a higher stack of patents". Companies with very little patents started buying patent portfolios in bulk, sometimes without even analyzing the portfolio. Such "exuberant" period for patent transactions has passed. Currently, due to the changing Patent Law and recent court decisions in US, as well as PTAB's high invalidation rate, IP strategies have changed for most companies. Nowadays, when a company receives a patent infringement notice, instead of caving in and paying up to get rid of the so-called IP "annoyances", companies tend to chose fighting for as long as they can, either through filing IPR or simply drag on the negotiation to drain out the other party's financial resources. As a result, many smaller non-practicing entities ("NPE"s) are having a hard time surviving. However, if an NPE has high quality patents that can survive the invalidity challenges and are truly infringed, it will continue moving forward in licensing operations. Therefore, for operating companies or NPEs, only when they have high quality patent portfolios on the patent supply side (more likely via patent acquisitions), will they have a fair chance to meet their IP demands.

Even for IP Demand D1 patent cross-licensing ("PCL") negotiations, if the other party doesn't feel that you have high quality patents that are real threats to their business, or can truly offer technical benefits to their business, they will not want to license out their patents to you without charging an appropriate royalty fee. As a result, the previous so-called "negotiation grade" patents intended for PCLs can no longer function well with just negotiation-grade quality. Instead, at least a portion will need to be at a higher quality in today's environment. In addition, in case the PCL negotiation falls apart and parties become confrontational, you must anticipate the other party going to court or trying to invalidate your patent via IPR or CBM at PTAB. You need to make sure that your patents most likely will survive such challenges.

For IP Demand D2 litigation/assertion activities, whether you are aggressively attacking other companies, or defensively responding to other's IP attacks, your patent quality must be "litigation grade", i.e. able to survive the challenges at court as well as at PTAB. In other words, the patents must have very high quality.

Even for monetization D3 such as patent sales, Company 3 wants to buy patents from Company 1 for the purpose of meeting its own IP Demands. Therefore, they need high quality patents in order to success-fully execute its IP strategy. As a result, patent purchasers are now also starting to focus on patent quality.

Chinese companies monitor US market closely. It has its own patent invalidity courts. Therefore, for Chinese and US companies, whether its IP Demand is targeted for US or China, they need to focus on patent quality in order to have a successful IP strategy.

6.6.4. *Checklist for high quality patent development*

The following Table 6-1 summarizes issues relating to patent qualities under US and Chinese patent systems.

Table 6-1 Comparison of key considerations in high quality patent development and factors to focus on for China versus US.

Issues to Consider	US Typical Approach	China Approach: (Similar) or Different
Does the patent currently, or in the future is likely to, map onto unlicensed third party product?	• US system can leverage its discovery process to uncover infringement related Use of Evidence. The burden of proof standard is by a preponderance of evidence.	• Lacks a robust system for evidentiary discovery.[1] This makes patent enforcement difficult in China. On the other hand, the lack of discovery makes litigation process shorter and faster, often 6 to 12 months.
How hard is it to invalid the claim?	• USPTO PTAB currently has a high % of invalidity rate at 80%+.	• Chinese SIPO has a reported invalidity rate of 25% for invention patents and 38% for utility patents. Therefore, it is harder to invalid patents in China which supports patent enforcement.
Is the infringement significant and hard to work around?	• Product shipment volume information can be obtained from research reports. Some shipment info are publically available for publically traded companies.	• Shipment info difficult to obtain, but is getting easier due to many companies going public and are required to disclose financial information.

(Continued)

---

[1]"Report on patent enforcement in China", prepared by the U.S. Patent and Trademark Office, http://www.uspto.gov/ip/global/China_Report_on_Patent_Enforcement_(FullRprt) FINAL.pdf

Table 6-1   (*Continued*)

Issues to Consider	US Typical Approach	China Approach: (Similar) or Different
Is the infringement easy to detect?	• Can leverage discovery process as indicated above.	• Harder to gather evidence as discussed above. Plaintiff needs to (1) notarize purchase of an infringement product to authenticate the process; (2) use a judicially certified testing lab to generate the infringement report.[2] • Chinese infringement court is separate from invalidity by SIPO. Therefore, plaintiff can get an injunction quickly if they win infringement case in court in 6–12 months.

6.7. Recommendation on How to Build a High Value Portfolio

After accumulating enough patents in volume to reach a critical mass, it is advisable to follow vigorous process in controlling patent quality to achieve better ROI. Clear and comprehensive procedure enables optimum decision on whether to file a patent application, and ensures high quality patent drafting after deciding to file. In addition, special consideration must be given to different due diligence requirements by local laws and processes (e.g. US versus China).

In our previous Chapters, we touched upon the importance of IP for companies large or small. In fact, a holistic IP strategy should be one

---

[2]Erin Coe, "5 Tips on Art of Patent War in China", http://www.law360.com/articles/537964/5-tips-in-the-art-of-patent-war-in-china.

of the most important cornerstones of your company's overall strategy. As shown in Figure 6-10, IP strategy plays an important role in three key areas, (1) defending a company's existing business by fending off competitors' assertions or litigations and gaining design freedom by signing cross-license agreements; (2) capturing innovative ideas generated from your R&D investments and keeping competitions from copying your product features or taking away your market shares; and (3) providing financial contributions to your company's bottom line by generating high margin IP revenues.

However, none of the above three areas of IP actions are possible without a high quality patent portfolio. The era of simply comparing each other's sheer number of patents to determine who pays a royalty is over. Any successful IP action, regardless of whether its objective is defensive, offensive or revenue generation, requires clear evidence of use of the asserted patent. In addition, these asserted patents must be able to survive patent invalidity challenges. In the US, with several new or revised patent review processes established under the Americas Inventor's Act (AIA), such as post grant review ("PGR"), *IPR*, CBM review, it is much easier nowadays to invalidate someone else's patents. Therefore, patent owners

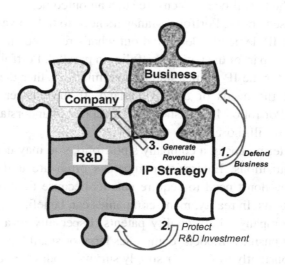

Figure 6-10 A holistic IP strategy should be a cornerstone of company strategy.

are required to pay significantly more attention to the quality of their patent portfolios.

6.7.1. *Build a strong IP strategy to fill in short-term and long-term gaps*

Often it is unclear whose responsibility it is to build a high quality portfolio. Inventors are usually focused on their own R&D projects, patent attorneys buried in claim drafting, licensing executives spend most time on potential customers, and litigation lawyers are constantly fire-fighting urgent cases. As discussed above, patent quality is similar to a chain built up by various links. The weakest link is where others will attack the patent first. Therefore, Companies should promote a situation where everyone in each functional area is cognizant about patent quality requirement and ensures that their areas do not contribute in any way to poor patent quality.

However, such concerted effort requires a champion or coordinator. Authors believe that it is mainly the duty of a Portfolio Manager to build a high quality patent portfolio for your company. As a result, portfolio managers need to monitor each step that lead to a final high quality patent and demand the best process to ensure such an outcome.

As discussed above, Portfolio Managers need to talk to various stake-holders on the IP demand side to find out what's required short term and long term on the part of the patent portfolio. In parallel, Portfolio Manager needs to monitor the IP supply side to determine whether they are sufficient to meet the needs of the IP demand. If the answer is "no" or "unsure", the Portfolio Manger should take actions to understand the gaps and promptly to fill those gaps.

For short term gaps in a company's portfolio, you may need to resort to patent acquisitions. Enterprise companies often are under the false belief that they don't need to acquire patents because they have a large number of patents. In reality, many companies can benefit from acquiring some other company's high quality patents. Especially in a world with ever changing business models, companies large or small have to reinvent themselves constantly to thrive or simply survive. Today's relevant patent portfolio might become less relevant a few years later. Therefore, fresh patents in new chosen technology areas are required and acquisition fills this need well.

For longer-term gaps, organically grow one's own patent portfolio often is cheaper and under greater control. Portfolio Manager, with a clear picture of what are needed to build a high quality portfolio, should start first by ensuring your inventors generate ideas in the right areas to be in good alignment with your company's IP strategy. This could include ideas covering competitor's future products, or ideas covering your own current and future products. It could be thoroughly thought-through blocking patents or breakthrough technologies. In either case, there are abundant opportunities to come up with high quality patents.

6.7.2. *TRIZ approach for breakthrough ideas or blocking patents*

Once in a while, it is necessary for companies to conduct brainstorm sessions to generate patentable ideas. This is particularly important when you want to control the budget for patented ideas so that you get the "most bang for your bucks". If your company is a technology leader in your industry, your company's products are likely copied by others and thus you need to protect your own technology vigorously. Portfolio Manager may feel less equipped in leading such a brainstorming session because the discussion may appear more technical and requires deep domain knowledge. However, Portfolio Managers can actually use their patent knowledge to help technologists to break through mental barriers by leveraging patent information, thus using IP strategy to drive innovation. The following TRIZ methodology is one of the IP tools that may help your invention brainstorm workshops.

Karen Tate and Ellen Domb classified[3] innovations into 40 Inventive Principles. Table 6-2 summarizes these 40 Principles in a condensed 4×10 array. Based on the hypothesis that "somebody someplace has already solved this problem (or one very similar to it); today, creativity involves finding that solution and adapting it to this particular problem", They are able to classify most inventions into one of these 40 Inventive Principles. Each category has a self-explanatory definition and the 40 Inventive Principles have plenty associated examples provided by Tate and Domb with the following caveats.

---

[3] "How to Help TRIZ Beginners Succeed", TRIZ Journal, April 1997.

Table 6-2   TRIZ 40 inventive principles.

	A	B	C	D
1	Segmentation	Beforehand cushioning	Skipping	Porous materials
2	Taking Out	Equipotentiality	"Turn Lemons into Lemonade"	Color changes
3	Local Quality	"The other way round"	Feedback	Homogeneity
4	Asymmetry	Spheroidality-Curvature	"Intermediary"	Discarding and recovering
5	Merging	Dynamics	Self-service	Parameter changes
6	Universality	Partial or excessive actions	Copying	Phase transitions
7	"Nestled Doll"	Another dimension	Cheap short-living objects	Thermal expansion
8	Anti-Weight	Mechanical vibration	Mechanics substitution	Strong oxidants
9	Preliminary anti-action	Periodic action	Pneumatics and hydraulics	Inert atmosphere
10	Preliminary action	Continuity of useful action	Flexible shells and thin films	Composite materials

— Each of the category names are self-explanatory, but the actual examples can be functional equivalent. For example in Column A, row #1 "Segmentation" category is defined as dividing an object into independent parts, such as multiprocessors with a CPU handling main complex calculations, and a graphic processor handling just image processing.
— Similarly for Columns B, D, and D, each row represents a unique technology category. For example, Column C row #3 "Feedback" means introducing feedback to improve an action, such as surface emitting laser using reflected light by the header to determine whether to increase or decrease the electrical current to keep the laser beam stable.

Readers interested in such subject matter, whether or not you completely agree with the above 40 Inventive Principle methodology, may want to investigate this approach further or even take relevant classes from

TRIZ experts. Although the majority of the above 40 Inventive Principles appear to be hardware related, software ideas should be capable of being classified into certain principals as well. Authors believe that the majority of today's inventions are evolutionary improvements instead of revolutionary breakthroughs. Therefore, such a TRIZ hypothesis, more often than not, is adequate in handling problems at hand. However, on rare occasions, completely new types of innovations may be created and then new Inventive Principles will need to be added into Table 6-2.

In the following, we attempt to apply the above TRIZ methodology to the previously discussed pencil and eraser combination example (where a US inventor filed a patent in 1858 which was unfortunately invalidated later due to a German factory's prior art). In this case, assuming the inventor was trying to solve a problem of having to carry separately a pencil and eraser where it was too easy to forget the eraser. Of course the assumption was also that there were no prior arts at the time of invention which is the reason why the invention was needed to solve a pain point suffered by the market. Using a graphic illustration to depict this invention, in Figure 6-11, part A is the pencil, part B is the eraser. Looking at the 40 invention principles, one could potentially leverage either A1 "Segmentation" dividing an object into separate parts, i.e. creating an object including pencil A and eraser B joined together by C. Initially, one could potentially contemplate using a string as object C to merely link eraser B with pencil A all the time, as shown in Figure 6-11(a). However, after experimenting with the corresponding implementation, one would discover that it is more convenient if C is rigid so that one can flip the pencil upside down and apply pressure to the eraser to erase pencil marks. As a result, a better embodiment would be the design in Figure 6-11(b).

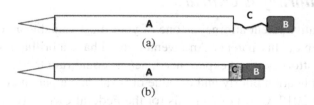

Figure 6-11   Applying TRIZ Inventive Principles to an exemplary pencil eraser combination invention.

In Lyman's 1858 invention, he used glue as object C. On the other hand, the German manufacture used a metal ferrule as object C to hold pencil A and eraser B together. Each design has its own pros and cons. Market reception is based on various factors, such as ease of use, scalability, pricing, branding, etc. Apparently, the German metal ferrule was more commonly adopted than the glued version.

Again as an illustration point, we can also try to apply TRIZ 40 inventive principles to the above pencil and eraser combination to explore an optimum design. An alternative possible applicable principle is C4 "Intermediary", i.e. using an intermediary carrier article. One could invent a temporary holder C that temporarily holds pencil A and eraser B together that can be removed easily. The advantage is reusability, but the disadvantage is probably difficult to match different sizes and shapes of pencil and easer, and possibly much more expensive than current designs. However, by familiarizing yourself with these 40 different inventive principles potentially could enable inventors try various approaches and more quickly find an optimum solution.

Similarly, one can also use these TRIZ inventive principles to search for blocking patents. Again using the previous pencil and eraser combination idea as an exemplary case, assuming your competitor is making pencil as their main products. By analysing the problems they face, i.e. users easily lose erasers, you can brainstorm with your inventors and come up with various possible solutions (such as those in Figure 6-11) and file patents including all the possible embodiments and thus block your competitors' future products.

6.7.3. *Producing high quality patent — patent attorney is critical*

A high quality patent attorney is one of your most valuable assets in generating high quality patents. An inventor could have a brilliant idea, but if the patent attorney is not experienced, he/she could ruin the case by drafting the application poorly and devalue or invalidate a patent completely.

In late 2012, Court of Appeals for the Federal Circuit (CAFC) ruled against Apple (Apple v. Samsung) in its claim construction. Apple's patent claimed a method of searching on a mobile device, requiring that the device comprise "a plurality of heuristic modules", "each heuristic module corresponds to a respective area of search and employs a different, predetermined heuristic algorithm." Apple argued that it means "some heuristic modules may use the same algorithm", but Samsung claimed that it means "each module must use different algorithm". The CAFC agreed with Samsung and suggested Apple should have written the claim as "each **of the plurality** of heuristic module corresponds to ..." by adding the highlighted underlined three words which would have avoided the different interpretation. Although some courts may agree with Apple's interpretation and disregard CAFC's ruling, this case illustrates the importance of the patent drafter to the patent quality.

A properly motivated patent attorney will work closely with the inventors to draft a very high quality patent application. How the drafter is compensated may affect the patent quality. For example, some companies use largely internal resources to draft their patent applications. The advantage of such practice is that the in-house lawyers have to worry about the long term effect of what they write. If they are still with the company 3–5 years later when the patent is granted, it is to their best interest to write a solid patent. However, some companies prefer to use external law-firms to write patent applications partly because they can control the cost better, especially for uneven production of patentable ideas. External law-firms may generate high value patents if they are experienced with the particular technology. However, one needs to be cognizant of outside law-firm's behaviour based on billing model. If law firms are paid per patent, they have less incentive to work on expansion of the ideas and covering all work arounds. On the other hand, if the reward is tied to the percentage of granted patents, then claims might be written overly simple or narrow. The most effective model is probably a long-term partnership between the idea generating company and the outside law-firm where outside counsels are deeply engaged with inventors. Such an outside law-firm needs to worry about long-term results due to the close partnership, and meanwhile should be able to generate high quality patents due to the familiarity with the technology.

Table 6-3 summarizes each aspect that requires close attention by the patent drafter.

To ensure high quality patents, one needs to first determine in Step 1, the pre-filing stage, whether a patent is worth filing, i.e. whether a patent

Table 6-3 Parameters which require close attention by Portfolio Manager, inventor, patent application drafter to ensure high quality.

Step 1: Pre-Filing	Key Factors	Step 1: Pre-Filing	Step 2: Drafting/Prosecuting
Approval Considerations ↑	PTO likely to grant – Prior Art search	✓	✓
	Others likely to use	✓	✓
Step 2: Drafting /Prosecuting ↓	TCA-Broadness		✓
Total Cost of Avoidance ("TCA") Considerations	TCA-Workaround		✓
	TCA-Market Size		✓
↑	TCA-Standards		✓
↓ Evidence of Use Quality ("EoUQ") Considerations	EoUQ-Maps to product well		✓
	EoUQ-Easy to Detect		✓
	EoUQ-Good draft		✓
	EoUQ-Clean file history		✓

is likely to grant and others likely will use the invention. High quality patents mean that they have strong Evidence of Use characteristics and total cost of avoiding the infringement is very high. Proper control during patent drafting, Step 2, is required to ensure generation of high quality patents.

As shown in Table 6-3, in Step 2, patent drafters should keep in mind the two key questions asked during Step 1. At the same time, detailed attention should be paid to TCA, which includes claim broadness, possible workarounds, market size, and relevance to Standards. In addition, proper attention must be paid to EoUQ, which includes mapping well to products, easy to detect, well drafted claims, and clean prosecution history.

Creating and maintaining a high quality patent portfolio takes a lot of money and efforts. We propose the above methodologies for a more effective process and better ROI.

6.7.4. *Action item checklist for high quality portfolio*

In Table 6-4, we summarize issues that need to be considered for a high quality portfolio in US and China.

Table 6-4   Comparison of steps when building a high quality portfolio in US versus China.

Issues to Consider	US Typical Approach	China Approach: (Similar) or Different
To obtain high quality patent, one must first determine to only file the following patents: • PTO is likely to grant a patent; and • Others are likely to use the invention.	• Perform prior art searches guided by patent attorneys under attorney client privilege to avoid being accused of willful infringement.	• Lack of attorney client privileges, but also lack discovery process.
	• Refine patent claims while monitoring competitor's products closely for potential infringement.	• Ensure high quality even for utility model patents.
You should control the choke point at the patent drafting stage vigorously to increase patent quality: • Will the patent likely to read onto third party products; • How to increase PTO likelihood to grant a patent; • How to make the claims broad yet allowable; • How to make it difficult to work around the solution; • How to increase the market size; • Whether it is possible to make it relevant to desired Standards; • How to make claims map well onto 3rd third party products; • How to make infringement easy to detect; • How to make sure claims language are well drafted so there are no ambiguities in interpretation; • How to avoid or reduce undesirable estoppels in the file history.	• Follow the USPTO interim guideline when filing patents to overcome §101 rejections. • Write claims with prior arts in mind so that the claims are not unreasonably broad. • Brainstorm various embodiments with inventors to cover all possible workarounds. • Check claim quality utilizing available tools such as TRIZ. • Conduct examiner interviews.	• Follow SIPO guidelines.

Chapter 7

For IP Transaction Practitioners and IP Managers (Relating to Deal Structure of Patent Acquisitions, IP Monetization, Patent Cross-Licensing, or Technology Transfers)

The ultimate goal of getting a patent granted is to leverage it to accomplish your final business objectives. In the following, we'll walk through some commonly encountered legal and business issues when conducting various intellectual property (IP) transactions. Such transactions include patent acquisition, patent sales, patent cross-licensing, and technology transfer.

7.1. Patent Acquisitions — Typical Issues

As discussed in Chapter 2 and Chapter 6, in order to fill the gaps in a company's patent portfolio, besides internal strategic patent filings, patent portfolio managers should also consider patent acquisitions, especially when trying to fill gaps within a short time window or in an area that is not in alignment with your R&D directions but maps to potential aggressor's product lines. There are various deal structures one can use for patent acquisition transactions. We'll discuss those and specific areas/steps which might go wrong, and how to avoid these issues when structuring the deals while at the same time seeking proper legal protection.

7.1.1. *Deal structure and associated issues*

Figure 7-1 depicts a typical patent acquisition structure where patent Buyer pays patent Seller money to buy Seller's patents. As indicated by Arrow #1 in Figure 7-1, Buyer transfers cash, $, to Seller. In return, Seller transfers patent assets to buyer as indicated as Arrow #2, together with warranties and representations. Issues often encountered are analyzed below from Buyer's perspective.

(i) <u>Grant back license to the seller</u>: If Seller is an operating company, Buyer must be prepared to grant a license to the Seller to the acquired patents. Buyers dislike this clause because they are concerned that the "grant-back" license will be passed on to a third party that they need to assert against in the future. Such transfer of license could happen due to spin-off, merger and acquisition, technology transfer, sub-licensing, or even intentional pass through for the purpose to avoid patent infringement. If the seller is an individual, no grant-back license is required and Buyer can insist on refusing the grant-back license. For operating companies, you can try to limit the grant-back license to Seller's internal use only initially, but expand to products/services **sold by the Seller**. Sometimes Seller will request grant-back license to cover products related to new entities from future merger and acquisitions, or spin-offs from

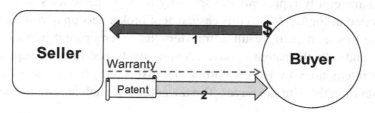

Figure 7-1   Typical patent acquisition deal structure.

the company. The former is reasonable, but the latter is usually not provided. In addition, seller may want to be able to provide "foundry service" to other companies. If there are no other ways around this issue, such right could be limited just to designs by the seller.

(ii) <u>Representation and warranty</u>: Seller often wants to include a "knowl-edge qualifier" to their representation and warranty, e.g. "to the attorney's knowledge, there are no encumbrances associated with this patent". Buyer should try to avoid such knowledge qualifier, especially the very narrow ones. Seller may also try to exclude certain aspects from their warranty and representation, such as whether the patent is encumbered by standards or open source. For large corporations, it is hard to determine whether the corporate has committed to certain standards or contributed to open source because it is hard to track the large employee base. As a result, seller doesn't want to bear the risk of misrepresentation. However, buyer should not be asked to bear such risk since they are in a worse position than the seller to determine whether such encumbrances exist.

(iii) <u>Encumbrances</u>: Seller sometimes may be inexperienced or make mistakes so buyer must beware. For example, even if the seller has a cross-license with an entity, it is possible that license is time based and the license expires at certain time. On the other hand, some seller may have committed a "covenant to not sue" to other entities. These are not necessarily personal to seller. They could be treated as patent licenses and follows the patent as it is sold.[1]

(iv) <u>Other issues</u> involve who pays associated withholding tax, whether the agreement should be assignable.

Another scenario is a patent acquisition deal structure where a patent broker materially represents the seller by owning the seller's patents, as illustrated in Figure 7-2. In this case, patent broker sets up a trust (assuming the trust is named "Vault"), transfers the seller's patent into the trust Vault, and sells the patent to buyer. Again, the dashed line box represents direct interactions by parties within the box. Seller, in this case doesn't interact directly with the buyer. The advantage of such an arrangement is

---

[1] *Transcore, LP v. Elec. Transaction Consultants Corp., 563 F.3d 1271, 1274 (Fed. Cir. 2009).*

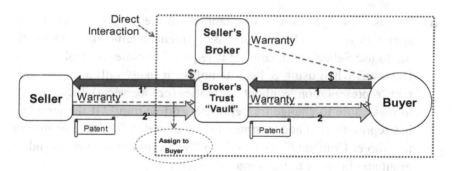

Figure 7-2 A patent acquisition deal structure including a deeply involved broker.

that the broker has more control over the deal closing and has greater incentives to sell. The disadvantage is that a lot of confidential information is unknown to the broker so they have to go back to seller to get more information. In addition, warranty and representation becomes overly convoluted. As shown in Figure 7-2, Broker via trust Vault transfers $' to Seller, Seller then transfers patent ownership in assignment 2' to Vault, including certain warranty and representation, Warranty'.

After Broker found and reached agreement with Buyer, Buyer transfers money $ via arrow 1 to Vault, Vault assigns patent to Buyer, via arrow 2 including a warranty and representation. However, because Vault is not a physical person or true entity, but a trust or empty shell, Buyer would need Broker to also provide a warranty and representation. In addition, grant-back license becomes complicated because the grant-back license from Buyer to Vault has to match exactly the grant-back from Vault to Seller. An additional issue is related to knowledge qualifier in the representation. It has to be the knowledge of Broker, Vault, **and** Seller. It is also important to make sure Broker and trust Vault take joint liability. You also have to consider the situation when Seller is sold to another company in the future, then the grant-back license can only be transferred one time, and only covers Seller's product at the time of transfer, Seller must provide notice to Buyer, and grant-back license terminates upon Seller's bankruptcy or insolvency.

Buyer usually wants to take control and dislikes risks. However, in order to obtain high quality assets, buyer can take a few calculated risks. For example, the following are a few suggestions.

(i) Parties often fight over whose template to use. Buyer should always start with your own Patent Purchase Agreement template, but be willing to use Seller's template if it is required to close the deal.

(ii) However, when using Seller's template, it likely only includes certain "representation" without warranties (or vice versa). Buyer needs to make sure to change to "represent **and** warrant". If the template has representation and warranty that "Seller didn't grant a license to the Target Company", change it to "Seller and prior owners didn't grant any licenses to the Target Company".

(iii) Agree to the following conditions only when absolutely necessary, with full awareness and analysis of potential risks in the future: (a) if seller makes products for other parties, those products get a grant-back license; (b) certain licensees may have "foundry rights".

7.1.2. *Business structure-related learning*

Many things could go wrong in a partnership. Getting the legal language right at the first place will provide better clarity on how to resolve issues/disputes when things do go wrong. The follow are a few areas to watch out for:

(i) Covenant to Not First Sue encumbrance: This covenant requires Buyer to use patents only for defensive purposes. Buyer can agree to this cumbersome obligation by implementing a clear process for future management of these assets, and may use the lowered valuation to obtain additional good quality patents.

(ii) Seller has foundry right: Narrow the Seller's name as much as possible. If only the Seller's semiconductor subsidiary has foundry right, make sure Seller's non-semiconductor subsidiaries are on the Non-Licensed Entity list to avoid misinterpretations.

7.1.3. *Contract-related learning*

It is easy to misinterpret contract language; some could be intentional misinterpretation by the other party. Therefore, it is important to make sure to avoid such confusions. In addition, there are administrative related issues which may derail the deal. For example, the typical signing of an agreement involves:

(i) Party A signs electronic version of the patent purchase agreement ("PPA") and sends the signed pdf to Party B;

(ii) Party A also sends B the original signed document in parallel;

(iii) Party B signs the electronic version;

(iv) Party B then receives the original and signs it, too.

A potential issue is that Party B signs the electronic version, dates it, and then signs the original and dates it. The problem is that you've got two sets of PPA floating around with two different dates. The solution is to make sure that there is a separate "Effective Date" independent of the signing date. One can also state in the Agreement that electronic version is equivalent to original for cases that originals are not necessary.

For counterparts, use language such as "Each Party will sign the print out of the original document, together they form the fully executed agreement" so that there is no need to wait for the other Party to send you the original signed document.

In addition, you should watch out for liens on the patent assets. Make sure to remove them before assets are transferred to you. Only after a lien is removed can the Buyer proceed to record Patent Assignment with US Patent and Trademark Office (USPTO) first, then pay the full amount.

Your team should conduct full due diligences and not let small things cause your deal to fall apart. In addition, when negotiating agreements, always redline your changes, unless both parties agree otherwise so that the other party doesn't mistakenly think you are trying to intentionally deceive them when you make changes. It is also helpful to use comments to document your unresolved issues so that there are no misunderstandings that you've accepted the proposed changes. When delivering the original signature from the other party to you, always provide your address, contact person, and phone number, especially for cross-border deals. You may also want to provide step-by-step detailed instruction on how to sign, what to sign, and how many copies to sign. When sending electronic signed documents, divide file into smaller total size in case there are email size limitations on the recipient's side to ensure your partner gets it. In addition, you should follow up and double check that the partner has received the electronic document.

7.1.4. *Recommended patent acquisition process*

Figure 7-3 is a recommended patent acquisition process flow, where the left column represents suggested steps, the middle column depicts the involved activities, and the right column lists key team members required for these activities:

(a) The first step is identifying target patents. Many companies may prefer to wait for the right patent portfolio come to them without much effort. If there are good patent brokers who understand your business needs, you can probably eventually purchase some good patents with such an approach. However, there are very few good brokers today who can deliver high quality patent analysis supported with adequate

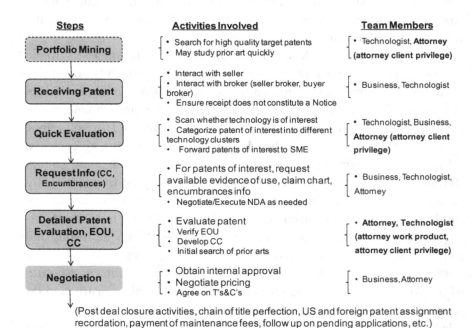

Figure 7-3   Patent acquisition process steps, activities, and team members.

evidence of use ("EoU") analysis. Therefore, your team might be better off using the alternative approach of portfolio mining, which is represented by a dashed lined box because it is optional. There are risks associated with such approaches so you should only carry out this step with protective procedures in place. You need to determine technologies you want to acquire based on your IP strategy, keeping in mind the target company's products and the related technology areas. The following are some of the specific activities involved:

— Search for all the relevant patents in that technology area, meaning patents that read or map onto the specific technology. You may need to conduct prior art searches to determine whether certain patents are high value.

— Identify patent owners that are good fits with your high standard for value patents.

— The team involved in this step consists of technical folks performing analysis and searches under the guidance of attorneys to maintain attorney–client privilege for sensitive communications. However, as discussed previously, Chinese attorneys do not have attorney–client communication privilege, you need to make sure to include a qualified US attorney.

(b) The second step is obtaining and receiving patent list from potential sellers. The detailed activities involved are:

— Approach target patent owner(s) to inquire whether they are willing to sell the patents you are interested in buying. This is particularly effective if you have an existing good relationship with the head IP and she/he was already interested in selling patents.

— If you want to initially stay anonymous until you know the seller is willing to sell target patents, or simply to avoid seller asking unreasonable high pricing, you may make the inquiry via intermediaries such as patent brokers, law firms or individuals.

— An important potential issue to watch out for is that if you or your intermediaries don't handle it correctly, the patents sent to you might be later treated as a notice of infringement. Many licensing entities, especially non-practicing entities (NPEs) use patent sales as a "door opener". After you started evaluating these patents and decided that you might be interested in purchasing them, the seller will turn the conversation into a patent licensing deal, claiming the patent is very expensive, or seller decided to not sell any more, etc. They may later use the fact that you have reviewed their patents as having received their notice of infringement. To avoid such potential issues, you should make sure you have a non-disclosure agreement (NDA) which states that such receipt of patents does not constitute a notice for future evidences to support or substantiate any willful infringement claims.

— Team involved at this step are usually the business lead who spears ahead communications with the seller, and the supporting technology teams who provide target patent list and revise the list as needed.

(c) The third step is a quick evaluation of the patent portfolios received. This is particularly important if they are not the result/outcome of your portfolio mining, but are simply the portfolios on the market at the time for sale. Even for portfolio mining efforts, the seller most likely will not sell you all the patents you've picked. Instead, they may send you some in your "pick list", together with a portion that are not on the list. The detailed activities involved are:

— Scan whether the technology covered by each patent is of interest to you. Drop those that are not of interest.

— Categorize the remaining patents into different technology clusters. You should try to be as specific as you can so that you can forward the clusters to the most suitable subject matter expert (SME) for further evaluation.

— Team members involved at this step are technologists, the business manager, and the attorney to provide attorney–client privilege.

(d) The fourth step is requesting information from patent seller assuming your SME found some patents worth further evaluation. The detailed activities involved are:

— If you have not received evidence of use (EoU), this might be a good time to request them. Even if you have already developed some yourself, it is still worthwhile to see if the seller or broker has a different perspective on EoU. Some people even provide claim charts which typically refer to evidence of infringement document that are essentially ready for legal usage. In addition, you may already know about the encumbrances, i.e. your target company is not licensed. However, you should find out whether other key companies of interest to you are also not licensed so that you have an idea about the total value of the patent. These are called encumbrances associated with a patent.

— If you have not already signed a NDA at this point, you should consider signing one. The seller probably will request one as well in order to properly disclose encumbrance information to you. An alternative approach is to provide seller a "white-list", i.e. a list of companies that you want to know whether licensed. Seller will only return to you a list of companies that are NOT licensed, thus the name of "white-list". Since these companies have not signed any NDA or contract with the seller, the seller has no obligation to keep their names confidential. Accordingly, black-list means that companies on the list are licensed. Many sellers can't disclose the black-list because some cross-licensing agreements include a clause requesting them to keep the existence of the agreement confidential. Therefore, seller would be breaching its confidentiality obligation if providing that company's name on a black-list, i.e. encumbrance list.

— Team involved at this step consists of the business lead, technologist, and attorneys.

(e) The fifth step is developing detailed claim chart, EoU so that you have a good understanding about the patent value and be able to justify to your management on how much to pay for the patent. The detailed activities involved are:

— Verify EoU, develop claim chart if needed. You may need to conduct prior art searches thoroughly at this point and study the file history of the patent.

— Based on the claim chart or EoU and prior art searches, you have a good understanding about which products the patent maps onto, and whether the patent is likely to survive any invalidation challenges. You will also have a good feeling about possible workaround, ease of detection, and encumbrances. These are all the key information you need to value a patent.

— Team involved at this step consists of attorney and technologist. If the patent also reads onto your product, the work should be performed under attorney–client privilege and attorney work-product protection.

(f) The sixth step is obtaining internal approval, then negotiating price, and contract terms and conditions if pricing is agreed upon. The team involved at this stage is typically just the business lead and attorney.

7.1.5. Advantage and disadvantage of portfolio mining

Although the portfolio mining approach tends to yield patents in better alignment with your IP strategy, you need to balance the advantage and disadvantage associated with this approach. In other words, you should be fully aware of the trade-offs so you can make well-informed decisions.

(a) **Advantage**
   — Patents are exactly what you want. Instead of waiting for the right patents to fall into your lap, this approach is more proactive and should enable you to accomplish your goal faster if done properly. It also provides better ROI because your team doesn't have to waste time on many portfolios not aligned with your strategy.

(b) **Disadvantage**
   — High legal risks due to the potential of being put on notice. You can use a NDA to remedy this risk and use attorney-client privilege to guide such analysis.
   — Most patents you picked out are not available for sale so that your team's efforts are largely wasted. To ensure higher yield of obtaining your desired patents, you should build strategic partnership with target companies before such portfolio mining so that you are more likely to obtain the patents you want to buy.

7.1.6. Checklist for patent acquisition

Table 7-1 summarizes issues to consider for patent acquisition actions.

Table 7-1   Comparison of patent acquisition issues for China versus US.

Issues to Consider	US Typical Approach	China Approach: (Similar) or Different
Prevent seller putting you on notice	• Sign an NDA with specific clause stating that evaluating these patents can't be used for future evidence of willful infringement	• (same)
Prevent discovery of your analysis results, especially if the patent read onto your product.	• Perform analysis under attorney client privilege. • Treat legal analysis as attorney work product.	• Chinese lawyer doesn't have the communication privilege. Make sure to use a qualified US lawyer.
Obtaining encumbrances information from seller.	• Sign NDA. • Provide white-list rather than black-list.	• (same)

7.2. Patent Sales

Although patent sale is on the opposite side of patent purchase so one might think you can easily do patent sales if you know patent acquisition. However, the approach and mentality requirement needed to be successful for patent sales is quite different from that for patent acquisition. We'll highlight some of these differences in the following sections.

7.2.1. *Due diligence*

For patent acquisition, buyer wants to make sure he can use the patent for litigation, assertion, or negotiation. With today's IP environment in US, he must be prepared that his patent will be challenged at PTAB in the future as invalid. As a result, before purchasing a patent, buyer usually conducts a thorough prior art search.

For patent sales, seller typically doesn't do any prior art searches. If a seller ("Seller") becomes aware of certain prior art issues for his for-sale patents, he will be morally obligated to inform the buyer of the defects, especially if asked. If the patent sales business team is aware of such issues, their sales pitch will be dampened even if subconsciously. Sometimes a patent purchase agreement may include a warranty and representation clause by the Seller that none of the patent is invalid to Seller's knowledge. Therefore, many sellers choose to not conduct any prior art searches for their for-sale portfolios.

However, other due diligences must be diligently performed before a patent sale portfolio is made available to the market. This will prevent future issues for your company and your buyer.

7.2.2. Ownership?

First, you should check patent ownership to ensure there is a clean chain of title without any breaks, gaps, or mistakes.

7.2.3. Is the patent seller the current owner for the US assets and non-US assets?

When companies acquire other companies, they sometimes don't record assignment of patents from the acquired company to themselves, either due to negligence or to save money (e.g. the assignment of an US case costs ~US$40). This may cause a huge issue when selling patents because seller needs to make up the missing assignment from the acquired company to seller to perfect the chain of title before assigning the patent to buyer. To get an officer from the original acquired company to sign the patent assignment agreement, it may be an impossible task especially after years passing by and people from the acquired company having moved on.

Some companies choose to only assign US assets to themselves, and leaving the foreign counterparts AS IS. The same issue as mentioned above will need to be dealt with when patent is sold. Even worse is that some foreign countries have stringent requirement on who can sign such a patent assignment document, and some countries require one original signature for each individual patent, and others require a corporate certification to authorize the person signing. Again, these tasks become much more difficult years after the merger or acquisition.

7.2.4. Is any patent jointly owner?

One must be keenly aware that some patents might be jointly owned. For example, when a company collaborates with a university on a project, the joint development agreement may have stipulated that the resulting patents are to be jointly owned by the two parties. Therefore, your team must check the PTO database ahead of time. However, you should be cognizant that sometimes the USPTO assignment record might be wrong due to mistakes by assignees or the PTO. Therefore, you want to make sure any joint ownership relationship is accurate.

Jointly owned patents are typically not good candidates for patent sales. First of all, a buyer who wants to use the patent sue/countersue another party could be severely compromised if the joint owner offers a license to the other party. In addition, there may be restrictions on selling patents in the joint development agreement ("JDA") because the JDA partner would not want patents it might use to fall into the wrong hands.

7.2.5. Does the patent seller have the authority to sell?

Seller needs to double check whether itself indeed has the right to sell the patents. There are a few cases which may prevent seller from selling patents:

(a) Exclusive license — some exclusive licenses are equivalent to near full ownership of the patent right, and thus allow the licensee to assert, or even sue, using those assets. The license agreement likely explicitly forbids licensor or seller from selling the patents.
(b) Liens on the patent asset — when patent portfolios have liens on them, they are not available for sale or to be assigned to another until the lien is removed.
(c) Joint ownership — as discussed above, certain jointly owned patents may not be available for sale. Some may require seeking the other party's consent before being made available for sale.

7.2.6. Can you use "black-list" approach for encumbrance disclosure or you must adopt a "white-list" approach?

Companies often sign cross-license agreements or license out one-way agreements. These patents are encumbered because buyers can't use these patents against licensee if they already have a license to these patents.

As a result, one of the important information buyers need to know is encumbrances.

However, most patent cross-licensing agreements require that both parties keep the terms of the agreement confidential. Usually such cross-licensing agreements don't try to prevent disclosure about the existence of such agreements because the licensees want people to know that they are licensed so that they are not bothered again by subsequent patent owners to license out or assert these assets. Licensor also want to disclose licensees' names because they want other companies in similar situation to know someone took a license which may be considered a validation of the patent value and quality. However, there are companies that insist on keeping the existence of such cross-licensing agreements confidential, perhaps due to some previous bad experiences or other reasons. In such cases, seller will not be able to disclose to buyer that they have cross license agreement with the licensee, i.e. they can't use the "black-list" approach to disclose encumbrances. Instead, they need to use the so called "white-list" approach. This approach requires the buyer to provide a list of companies for which they desire to learn about the encumbrance situation, seller will then list the ones that are not licensees to these patents. As discussed above, seller can disclosure non-licensee names because they have no confidentiality obligations to these non-licensees. However, by removing certain companies from the white-list, it could be an implied admission that there are cross-licensing agreements with the parties removed from the list, or some other arrangements. Therefore, you want to be careful and only disclosure such information under a non-disclosure agreement (NDA).

7.2.7. *Make sure your team check all possible encumbrances*

You need to check the encumbrances because it affects the value of these patents. If all potential licensing target companies have a license to these patents, then there are very little or no value left to these patents. Therefore, you should ask your team to provide details for the following type of agreements:

(a) Bare patent license agreements: licensed patent, capture period, scope, licensed period;

(b) Product license agreements;
(c) Joint development agreements;
(d) Sublicense rights.

7.2.8. *Are you able to track and thus disclose company participation in any open source communities?*

Some companies are so big (or small but disorganized) that they don't know when their engineers participate in certain open source committees and contributed codes to the open sources. If your company falls within this category, then you may need to disclaim such disclosure obligation expressly in the patent sale agreement so that there are no misunderstandings by the buyer.

7.2.9. *Are you able to track and thus disclose company participation in any standard committee, and what are the obligations?*

Similarly, some companies are too big to track their engineers' activities. Therefore, if someone commits company's participation to a particular standard, others may not even know. In that case, you'll need to disclaim such disclosure obligation expressly or limit to a "knowledge based" representation if the buyer insists on such a representation.

7.2.10. *Look for patent disclaimers*

Disclaimed patents typically cannot be owned separately by two different owners. They must be sold together or not sell at all. If one of the disclaimed patents has been lapsed, you are recommended to sell the lapsed case together with the disclaimed active patent to buyer so that there are no issues later regarding whether the two disclaimed patents are commonly owned by the same owner. There are various places to look for patent disclaimer information. The following few sections address them individually.

7.2.11. *USPTO provides some info in the electronic image of file history*

(a) You may need to make special orders from USPTO;
(b) Check front page of the patent;
(c) Your internal database might have some information;
(d) Common inventor and similar specification might be a helpful clue;
(e) Specialized due diligence services can check disclaimers for a fee.

7.2.12. *Check whether a disclaimed patent is a parent or child which might affect the patent active status*

(a) You must locate the disclaimer document for the child patent. It should list all the disclaimers in exchange for getting the child patent allowed.
(b) Typically, the disclaimer requires common ownership between the child and the parent patent.
(c) The question is if the parent patent is lapsed intentionally or unintentionally, does it render the child patent inactive, or vice versa? Our understanding of most disclaimer language is that it doesn't, but one should watch for cases in the future for this issue.
(d) If the parent patent has naturally expired, then the child patent expires with it.

7.2.13. *Check patent family members*

(a) Buyers would want to obtain all the foreign counterparts together when they buy patents. As a result, your patent sales due diligence should include searching for active foreign counterparts in a patent family. As stated above in the disclaimer section, some companies may want to transfer lapsed patents as well.
(b) For US family members, find out all the continuations, divisional, continuation-in-parts. Some buyers will insist on acquiring the entire family because they believe courts will deem them lack of standing if they don't own the entire family. Other buyers may only insist on acquiring all

continuations, while divisional cases are OK to leave out since they address different invention points.

(c) Seller should also conduct due diligence on equivalent family members. Some companies may utilize so-called "master specification" techniques, i.e. patents in different families use identical or near identical specifications, with the same inventor and the same filing date. These could be viewed as one family even if they are not filed as one family. Certain buyers may insist on buying those together as well.

(d) Seller also needs to perform due diligence on all the published applications, unpublished pending applications. Buyers often want the seller to transfer all the cases together to the buyer. Some buyers are particularly interested in pending applications so they can modify the claims of pending applications after purchase. Some buyers insist on seller transfer the associated invention disclosures. This could be problematic because certain information disclosed in the original invention disclosure might not have been included into the patent application specification, either because the seller intentionally wanted to keep it as a trade secret, or it has a different invention point which doesn't fit too well with the current application. In such cases, seller may not want buyer to have access to those invention disclosures AS IS, but instead can redact the invention disclosures such that they only include portions that have incorporated into the patent applications. Buyer may insist on seller to either turn over a redacted version at the time of deal closure, or at a later time when issues regarding the patent priority date surface. As a result, buyer may request seller to promise to not destroy the original invention disclosure record even though seller no longer owns the resulting patent. These will impose significant burden on seller and seller must be aware of the costs associated with maintaining these documents and the risks associated with breaching the contract if someone in the company later accidently destroys the documents.

7.2.14. *Other potential defects in the chain of title*

(a) <u>Assignment from inventor to employer</u>. It is a good practice to ensure the Assignment document from inventor to employer is signed and

collected before patent filing. Otherwise, after an employee leaves the
company, it becomes much more costly or impossible to collect the
signature. In a particular case, the employee's personal email no
longer worked, or he wasn't checking it. Patent sales team had to use
LinkedIn to track him down, or ask friends who knew him to find his
new contact information. However, some ex-employees simply don't
reply either being too busy, or in a worse scenario, resent their
ex-employers and therefore are intentionally not responding. In such
a situation, company would have to resort back to the original employment agreement and hoping that there was an IP Ownership clause
stipulating that IP generated by employees while employed by the
Company belongs to the Company.

Collecting the assignment form from inventor to employer in a
timely manner also prevents subsequent issues in litigation. One company reported that German law doesn't recognize patent ownership
unless there is an assignment in the current tense (e.g. "I hereby
assign", rather than "I will assign") from inventor to the employer. In
addition, the assignment form needs to be executed prior to entering
into Germany. Signing the assignment form by inventor after national-
izing in Germany was deemed invalid. The company had to resort to
the employee's employment agreement at the time of being hired by
the company to show the ownership by the employer.

(b) <u>Defects in the chain of title</u> — <u>Intentionally, delayed execution of
assignment agreement by employer</u>. Some companies don't want
other people figure out their future product directions. However, they
can't risk the chance of not protecting their new inventions. Therefore,
they try to disclose as late as possible by not executing the assignment
agreement from inventor to employer until patent grant. As a result,
certain pending patent applications are not associated with any companies, but under the inventor's name only. The risk of such practice
is that if the inventor leaves the company before patent grant,
employer may need to locate the ex-employee and ask him/her to sign
the assignment agreement. The additional risk is that if the grant happens after the case enters a foreign country; assignment agreement
signed then may not be viewed as valid under the local law. Therefore,
the best practice is to get the assignment agreement signed by inventor
before or at the same time as the patent filing. In addition, before an

employee leaves a company, make sure he/she signs all related assignment agreements before his/her departure.

(c) <u>Defects in the chain of title</u> — <u>Partially collected Assignment document</u>. This is a scenario where among multiple inventors, some assignment documents are completed but one or more were not collected either due to the fact that those inventors were not available at the time of filing or other oversights. The risk is similar to that described in (a) and should be avoided as much as possible.

(d) <u>Defects in the chain of title</u> — <u>Misspelled inventor name or employer name</u>. Sometimes inventor names are spelled wrong, such as Jon Smith rather than the correct spelling of John Smith. Assignee name might be spelled wrong, such as company name NewCo is mistakenly spelled as New_Co. These all require corrections when selling patents and are much easier to correct early than late. Companies should try to avoid such mistakes up front at the time of patent filing.

(e) <u>Defects in the chain of title</u> — <u>No assignment document from inventor to employer for a continuation case</u>. This is not a defect necessarily but seller must ensure parent case assignment document is included in the patent sale deal so that the continuation case has no defects in its chain of title.

(f) <u>Defect in Assignment from acquiree to acquiror for an M&A transaction</u> — <u>not registered with PTO</u>. Often after a merger and acquisition transaction, people are too busy to bother with patent assignment from the acquired company to the acquiring company. Another reason for not doing such assignment registration/recordation is to save money because each assignment costs ~$40 at USPTO. However, such assignment could be much harder to perfect at the time of patent sales because the executives for the original acquired company might have left the acquiring company and are hard to find. Some countries require signature by the company officer with a certificate that the signatory is indeed such a high level executive.

(g) <u>Defect in Assignment from acquiree to acquiror for an M&A transaction</u> — <u>misspelled company name</u>. Sometimes, company name is spelled incorrectly in a minor way which still requires fixing, e.g. NewCo, LLC versus NewCo LLC. It is much harder to fix these defects years later at the time of patent sales. The best practice is to do it correctly immediately after M&A transaction.

(h) <u>Defect in Assignment from acquiree to acquiror for an M&A transaction — not following local registration procedure</u>. Certain countries have specific requirement on assignment document, e.g. ensure to list patent numbers.

(i) <u>Defect in Assignment from acquiree to acquiror for an M&A transaction — foreign asset registration not done</u>. This might be due to the fact that some foreign assignments are expensive because they may require translation. However, such issues are much harder to handle later when doing patent sales transaction.

(j) <u>Company name change or setting up patent holding subsidiary — not registered with PTO</u>. This could be due to cost concerns or some companies may intentionally not register to hide a non-public event. This will cost similar issues as discussed above.

(k) <u>"Dangling branches" in the assignment history</u>. A perfect chain of title starts with the individual inventor, potentially goes to a corporation, then eventually assigns to the patent purchaser. There shouldn't be any missing links, or additional branches that don't close the loop leading eventually to the patent purchaser. These defects are referred to as the "dangling branches". They might be mistakenly recorded assignments either by other companies or by USPTO. Sometimes it could be a registration of a non-exclusive license to a licensee rather than an outright sale. Alternatively, it could be a lien by a bank. Therefore, one must study the documents associated with each assignment carefully to assess the exact situation and whether it should be a concern.

7.2.15. *Check patent/application status*

First of all, it is important to ensure that the patents you are trying to sell are still active. If a Seller sells "dead" patents, a buyer may be entitled to refund or additional compensations. Therefore, it is to the mutual benefits of both seller and buyer to confirm patent status before transaction.

(a) For a granted patent, seller needs to check whether patent has expired.
— Check priority date. Patent expires naturally 20 years from the priority date.

— Check whether it was filed before June 8, 1995. If the answer is YES, then patent expires 20 years from the priority date or 17 years from the grant date, whichever is later. Therefore, your patent may still be alive if using the 17 years from grant date rule.

— Check whether the patent is lapsed due to unpaid maintenance fee.

— Check whether patent owner expressly donated it to public.

— Check whether there are any cases where the patent was reinstated by petition. The maintenance fee typically has a Due Date, and the date after Due Date is called Surcharge Date. There is a grace period to pay the maintenance fee within 6 months from the Surcharge Date ("Grace Period") by also paying a late payment fee. If seller negligently forgot to pay the maintenance fee after the Grace Period, the patent is deemed lapsed. However, if the company can truly prove that the failure to pay was unintentional and the lapse is no more than 2 years from the Surcharge Date, then it can reinstated the patent by a lawyer's petition to USPTO under "unintentional failure to pay" category. Alternatively, the patent can be reinstated by petitioning "unavoidable failure to pay" category. However, this standard is much harder to meet. Buyers may need to check the facts carefully before purchasing such reinstated patents to ensure the "unintentional failure to pay" was truly unintentional, and the "unavoidable failure to pay" meets the required standard if challenged in court.

(b) For pending applications, it is abandoned if patent owner does not respond to an office action, not paying fees due, or expressly abandons the case. Seller may revive a previously abandoned case via a petition of "unintentional abandonment". However, buyer should ensure that the circumstances truly meet the "unintentional" definition if later challenged in court.

7.2.16. *Check the patent history*

(a) File wrapper: Seller should understand whether there are any estoppels in the file history so that it can answer questions from buyers knowledgably and truthfully.

(b) Litigation or assertion: If any patent has been used in a litigation, seller needs to disclose whether there have been any invalidity challenges, whether there have been Markman hearing in claim construction and how did those turn out. If a patent has been used in an assertion, seller needs to disclose to potential buyer the materials used because the asserted companies may be deemed to have been "on notice". They may have the right to file a declaratory judgment (D.J.).

7.3. Risk Mitigation Related to Due Diligence Efforts

Even if Seller's team performs due diligences carefully, there may still be risks that Seller should try to mitigate by taking precautions.

7.3.1. *Conduct due diligence using external specialized services*

Even large corporations may not have access to all the information of their own patents. As a result, it might be necessary to hire external experts to perform due diligences. Companies that provide such due diligences include CPI. The purpose is to make sure the following areas are properly and adequately addressed:

(a) Include US assets and foreign counterparts in a family;
(b) Remove jointly owned assets;
(c) Remove patents with a disclaimer without all related patents;
(d) List any US family member patent number individually if they are part of the transaction;
(e) Include all foreign counter patent numbers;
(f) Include parent cases that have been lapsed or abandoned in the assignment.

7.3.2. *Conduct due diligences internally*

Some companies might be well equipped to conduct their own due diligences. It is to seller's best interest to provide buyer with available information so buyer is more confident about the asset they are buying.

(a) Seller can order file history from USPTO to help buyer's due diligence;

(b) Seller may also provide internal file history to buyer;

(c) Seller might be willing to provide invention disclosure or redacted copy of invention disclosure to establish earlier invention date in case buyer needs it in the future.

7.3.3. *Ensure no additional encumbrances are added later*

(a) <u>Between the signing of a patent purchase agreement ("PPA") and the deal closing</u>. Seller may induce additional encumbrances to the to-be-sold patents and must disclose these to buyer. For example, if seller executes a licensing agreement after PPA signing, the licensee is licensed to the patents to be sold because the patents are deemed to be owned by seller before closing and thus are "swept into the licensing agreement".

(b) <u>After closing</u>. Seller may have signed certain agreements that can encumber the to-be-sold patents even after closing. Seller must disclose such encumbrances to buyer before deal closing. For example, if Seller has signed a "springing license agreement", i.e. a license to licensee which is triggered by the patent being sold to another party, then such arrangement must be included in the encumbrance disclosure. There are also certain Standards obligations or Open Source obligations that may put certain requirement on the to-be-sold patents. Seller should study the technology the patents cover and conclude whether such technologies are subject to such Standard or Open Sources commitments that Seller made.

7.3.4. *Limit seller's representation and warranties*

(a) You as a Seller, unless necessary, should only offer warranties, but not representations, in the Patent Sales Agreement. Warranty provides remedies specified in the contract, but representation imposes a higher burden on the lawyer so he/she must perform additional due diligence in order to make such a representation.

(b) You may agree to a language which lists specific remedies for breach of warranty, but warn buyer that they should be aware of appearance of penalty which may become unenforceable.
(c) Seller should be prepared to include the following in the warranty and representation:
— Both US and foreign counterparts are active with maintenance fees paid by certain date;
— Encumbrances information are accurate;
— Marketable title, authority to executive the agreement, no liens;
— Patent not subject to open source license;
— Patent not subject to standards license.

7.3.5. *Specify who is responsible for how long*

As a seller, you should make sure you and buyer agree up front who will take care of the following activities and for how long.

(a) Buyer may request assistance in recordation and perfection for X months. Seller can request a fee if the X period is unreasonably long (e.g. greater than 3 months);
(b) Who will pay unpaid maintenance fees;
(c) Which law-firm will be responsible for the correspondences sent out by PTO for pending applications;
(d) Who is responsible for missing statutory due date:
— US applications;
— Foreign filings.

7.4. Fixing Issues After Closing

7.4.1. *Missing assignment from inventor to employer*

If there are still missing assignments from inventor to employer after the deal is closed, seller may try the following approaches.

(a) Track down inventor via LinkedIn, their friends, etc;
(b) Provide buyer a copy of employment agreement of the inventor with the Seller;

(c) Rely on specific country law if it stipulates that IP belongs to the employer;

(d) Provide parent assignment to buyer if available.

7.4.2. *Missing assignment from entity A to entity B*

(a) Your company can try to certify that it has the power to represent Entity A to fix the defect, if A is a subsidiary of your company.

(b) Fix assignment before buyer registration.

7.4.3. *Strategy to deal with hard to fix defects*

(a) <u>Inventor not found or unwilling to cooperate</u>: use financial incentive, employment agreement obligations, or country law of IP ownership.

(b) <u>Certain countries may require original translated document</u>. Use petition to overcome such issues. Can also consider Apostille system.

7.5. Educate/Warn Buyer of the Different Registration Requirement in Different Countries

Many patent purchasers are "new to the game". You, as a seller, can help the purchaser/buyer to watch out for certain issues during patent assignment recordation so that your patent sale transaction concludes smoothly.

7.5.1. *USPTO*

(a) Electronic assignment document is acceptable.

(b) All patents can use one assignment document by listing the patent numbers.

7.5.2. *Japan (some European countries as well)*

(a) Must have original signature on assignment document, electronic assignment document is not acceptable.

(b) Each patent must be listed on different document. If you are selling lots of Japanese patent, your signatory will have to sign many original assignment documents.
(c) Need to provide power of attorney ("POA") of local lawyers to handle the subsequent communication.
(d) Need to provide translation of the assignment document.

7.5.3. *South Korea*

(a) Must have original signature on assignment document.
(b) Need to provide POA.
(c) Need certificate of corporation to prove that the signatory has the authority to sign the patent sale agreement on behalf of your company.

7.5.4. *Other countries*

(a) Mexico: need original document and must be translated.
(b) China: need translation.

7.6. Patent Brokers

Patent brokers play a role in the IP transaction market. Figure 7-4 depicts their potential role. Unfortunately, many brokers want quick and easy profits without putting in necessary efforts or investment. As a result, many

Figure 7-4   Potential roles that could be played by a competent patent broker.

only focus on transaction brokering without providing EoU. Therefore, there is a need for brokers that provide more high quality value such as claim charting or developing solid evidence or use.

As shown in the above Figure 7-4 brokers function as a connecting service to link buyer, seller, patent technical analysis service provider, and other brokers together. If done correctly, it could add significant value in IP transactions. However, many brokers don't have the resources to provide high quality claim chart work, but merely using their client base as the only value-add. Even so, many still demand to either have up-front fees as well as high success fees, some demanding 25% or more broker fees. For sellers without much technical resources, it is important to find a broker that is capable of developing high quality claim charts. For companies who have long-term plans to sell patents regularly, they might get better ROI by developing internal high quality technical teams to support patent sales effort.

There are disadvantages using patent broker to sell portfolios. Your portfolio could change any time, such as a need to pull out a few key patents from the previously for-sale portfolio in order to support your negotiation team. However, you likely will not inform the broker immediately because you may not know whether the other negotiation will materialize eventually. In addition, encumbrances are usually shared in the form of white-list. Brokers want to know up front which companies are licensed, while you don't want to or cannot disclose confidential information unless the broker finds a real interested buyer who provides you a white-list first.

On the other hand, there are significant advantages in using patent brokers to sell patents. You have a greater reach to potential buyers via brokers because the conversation is conducted at arm's-length so the portfolio may reach competitors or companies in a completely different industry that you are unfamiliar with. In addition, it allows you to free up bandwidth to work on other important projects. Some brokers are really good at finding out who needs what type of patents and can close deals well. Therefore, with the right broker, it could work out wonderfully for everyone.

Even for patent purchasers, a good patent broker can play an invaluable role. A high quality broker can perform the patent mining or portfolio mining on behalf of the buyer, thus shielding the patent buyer from potential legal risks of being put on notice or being accused of willful infringement. In addition, some buyer companies don't want to disclose their name before knowing that the seller is willing to part with the target patents. Other buyers want to stay anonymous even after signing the patent purchase agreement. They may use a broker to hold the acquired patents, and then direct the broker to transfer the patents to them only when necessary.

To formalize the relationship between a patent seller and a patent broker representing the seller, a patent sales broker agreement is required. Similarly for brokers representing patent buyer, a formal agreement needs to be signed between the parties. The following are typical business structure related issues to watch out for in a broker agreement. In Chapter 8, we'll cover the contract language-related issues for a broker agreement.

7.6.1. *Patent seller and broker deal structure*

Patent sale broker deals are typically structured as contingent payment, i.e. they are paid a certain percentage (10–30%) of the patent sale price after the portfolio is sold. A few new brokers might be willing to accept 5% if all they do is to forward a portfolio to someone. For such a case, it is more like a referral fee. For very large patent sale deals, broker might be willing to accept a low percentage or a fixed fee. Similarly for very small deals, broker might want a large percentage or a fixed fee simply to cover their cost.

In addition, some brokers want to be paid before the sale, especially if they spend a lot of time and money on developing claim charts. Sellers usually don't agree to such arrangement because they want to make sure broker is motivated to sell the portfolio by compensating them contingently.

Other issues include how long to set the broker agreement contract terms. The patent sale cycle is getting longer nowadays, too short a term is not fair to the broker if broker doesn't get credit after spending lots of efforts developing the sales material. On the other hand, too long a term is not fair to the seller, especially if the broker is not performing and the seller could have sold the portfolio quickly if using another broker.

(1) <u>Preamble</u>: For an Agreement to be effective, it is advised that there are "considerations". Therefore, the preamble paragraph (e.g. the paragraph

starting with "whereas") should list services the broker offers so that the payment it receives later is in exchange for its valuable service.

(2) <u>Definition of purchase price</u>: Patent sales broker that provides claim chart service for the patent seller often takes a success fee, typically between 10% and 30% of the purchase price. In corner cases, patent seller needs to consider when a patent sale transaction is conducted not purely with cash, but partially or completely with non-cash assets, for example exchanging patents without any cash flowing in either direction. Another example is that if a patent sale eventually becomes a spin-off of a business unit to the buyer broker introduced, how do you calculate the patent portion as the base for broker's commission? When seller and broker have a good relationship, these are not issues to be bothered with because you don't want spend too much time on negotiating a broker agreement or let the broker agreement prevent you from utilizing the broker to sell your portfolios. However, for brokers you don't have a close relationship yet, you may have to resort to dotting the i's and crossing the t's in the Agreement to protect your interest. Seller would try to use pure cash that's solely associated with patent sales as the base for calculating commissions, while broker would use the cash equivalent attributable to the patent value in a transaction as the base. Parties likely will settle somewhere mid-way.

(3) <u>A common issue for broker agreement is whether the relationship is exclusive</u>. Broker always want to have the exclusive right to sell a portfolio, but companies are concerned that they'd be stuck if a broker can't sell in a timely manner. At a minimum, company should always have the right to sell the portfolio themselves in parallel with the broker.

(4) <u>Another common issue is which ones are the patent sale leads brought in by the broker and thus entitle the broker a commission fee if the deal successful transacts within the agreed upon time frame</u>. A simple verbal or written communication from a potential buyer does not qualify as a successful lead. Broker needs to bring in a written offer and ensures the offer converts to a successful patent sale deals in a timely manner. Only then, broker is entitled to receiving a commission.

(5) In the Warranties, Indemnification & Limitation of Liability sections, Company may require broker to indemnify and hold Company against liabilities related to broker's misrepresentation or incorrect material

provided by broker to potential buyers. For example, some brokers may become overly aggressive in presenting claim charts using company's patents. It could trigger a DJ (see discussion in the next section). Under such circumstances, seller could become a defendant of a DJ suit that was inadvertently cause by the broker. It could be disruptive to Company's business operations. Therefore, Company wants certain clauses in the broker Agreement to prevent such situations. However, broker will resist accepting such clauses because small operations often don't have insurance, or only insure a small amount. The cost associated with a DJ would be beyond their financial capability. Company may limit such clause to intentional misrepresenting the Company, etc. so to move the deal forward.

7.6.2. *Patent buyer and broker deal structure*

Patent buyer may also employ patent brokers to help them acquire patents. The service offered by such a broker could range from merely making a phone call to a seller company asking if they are willing to sell a particular patent, to conducting thorough portfolio mining to look for patents in alignment with buyer's IP strategy, develop claim charts, inquire patent encumbrances information, and even negotiate patent purchase agreement on behalf of the buyer. As a result, the commission structure varies as well. Again, brokers prefer to be paid up front for their work such as patent selection and claim charting, at least for the time and material in portfolio mining. Buyers, on the other hand, prefer to only pay when the portfolio is purchased. If broker is not willing to proceed unless some fees are paid up front, buyers may consider a milestone payment arrangement. For example, installed payment can be made at: (i) when buyer approves patent selection and the associated claim chart; (ii) upon broker's obtaining a pricing within buyer's expected range; and then (iii) upon deal completion. The following are additional issues one may encounter for such a buyer broker relationship.

(1) Some of the above issues outlined for seller broker Agreement also apply to buyer broker relationship, e.g. including "consideration" in the preamble, broker's desire for exclusivity, etc. Exclusivity in this

case is reasonable. Otherwise, if two different brokers uncovered the same patent and try to buy it around the same time, it might start a price bidding war between buyer's two brokers.

(2) Another issue to consider is if you agreed to pay for the time and material of broker's portfolio mining and claim chart development work, who owns the material, can broker use it for other purposes.

7.7. Utilizing Disclaimer/Avoid Triggering DJ

For patent sales team, it is important to handle portfolio marketing tactics carefully. Due to the fact that the criterion to trigger declaratory judgment (DJ) has decreased significantly (*MedImmune, Inc. v. Genentech*, 127 S. Ct., 2007), careful handling of patent sales pitch is required to manage the process. Although due to recent popularity of invalidity in front of PTAB via *IPR* process created by AIA, DJ is still utilized by litigants in search of favorable venues. Companies being accused of patent infringement may file a DJ motion in a court that is favorable to them, asking judge to declare that (i) the patent is invalid; and/or (ii) their products don't infringe. This is the so-called "first mover" advantage because you can choose the venue advantageous to you. Often the accuser doesn't want to go to court because they simply want to quickly get licensing money. Therefore, such tactics of filing DJ (or *IPR*) could force them to settle for very low fees or simply walk away if they don't want their patents to be challenged. Previously one has to prove that an aggressor provided a patent number in combination with a specific product in the form of a claim chart to demand DJ. Due to the recent case (*Medimmune*), a DJ can be easily triggered, sometimes simply with a patent list plus some indication of products.

More recently, companies routinely use *Inter Partes Review* (IPR) to challenge the validity of asserted patents due to the high invalidity percentage (80%+) of USPTO's patent trial and appeal board (PTAB). As a result, patent sale teams need to be extra careful to not inadvertently be dragged into a litigation suit.

Based on the above concerns, material to be sent out for patent sale programs should include a clear statement such as "THE INFORMATION PROVIDED HEREIN AS PART OF COMPANY'S PATENT SALES

PROCESS IS NOT INTENDED TO CONSTITUTE LEGAL ANALYSIS, NOTICE OR AN ACCUSATION OF INFRINGEMENT WITH REGARD TO ANY OF THE PATENTS OR APPLICATIONS OFFERED FOR SALE. COMPANY MAKES NO REPRESENTATION OR WARRANTIES REGARDING THE PATENTS, APPLICATIONS, OR THE SALES PROCESS, AND RESERVES THE RIGHT IN ITS SOLE DISCRETION TO MODIFY OR DISCONTINUE THE SALES PROCESS AT ANY TIME WITHOUT PRIOR NOTICE."

In addition, claim charts or EoU documents should only be provided under NDA which should include a clause stating that the patent sale company will not use the fact that the recipient reviewed the patent list to substantiate any willful infringement accusation against the potential purchaser, and in return the potential purchase will not challenge the validity of the for-sale patents, and will not file DJ or *IPR* proceedings against the reviewed patents during the evaluation process.

7.8. Patent Cross-License

For operating companies, patent cross-licensing agreement is an effective tool to reduce future litigation risks and gain freedom of operation or design freedom. Fifteen years ago, such patent cross-licensing negotiations were often conducted by comparing the height of each party's patents if you actually pile up the paper patent documents. This caused many companies to boast the total number of patents they have. For example, HP's ex-CEO used to, and still does today, publicly announce proudly that HP tripled its innovation and was generating nearly 15 patents a day during mid-2000's.[2]

Now more than a decade later, patent quantity is no longer a key factor after reaching certain critical mass. Instead, patent quality is the most important factor when parties negotiate cross-licensing agreements. One might argue that assuming each party has a yield of generating 1% high quality patents, in that case comparing quantity should be equivalent to

---

[2]Ellie Shechet, Carly Firina to Interviewer: 'I Don't Accept Your Premise That HP Had Misfortunes', 2016, can be found at http://theslot.jezebel.com/carly-fiorina-to-interviewer-i-dont-accept-your-premis-1751570204.

comparing quality. The reality is a very different picture. The reason is that companies have different approaches in filing patents. Some conduct thorough prior art searches and thus their high quality patents likely constitute a high percentage of the total population. On the other end of the spectrum are some companies who don't allow inventors or lawyers to search for prior arts. In such cases, most patents probably are entangled with prior arts and thus can be easily invalidated. In addition, some companies file patents that read onto their own products, but may not map onto any third party products and not in alignment with any third party product roadmaps and thus have no cross-licensing value. The more experienced portfolio managers will spend a large amount of efforts trying to ensure their patents read onto third party's current or future products.

With such vastly different approaches, companies could display a significant difference in the percentage of their high quality patents. When negotiating cross-licensing agreements, each party will look at how much of their own products are, or will be, exposed to the other party's patent portfolios and assign a value to that risk. If the amount of risks to each party is not in a similar range with each other, then the party with more risk exposure needs to pay on-going royalties or a one-time lump sum payment (or installed payment) to the other party.

Some companies tend to combine patent cross-licensing negotiation with other type of business deals, such as patent sale, patent purchase, technology transfer, joint R&D development or even business sale. For example, if target licensee is a large supplier to your business, then you have some leverage over the supplier during a patent cross-licensing negotiation, especially if the supplier really wants to continuously win your business deal.

The following are some key parameters to pay attention to during a patent cross-license agreement negotiation:

7.8.1. *Licensed patents, capture period*

Licensed patents mean patents to license to each other. It could be a list of patents, a technology description, all patents excluding a few areas, or all the patents you have the right to license. For example, if you want to just license out patents in the storage area, you may state that licensed patents are "all the <u>storage patents</u> that you have the right to license out by the

Effective Date". This way, if you have sold some patents, even if you are still holding the title for those patents, you have already relinquished the ownership through a patent sales agreement and thus can no longer license out that patent.

You need to be cognizant that some patents cover multiple technology areas. For example, you may have a storage patent which also covers certain server technology. Such a description would inadvertently license out your server technology as well. This is particularly troubling if licensee insists on taking a license to all family members, such as Continuations, Continuations-In-Part, and Divisional. Therefore, the least confusing approach is patent list.

Even with clearly listed patents for licensing, if you truly want to prevent inadvertently licensing out some core technologies, you can specifically exclude those. For example, you could state that "licensed patent is the list, but expressly exclude any server related technology". Such "carve-out" can also be handled using the field of use restriction, but you can restrict in both places if the technology is extremely critical to your company.

Another key concept is the capture period. This is the period that if certain date associated with a patent falls within it, then the patent is a licensed patent. You can use priority date, filing date, grant date, etc. However, priority date is the most natural if you want to include all family members. One needs to be careful about the definition of a family, is it just the parent patent and all the continuations, or including all related continuation-in-part as well as divisional. The clearer you are in the contract, the less confusing in the future when there is a dispute.

7.8.2. *Licensed product or field of use (or license scope), merger, spin-off*

Licensed product means which product licensee is permitted to use the licensed patented technology for. This is also called the field of use or license scope because it limits the usage of licensed patents to a specific scope. You want to be extra diligent here to clearly specify what's licensed and what's not. Using the above storage and server example again, you could define that licensed products are storage products. To avoid any doubt in the future, you may specifically indicate that the licensed product does not include server products.

You also want to look carefully at licensee's business model and potential changes that might happen in the future when defining the licensed product. Is the license worldwide or just a specific jurisdiction? Does the field of use only cover the product and services licensee sells under its own name? Have-made right is typically included, i.e. the product is designed by licensee but made by another party for licensee. What if someone else does all the design and manufacturing while licensee only puts its name on the box? What if you are in the middle of litigation with a third party which funnels all its storage products through this licensee, i.e. the so-called patent laundering? We'll go into more details in Chapter 8 to recommend certain language to deal with such issues.

Another factor to consider is whether licensed products include those of companies that licensee purchases or merges with in the future. For example, if licensee A purchases another company B, and B also sells storage products. Will the license scope cover B's storage products? The final outcome depends on each party's negotiation bargaining chips. If you are the licensee, you will try to include all future subsidiaries into the licensed scope. However, if you are the licensor, you'll not want to include future subsidiaries in the licensed products. Your concern would be if you are in litigation with a company, that company gets acquired by the licensee and then your IP weapon immediately becomes neutralized. If you are addressing cross-licensing arrangement for which most clauses are bilateral and go both ways, then you should balance the pros and cons of each option and chose intelligently based on your needs.

Similarly for spin-off subsidiaries, business units, or simply a product line, should that spin-off continuously enjoy the previous license? It is common practice that the new acquirer's product line doesn't get a license. A typical approach is that only the spin-off's product line at the time of spin-off is licensed. Each year, the volume of such spun-off product line can increase a certain percentage point. The problem is that if the acquirer takes over the acquiree's product line and modifies it significantly; then will the licensed scope include those modified products? If you are the licensor, you should probably try to exclude them.

7.8.3. *License period — patent life time versus guillotine license structure*

How long should the license period be is a tricky parameter to carefully consider. There are two commonly seen practices:

1. license period is patent life-time; or
2. license period is a fixed number of years (e.g. 5 years) and the license terminates the day after license period so that all previously licensed products suddenly become unlicensed. This is the so-called "Guillotine license", i.e. it cuts off sharply at certain date.

If Licensee believes that its future business prospect is very good, then it will choose patent life-time. However, if future is unsure or if you would like to have a chance to renegotiate the agreement or royalty rate, than a Guillotine license is the most appropriate.

7.9. Patent Assertion

Patent assertion means one party claiming the other party infringes its patents and demanding a payment. The issues encountered are similar to that in cross-licensing negotiations with some different characteristics. The following discusses a few main distinctions.

Patent licensing is difficult today as a profitable business; it was easier a decade ago due to a friendlier IP environment toward licensors but was still very challenging. Licensors have to be prepared to enforce their patents via litigation or shutting down licensee's business in order to have a reasonable licensing program. If the licensee already has an existing business relationship with the licensor, licensee will more likely take a patent license from the licensor for fear of otherwise losing its business relationship. Without any, or with very little, existing business relationship, licensors often need to resort to the threat of litigation to entice licensees taking a license. This is a common tactics regardless of whether in USA or China. As a result, licensors often pick a licensee to bring to court to show other potential licensees the consequence of not paying the royalty. It is an art to decide which licensee to bring to court. Some licensors believe the best strategy is picking a weak licensee that licensor knows pretty sure will lose in court or agree to take a license. This is described in Chinese idiom as 杀鸡警猴, "killing a chicken to warn the monkeys". Alternatively, other licensors intentionally pick a tough strong licensee to bring to court, believing that if this lead licensee folds, all others will fold. This is expressed in Chinese idiom as 打蛇要打头, "to hit a snake, start with the head". Depending on the strength of your patent portfolio and the type of licensees, each strategy has its own pros and cons.

7.9.1. *Timing of notice — latches*

Licensors' objective is to maximize the royalty payment by the licensee. They will likely choose an optimized timing to send a notice to licensee, alleging them infringing licensor's patent ("Notice"). Typically a Notice includes at least a patent number from licensor and a product name by licensee, and this is considered an "actual notice". There is also a "constructive Notice" where licensor has put patent number on most of its products declaring that the product is covered by the patent.

Providing Licensee a Notice may entitle the Licensor seek past damages from Licensee up to 6 years before the date of Notice. In addition, Licensor may seek willful infringement damage award after Notice which could treble (three times) the damage award amount. Therefore, Licensors would want to put a licensee "on notice" to start the time clock for past damages and willful infringement. However, there are other factors that Licensors need to consider, such as potentially triggering declaratory judgment which will be discussed in a later section.

Licensor may delay putting a licensee on notice due to various business or legal reasons. If a licensee is still ramping up the product that licensor wants the licensee to pay royalty on, licensor may want to wait until the volume is significant or the product becomes more strategic to the licensee so that licensee is more likely to pay the royalty fee. For example, if licensee's customers like a feature a lot, then it becomes harder for licensee to drop the feature. Even if the licensee is able to work around licensor's solution via a less convenient approach, licensee may choose to keep the easier approach due to customers' overwhelming liking. For example, if the infringing feature is a one click payment button, even if the licensee could use a two-click process for payment, licensee may opt to simply keep the one-click payment button by paying a licensing fee in order to keep customers happy.

However, licensors cannot wait for too long to take actions. Licensees may argue that licensor's right has latched if licensor waits for a long period of time. Typically, this is the same period as the past damage period of six years. Licensor probably will argue that it did not know about the licensee's infringement which caused the delay, but licensees will document that licensor knew about it more than six years ago and therefore forfeited its right to enforce the patent.

7.9.2. *Method claim versus apparatus claim for claim charting*

For patent assertion, licensors usually prepare claim charts based on a dozen strong patents that map onto licensee's products. Licensors need to be careful which claims to use for claim chart construction. A decade ago, the common practice was to use the broadest claim in your patent. In fact, there was a so-called "three fingers rule", i.e. you put up your index finger, middle finger, and ring finger together, if you are able to cover up the claim, then that is likely a good claim because it is so short.

However, in today's IP environment, a typical practice is that licensors will ensure that the claims used for claim charting are not going to be invalidated easily if challenged via *IPR* in front of PTAB or in court during litigation. Therefore, licensors will need to apply the high quality patent principles discussed in the above chapters.

One additional point worth mentioning is whether licensors will likely choose a method claim or an apparatus claim for claim charting. A decade ago, method claim was often favored because it doesn't require a "Notice" to recover past damages (up to six years prior to the Notice). Unlike apparatus claims which are more easily attached to a device and thus can be put onto the corresponding product as a "Constructive Notice", method claims can't be put onto a product easily and thus are deemed to have provided a constructive notice.

However, method claims sometimes are easier to work around. There were cases where method claims were by-passed by switching the order of one step. However, such approach only works if order of the steps is important to the invention outcome.

7.9.3. *Patent licensors — avoiding triggering DJ*

When a party approaches another company to enter into a licensing discussion, its main goal typically is to collect money, not to go to court. This is particularly true in today's US IP environment where injunctions become increasingly difficult to obtain so the assertors usually will walk away after being paid some royalty because they know stopping the other party's product shipment is not easily attainable. In addition, litigating in court is expensive to both sides, and the outcome is uncertain. Therefore, if possible, they will try very hard to avoid being dragged into court.

Assertors face a potential DJ complaint if the assertion effort is not handled properly. DJ gives the potential licensee an advantage because the venue is chosen by the licensee. Therefore, licensors prefer to avoid being DJ'ed. However, due to the lowered bar for DJ standard post MedImmune,[3] a licensor can find itself being DJ'ed without sending a patent number or specific licensee's product name to potential licensees. This is particularly true for NPEs due to the strong push-backs on NPE activities. Whether there is an imminent threat of litigation to the litigant is judged from the totality of the circumstances. As a result, many NPEs chose to sue first, ask questions later.

Interestingly, many operating companies nowadays have IP licensing departments. These operating companies simply want to recoup some of the R&D investment from their patent licensing programs by monetizing their IP portfolios. Therefore, they have no intention going to courts unless absolutely necessary. Litigation is painful for operating companies as well as non-operating companies. As a consequence, licensors trying to license out their patent portfolios should be fully aware of approaches which more easily trigger DJ, and take measures to avoid them.

Although there are no "safe havens" in avoiding DJ, the following precautions can reduce the chance of being DJ'ed if you are a licensor:

(i) Do not put your patent number and potential licensee's product name in the same context, especially in writing;
(ii) Sign a NDA before conducting detailed discussions and the NDA should include a paragraph regarding FRE408 (see the following section).

---

[3] *MedImmune, inc. v. Genentech, Inc.*, 549 U.S. 118 (2007).

7.9.4. *FRE408*

Federal Rule of Evidence 408 "Compromise Offers and Negotiations" was adopted in 1974 to help parties try to reach settlements rather than going to court. It enables parties to review infringement evidences, yet does not allow such evidences to be used for litigation purposes.

Licensor should label its licensing negotiation royalty rate analysis, claim chart material, presentation slides, regardless whether in powerpoint, word document format or excel spreadsheet, and clearly state that they are subject to FRE408, and not admissible as evidence for litigations.

7.9.5. *Patent licensees — how to neutralize the assertions*

For companies who receive patent assertions, there are various ways to handle it. The type of reactions by the defendant should not be, but often is, related to whether the licensor is an operating company or NPE. The key is to stay objective and choose the optimum approach for your company's short term and long term well-being.

One of the options is to enter into a negotiation. If the licensor is an operating company, you can use this opportunity to obtain a broad patent cross-license. It may afford you other benefits in addition to freedom of operation. For example, you'll already be licensed if the licensor sells some of its patent portfolios to NPEs. As a result, you'll have less nuisance suits in the future by NPEs because you have taken a preemptive strike by "neutralizing" the patents before their sale. If the patent portfolio strengths between the two parties exhibit significant gaps and you don't want to pay for a broad cross-license, you can try to agree upon a "springing license" arrangement (i.e. each party is automatically licensed to the other party's sold patents trigged by the patent sale event) which is similar to the License On Transfer "LOT" program Google has launched.

You can also fight and hope to win. Invalidating licensor's patents via IPR is a commonly adopted strategy by licensees nowadays due to PTAB's high patent invalidity rate (80%+). Meanwhile, while waiting for PTAB's ruling, you can try to work around licensor's patents.

We now use the pencil eraser example above to illustrate how to find workarounds. This case is overly simplified but we simply want to use it as an example to explain the general principles and approaches you can utilize. Assuming the asserted patent has the following claims:

Claim 1. A pencil eraser combination, comprising:
    a pencil;
    an eraser; and
    a metal band connecting said pencil and said eraser.

Utilizing the methodology of Claim Deconstruction discussed in Chapter 4, we can represent the above claim with Figure 7-5. By carefully examining the corresponding flowchart, there are several ways to attack this claim:

(a) First of all, there are three main elements: a pencil, an eraser, and a metal band. If your product is not exactly the same as these three elements (for example, you can change your product design into using a plastic band or hard rubber band, rather than the "metal band" as described in the claim), then you can argue that your current product doesn't infringe.

(b) Alternatively, you can attack any or all elements in the claim to show that the claim is not enabled and thus not enforceable. Here, it is apparent that the main novelty point seems to reside within the box "metal band connecting said pencil and said eraser". Since the claim doesn't

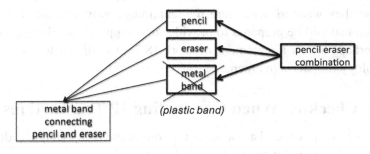

Figure 7-5   Flow chart representing an exemplary claim being asserted.

have specific description about how is the metal band connecting the pencil and eraser, you need to search within the specification to find out whether this element is fully enabled and what are the embodiments included.

(c) If the claim is functional limited (see Chapter 5), then you can leverage *Williamson* to invoke §112(f) and try to limit the claim narrowly to only the specific embodiments disclosed in the specification. If your connecting method is different from those described in the specification, you may argue that the claim does not correspond to your product.

On the other hand, if a claim maps onto your product, and you can utilize the Claim Deconstruction method to look for workarounds to avoid future versions of your product corresponding to the claim. This way, you can neutralize the asserted patent at least for future products.

7.10. Technology Transfer

Technology transfer (including hardware technology know-how licensing or software source code licensing) is a more friendly approach than "bare" patent licensing and is more readily accepted by licensees. Therefore, even NPEs nowadays are starting to try to work on or acquire technologies in order to bundle them with their patent portfolio.

However, technology transfer is much more complicated than patent licensing. Licensor needs to transfer "know-how" to licensee, and usually there is a training period to bring a licensee up to speed on the technology. In addition, licensee often wants continued support to the technology because they want to make sure the technology works in the long run. Licensors should be prepared to provide such support/consulting services and perhaps attach a statement of work (SOW) template to the master technology transfer agreement.

7.11. Checklist When Conducting IP Transactions

Table 7-2 is the checklist for reader's convenience to reference during IP transaction negotiations and due diligences.

Table 7-2　Comparing US and China approaches in conducting IP transactions.

Issues to Consider	US Typical Approach	China Approach: (Similar) or Different
Licensed patents	• Prefer a patent list. • May consider a specific narrow technology area, expressly excluding technologies not to be licensed. • May use capture period if patent list approach is not used.	• (Same) • SIPO's new rule on compulsory patent license was effective on May 1, 2012. It clarified procedures on granting compulsory licenses. The five conditions are: 1) patents not exploited sufficiently; 2) dependent patents; 3) monopoly; 4) state emergency; and 5) public health. • However, it is still unclear what factors SIPO will consider in granting a compulsory license; or how to determine royalty rates.
Licensed product	• Specific products by licensee, may include have made rights. • Prevent "foundry service" or "patent laundering".	• (Same)
Licensed period	• Patent life; or • Guillotine's license, i.e. a fixed period (e.g. 5 years).	• (Same)

Chapter 8

For IP Transaction Lawyers and Negotiators (Relating to Detailed Agreement T's & C's)

This chapter will dive deeper into various agreement terms and conditions. Again, this book is not intended to cover all basic foundations for each type of agreements. Instead, we'll only highlight areas that tend to be controversial or need special attention so that you are prepared when the issues come up during negotiations.

8.1. Non-Confidential Disclosure Agreement (NDA) Negotiation

NDA is a necessary tool for many business, technical, and legal discussions. Patent sellers, Licensors or Disclosers want to sign a NDA to ensure the recipient doesn't disclose their confidential information such as claim charts or other sensitive data without prior permission. In addition, they may add a FRE408 clause in the Agreement to refrain recipient from filing a declaratory judgment (DJ) against them.

However, certain information can only be disclosed under a NDA, such as patent encumbrances, claim charts, and royalty calculation. In addition, some recipients don't want to receive any confidential information unless there is a NDA. For example, patent buyers or licensees don't want to review claim charts unless there is a NDA and the NDA states that patent seller or licensor agrees that they will not use the fact that recipient has analyzed their patents as notice of infringement or evidence of willful infringement. However, for the recipient, NDA is like a double-edged sword, it can protect you but might hurt you in some situations. For example, if you are exchanging information under an NDA, then later your products have features resemble that of the other party. Even if your team invented the feature completely independently, the NDA record clearly shows that you've seen the other party's feature prior to your invention. You'll need a lot of documentation to prove that your R&D team did its work in a "clean-room" environment and was not contaminated in any way by the disclosure under the NDA. Therefore, our recommendation is that recipient should try to obtain information as much as possible without a NDA and only sign NDA when necessary.

8.1.1. *Battle of forms*

Whose template or form to start with is a common issue parties face and thus earned a nickname "battle of forms". Each party wants to use its own template because it is usually more favorable to the drafter and drafter is more familiar with potential pitfalls. If your company is a Seller, you should consider the following factors:

(a) How is the availability of legal resources to you, fairness of each party's template, how big an ego each party has, etc. If your legal team has a tight bandwidth, then you may have to insist on the other party reviewing your template and redline changes so that it is easier for your lawyer.

(b) Keep in mind that too simple a template (which, for example, does not address how to resolve issues, or whom to communicate with when issues arise) perhaps is not a good template to use regardless whether such a template is yours or the other party's. Stay objective and use the template that enables you to accomplish your goal with the least current and future issues.

(c) You also need to be cognizant that too complicated template wastes legal resources without ever getting business discussion going because both parties start "butting heads" about the template. Then the template is useless and should be avoided regardless it is yours or the other party's.

8.1.2. *Choice of law*

Choice of law is often an issue as well, because each party wants to adopt the law most favorable to them. Typically it depends on where the party is incorporated and usually one prefers "home court advantage". Generally, we recommend the following choice of law for your IP transaction or when there is a conflict of law:

(a) Corporation incorporated in Texas would typically choose Texas first;
(b) Then New York because it is supposed to be more business friendly;
(c) California is an alternative.

8.1.3. *Confidential information description*

The following are some best practices or lessons learned for NDAs.

(a) If there is no confidential information to be disclosed by a party, then state clearly "none" for that party.
(b) Narrow the purpose of NDA if you are the disclosure so the recipient can only use it for specific purposes.
(c) For the question regarding whom can the confidential information be disclosed to or share with, if you are the discloser, request that even for internal disclosure within the recipient's company, it should be on "need-to-know" basis. In you are the recipient, to avoid issues in the future, you may want to specify that you can disclose to contractors and consultants who are supporting you for the specific project.
(d) Usually there is a requirement of "marking", i.e. confidential information should be marked with "confidential", "proprietary" or legend of similar meaning. This makes it easier to manage the confidential information distribution. If you are not sure whether something is indeed confidential or not, it is hard to comply with sharing within the company only on "need-to-know" basis. Some NDAs define Confidential

Information as "any communication under typical business practice should be treated as confidential". Such definition is too vague, difficult to manage, and should be avoided if possible.

(e) If you have communicated verbally some confidential information to the recipient, you should follow up, within certain time period (typically 30 days), with a written summary and label it "Confidential Information".

8.1.4. *Subsidiary definition, is it 50%+ ownership*

Some templates define subsidiary as 50% or more ownership by the parent company. We recommend using "50%+ or more ownership" language to avoid confusion in the future if two companies co-own a subsidiary with a 50%/50% split.

8.1.5. *Affiliate definition, is control enough*

Affiliate definition is important to pay attention to, even for a NDA. On the discloser side, covenant to not use recipient's receipt of your confidential information for future evidence of willful infringement will bind on all your Affiliates. Therefore, as a Discloser, you want to narrow the definition for Affiliate for your company only if reasonable (usually clauses are bilateral or reciprocal), taking into consideration that you may want to cover other divisions within your company who also need to disclose confidential information to the same recipient. Some templates define an Affiliate as an entity that is "controlled by", "controlling", "under common control with" a party, intending to include parent companies, child companies, and sister/brother companies of the party. Such approach is likely inappropriate for purpose described in this paragraph.

On the recipient side, you want as many as possible internal divisions and business units to use the same confidential information to make the internal coordination seamless. Therefore, you want to enlarge the Affiliate definition. Perhaps the above "control" verbiage is appropriate for such scenarios. However, you should be cognizant that all Affiliate is subject to refraining from filing DJ against the Discloser and you should make sure to balance the pros and cons of your chosen language.

8.1.6. *Method of communication*

Some old contract language requires US registered mail for all communications. However, it doesn't work for foreign companies because they don't have US registered mail readily available. In fact, nowadays it is not commonly used in US either and you should be prepared if someday US Post Office decides to obsolete it or replace it. Therefore, you want to choose a delivery mechanism that has legal effect and yet is compatible with local common practice.

8.1.7. *Special contract clauses*

Some companies want to include the following clause into a NDA, while others don't like it. You should decide whether to incorporate based on your own specific situation which could be case dependent.

"The Company's patents for sale shall be provided to Recipient in confidence solely for the purpose of evaluating a potential purchase of same. Nothing herein shall be construed as any opinion regarding the actual use or functionality of the patented invention by any party, and does not constitute any legal opinion or representation of any kind."

8.2. Triggering DJ

As discussed above, patent sellers or patent licensors don't want to trigger DJ when they send patent list to potential buyers or licensees. DJ gives the plaintiff option to choose the venue most favorable to plaintiff and likely less favorable to the seller/licensor. Therefore, in the above NDA section, we covered ways frequently deployed by sellers/licensors to reduce the chance of triggering DJ.

8.3. Term Sheet, Letter of Intent (LOI), or Memorandum of Understanding (MOU)

Many business leaders are eager to get to the finish line and thus may want to start negotiating the final agreement as soon as possible. However, sometimes it is actually faster if you start with a term sheet, LOI or MOU. Term sheet is typically not signed, while LOI and MOU often are signed documents.

8.3.1. *Term sheet*

A term sheet is helpful when you have a complex deal where each party's contributions and deliverables need to be clearly identified. If parties wait until the contract negotiation stage to cover these aspects, you may end up renegotiating pricing and other terms caused by unacceptable imbalance and the misunderstandings at the beginning. When parties start "back-paddling", it frequently results in distrust which could lead to the deal falling apart. Therefore, having a term sheet upfront sometimes can save your time, and might even save the deal. Therefore, it is important to understand common issues encountered for term sheet.

Since a term sheet should not be treated as a binding agreement, we recommend users to include the following header or footer, or language with similar effect, on each page to clearly indicate that these are pre-liminary terms so that there are no misunderstanding by either party: **"Confidential Information — Draft Term Sheet, for Discussion Purposes Only"**.

The format of a term sheet should be informal. The more formal the language, the more likely the term sheet might be construed as an "offer" that's capable of being accepted and thus be treated as a binding agreement. Email format including bullet points listing each party's deliverable/ benefit is acceptable. However, Microsoft word document format is easier to keep track of, and clearer to redline so each party can see what the other party has modified.

A typical term sheet includes the following sections, and each section comprises relevant bullet points:

(a) Preamble — you should start with a statement upfront to reiterate that the term sheet is not a binding document. An exemplary paragraph is "THE PROPOSED TERMS HEREIN DO NOT CONSTITUE AN OFFER CAPABLE OF ACCEPTANCE AND ARE NOT BINDING UPON THE PARTIES UNLESS AND UNTIL MEMORIALIZED IN A DEFINITIVE AGREEMENT EXECUTED BY BOTH PARTIES".

(b) Parties — list each party's name, and place of incorporation, e.g. Party 1: NewCo, a Delaware company, having a place of business at xxx street, Mountain View, California 94043. Party 2: BigCo, a California company, having a place of business at xxx Street, Sunnyvale, CA 94086"

(c) Objective — briefly describe what are the parties negotiating for, e.g. "The Parties intend to negotiate in good faith a technology transfer and memorialize such transaction in a definite agreement by or before xx/xx/2016 based on the terms set forth herein".

(d) Key terms — use bullet points to list each party's deliverables such as licenses granted (exclusive or non-exclusive, world-wide or local), ownership of IP, support offered, licensee fee, payment term (30 days or 60 days), terms of the Agreement, termination clause, governing law, warranty, indemnification, limit of liability, publicity, etc.

Some term sheet templates include a signature block for each party at the bottom, which in format is more similar to a LOI, or MOU. We recommend not including such signature blocks in a term sheet. If a party needs a signature so that their management treats the discussion more seriously, then a LOI or MOU is a more appropriate format. If the term sheet is negotiated in China, US companies should be cognizant that liabilities may still be attached even though they have not signed any documents. Chinese Contract Law is similar to German contract law under which parties to a contract owe each other a duty of good faith. Article 42 of Chinese Contract Law (Pre-contract Liabilities) stipulates that the party that causes the failure of contracting may be liable to the other party for loss resulting from the party's misconduct during the negotiation.

8.3.2. *LOI/MOU*

A LOI sometimes is treated similarly to a term sheet, and other times similarly to a MOU. The format can be similar to a term sheet except that certain clauses are binding in the LOI, more similar to a MOU. Therefore, a signature block is required in a LOI/MOU. US companies often treat LOI the same as a term sheet because both formats are typically used for two-party negotiations, while MOU can be used for a multi-party negotiation. However, Chinese companies often treat LOI and MOU similarly because both are signed documents. In fact, some Chinese companies consider LOI/MOU as the final contract, which may come as a shock to many US companies. In the following, we will group LOI and MOU together in our discussions.

For press releases (PRs) of a partnership announcement, typical practice requires a signed agreement. Instead of negotiating and signing a fully fleshed out agreement which requires detail terms and conditions being agreed upon, LOI/MOU is sufficient for PR purposes. Most terms in a LOI/MOU are non-binding and only a few PR-related sentences are binding. Therefore, it is much easier and faster to reach an agreement on LOI/MOU. As a result, Chinese government and Chinese companies often utilize the LOI/MOU as a tool to make public announcements. Small USA companies and start-ups sometimes prefer using LOI/MOU to establish a business partnering relationship because it is simpler than a full blown agreement and requires less legal resources. However, as stated above in the Term Sheet section, sometimes it is better to spell out each party's obligations clearly upfront in a termsheet.

The structure of a LOI/MOU consists of bullet points. These points, as in Term Sheets, are non-binding "wish-list" points by each party. Meanwhile, there is a binding section. A LOI/MOU might have sections as described in the following.

(a) Preamble — an example could be "This LOI is intended to summarize the mutual understandings between Party 1 and Party 2 with respect to their possible collaboration in the technology transfer of xxxx. Parties agree to proceed at their own risk and expense until the execution of a formal Agreement.

(b) Non-binding provisions — this portion can be structured similar to those for a term sheet.

(c) Binding provisions — this portion usually involves parties agreeing to make a public release by certain date, or in contrast, keep the discussion confidential. The parties may also agree to negotiate in good faith to arrive at a definitive agreement by certain date.

(d) Signature block — the LOI/MOU includes a signature portion for both parties to sign. The signatory should be personnel on each side that are capable of representing that party.

As stated earlier, Chinese contract law requires good faith negotiation. Thus, parties are exposed to statutory liabilities even before entering a contract. A party faces even greater liability if the deal falls apart after detailed terms have been agreed upon in a signed LOI/MOU. US companies may consider LOI/MOU as largely non-binding because the LOI/MOU clearly states as such. However, Chinese companies may consider most clauses as binding such that direct and indirect damages apply when the other party causes the deal to fail. Therefore, US companies should exercise extreme caution when entering a LOI/MOU with Chinese companies, or with any company in China.

8.4. Broker Agreement

To formalize the relationship between the patent seller and the patent broker representing the seller, a patent sales broker agreement is required. Large enterprises often want the brokers to take on certain liabilities. However, due to the fact that many patent brokers are small boutiques companies, or even individuals, both parties need to be cognizant of unreasonable/unrealistic clauses written into the Agreement which may not translate into enforceable action. For example, brokers sometimes ask the limit of liability to be set as the amount of their insurance. Even if a large corporation "strong-arms" a broker into agreeing to take on a liability amount significantly greater than what they are able to pay, the enterprise company should be fully aware that they are unlikely to collect such amount should liabilities arise in the future. Most brokers are small entities, and would simply file Chapter 11 if they are required to pay. As a result, the best strategy for a large corporation to manage brokers seamlessly is to carefully select reputable broker, then wisely manage the relationship, how do they contact business, how do they approach potential clients, etc. This is probably the best way to reduce risks for your company (the broker benefit as well along the way).

8.5. Patent Sales Agreement and Some Frequently Seen Issues or "Trouble Makers"

8.5.1. *What each party is looking for — buyers*

(a) Obtain the patent assets free and clean from any issues so that buyer can readily use them in assertion or litigation;
(b) Incur no additional costs during and after the deal.

8.5.2. *What each party is looking for — sellers*

(a) Have no additional obligations: so Seller can recognize revenue;
(b) Not introduce negative impact to existing customers/product lines;
(c) Not impact or breach under existing patent cross-licenses;
(d) Incur no additional costs during and after the dal.

8.5.3. *Battle of form — whose template to start with*

(a) As discussed above, you should take into consideration the availability of legal resources, fairness of the template, ego, etc.
(b) Whoever does more transactions usually wins because they have a more readily available template.

8.5.4. *Choice of law*

(a) Typically start with the place of the incorporation;
(b) Then New York;
(c) Then California.

8.5.5. *Confidential information*

(a) Typically, most companies treat the terms and conditions of the Patent Purchase Agreement (PPA) as confidential;
(b) Some companies may even treat the existence of PPA as confidential as well;
(c) The assignment document, typically in the form of an exhibit to the PPA, is not confidential because the buyer needs to attach it to the PTO assignment recordation document.

8.5.6. *Grant back license*

Most sellers want a broad grant-back license while the buyer wants to limit the grant-back license scope. Parties should be ready to discuss and consider the following seller areas:

(a) Customer of existing products;
(b) Future products;

(c) Reseller;
(d) Trademarked products;
(e) Technology licensing; and
(f) Future acquisitions, spin-offs.

8.5.7. *Covenant to not sue seller customers*

Often seller is concerns about offending their customers and will ask buyer to agree to a covenant to not sue seller customers. If seller provides a small list of customer, it might be negotiable. However, when seller requests a large list of customers to be exempt from this obligation, then it might become an issue. Buyer and Seller should all be cognizant of this potential issue and be prepared to discuss it.

Some key questions to ask include the following:

a) Who is a seller customer, how many layers will you cover, what about seller's customer's customer?

b) Does the covenant to not sue seller customers cover combination products? What if seller insists that the combination is necessary in order to be compatible with seller's products?

8.5.8. *Representation and warranty*

a) Is "knowledge qualifier" acceptable for seller's representation and warranty? What scope is acceptable, attorney working on the case, attorney in the IP department, legal department, or the company?

b) Whether to include open source, standards into the warranty and representation.

8.5.9. *Assignment subject to encumbrances*

(a) What is the definition of encumbrances? Does it just include patent cross licenses, or also include certain commitments, such as covenant to not sue? In addition, technology transfer might also sweep some patent licensee in.

(b) Make sure no new encumbrances are induced after signing or closing the deal.

8.5.10. *Assignment of the PPA*

(a) Who can assign the PPA, both parties, or one party, or neither?
(b) Whom can it be assigned to: exclude competitors?
(c) Can rights be split, e.g. a portion of the family goes to entity A and another to B, especially if portfolio includes different technologies. What about the grant-back license right? Can it be split to the spin-off company and remain with the parent company, or should it simply be assigned, as whole, either to the parent company or to the spin-off?

8.5.11. *Remedy for breach of contract*

(a) Avoid penalty clause when using refund approach.
(b) If a portion is breached, e.g. encumbrance information was wrong for 1 patent out of a multi-patent portfolio, how much to refund to buyer? Would seller want buyer return the patent with incorrect encumbrance information? Does the buyer want to pick a replacement patent?
(c) If buyer got some benefits already, e.g. already sued another company successfully, how much to refund?

8.6. Patent Transaction Agreement — Case Study

Drafters of patent cross-license agreement should be cognizant of potential language issues that could cause huge adverse consequences. We use publically known Microsoft and Samsung[1] Patent Cross Licensing Agreement and Business Collaboration Agreement as an example to explore what went wrong and how might contractual language mistakes be prevented.

8.6.1. *Background information*

(a) Microsoft and Samsung signed a Patent Cross-Licensing Agreement (PLA) and a Business Collaboration Agreement (BCA) in July 2011;

---

[1]Microsoft Corporation and Microsoft Licensing GP v. Samsung Electronics Cor., Ltd. Case 1:14-cv-06039-JSR, filed 10/23/2014. Available at https://www.scribd.com/doc/244294495/Redacted-version-of-Microsoft-s-2011-contracts-with-Samsung-pdf.

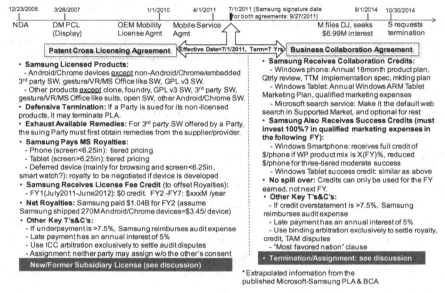

Figure 8-1 Summary of Microsoft-Samsung T's & C's based on published patent and business agreements.

(b) Samsung paid FY1 royalty on time in late 2012, but paid FY2 royalty of $1B+ 1.5 month late (citing Microsoft's acquisition of Nokia as the reason);

(c) Microsoft filed a claim in NY on August 1, 2014 for Court to: (a) declare its Nokia acquisition doesn't breach BCA, and (b) Samsung owes it a $6.9M interest on late payment;.

(d) Samsung initially sought arbitration in HK on October 7, 2014 on Success Credit, but filed a counterclaim in NY on October 30, 2014 asking Court to terminate PLA and BCA. Figure 8.1 summarizes main terms and conditions of PLA and BCA.

8.6.2. BCA — allows termination of PLA

The PLA included the following sections. We believe these might have contributed toward the disputes.

"**8.5 Termination of PLA.** If Samsung terminates this Agreement pursuant to Section 9.7, then Samsung may terminate the PLA by giving Microsoft written notice terminating the PLA as part of, or concurrently with, its notice terminating this Agreement in accordance with Section 9.7."

"**9.7 Assignment.** No party may assign this Agreement, ..., except as expressly provided in this Section 9.7. For purposes of this Agreement, an "assignment" ... includes **each** of the following: (a) a change of Control of a party; and (b) the **sale or other transfer of any assets that are material to this Agreement** (whether in a single transaction or series of transaction). In addition, an "assignment" also includes the following where the assignment is to **a competitor** of the other party: (x) ...; (y) **a merge** of a party with a third party, **whether or not the party to this Agreement is the surviving entity;** and (z)... Upon the occurrence of any prohibited assignment, the non-assigning party will be entitled to terminate this Agreement immediately upon written notice."

(a) The main issues in BCA drafting:
  — Not clarifying "merge": is acquiring another company a merge?
  — Allowing termination even when Microsoft is the "surviving entity".
(b) Other mistakes that might cause issues down the road for both companies (but hasn't been brought up during the 2014 contract dispute):
  — Not defining "competitor": might prevent Microsoft or Samsung from acquiring even a tiny company.
  — Forbidding sale/transfer of "any material assets": could it prevent Microsoft or Samsung from selling/transferring any key patents (especially if PLA and BCA are considered as one deal)?

8.6.3. *Discussion about MS/Samsung PLA T's and C's*

(a) **Former Subsidiary:** If a BU/division leaves a Party, its patents are still licensed to the other Party, but its license from the other Party is terminated. This differs from the reciprocity approach.
(b) **New Subsidiary:** Newly acquired BU/division is licensed as to the acquisition date. If a party is acquiring an entity which is in the middle of litigation with the other party, does the litigation dissolve automatically?

8.6.4. *Questions*

(a) Samsung/Nokia extended previous PLA on April 11, 2013 for 5 yrs. A question is: did the previous Samsung/Nokia PLA have similar Subsidiary T's & C's as in Microsoft/Samsung PLA?
  — If YES, then Samsung would argue that Nokia Device, as a "Former Subsidiary" to Nokia, is no longer licensed to Samsung patents. Microsoft, on the other hand, would argue that Nokia Device, as Microsoft's "New Subsidiary", is licensed. **Which argument will prevail?**
  — If NO, the previous Samsung/Nokia PLA might provide a limited License to spin-offs, then Nokia Device remains licensed to Samsung patents and there will be less to dispute about.

8.6.5. *Observations*

(a) First Scenario is likely true because Microsoft/Samsung have been arguing about whether Nokia is licensed since late 2013.
(b) If Microsoft prevails for Scenario #1, it puts Samsung in a difficult situation because Nokia Device gets a free license under Microsoft, while the remaining Nokia holds most patents with less product exposure and thus can demand higher royalty payment from Samsung.

8.6.6. *Lessons learned*

(a) Sometimes simpler deal structure works better, especially for fast evolving business.
(b) A good business deal structure may not work out if agreement is not drafted well. Engage legal team early on is critical to business team's success.
(c) It is important to insist on clear and well written key paragraphs even when under time pressure, such as Assignment, Termination, Subsidiary, Licensed Products, Licensed Patents, Indemnification, LOL.
(d) There are some creativity in the business deal structure for others to learn from:
  — Set a high royalty rate separately in PLA;
  — Entice Samsung to sign the deal using various Credits;

— Mandate Success Credits invested on Window Marketing;
— Control/monitor Samsung roadmap.

8.7. Patent Cross-License Agreement/Patent License Agreement

Patent cross-license agreements benefits both parties bilaterally so the clauses are usually fairer (or similarly unfair) to each party. A patent cross license agreement is between a licensor and its licensee so whichever party has more negotiation power or more experience will demand to use its template and thus can obtain a few more favorable clauses for themselves. We'll focus on the general portions for patent cross-license agreement terms and conditions here. Parties with the upper hand in negotiation can modify certain portions to suit their particular needs.

One distinct difference between patent cross-license (PCL) and one-way patent license agreement (PLA) is due to the fact that some attorneys strongly believe a valid agreement requires consideration. Therefore, for a PLA where party A grants party B a license to party A's patents, party B must pay certain amount in return. Even if it is a $1 payment, such payment terms need to be included in the contract language to make it valid. Alternatively, you can include certain business considerations such as providing marketing support, consulting, or products. Those are considerations and thus will make the agreement a valid and enforceable contract. In comparison, patent cross license could have no money changing hands. The patent license right granted to each other are the consideration.

PLA or PCL typically consists of preamble, license, payment (only if there is a balance payment from one party to another), representation/warranties, indemnity, the limit of liability, terms and termination, miscellaneous, and signature block. Parties usually get stuck at license, indemnity, and limit of liability portions. We'll cover these areas in the following sections.

8.7.1. *Licenses granted*

As stated above, cross-license agreements tend to be less complicated because the clauses apply to both parties. One party may want to limit the patent licensed to the other party by excluding certain fields. Then the other party would want to include some exclusion as well.

A typical license language looks something like "Each Party hereby grants a non-exclusive, non-sublicensable, worldwide license to Party's Licensed Patents, to the other Party to make, have made, sell, offer for sale, import the other Party's Licensed Product. Such license is effective on xx/xx/xxxx and ends on yy/yy/yyyy".

As discussed above, the art of negotiation lies within the definition of each Party's Licensed Patents, Licensed Product, and licensed period (yy/yy/yyyy ending date). Agreement drafter needs to pay close attention to these areas.

8.7.2. *Indemnity*

Indemnification is a contentious point for most Agreement negotiations. Each party wants the other party to indemnify them and hold them harmless from any damages or loss incurred. However, in a cross-licensing relationship, this clause is bilateral so the party believing the other party more likely to incur risks will insist on a strong indemnity clause.

8.7.3. *Limit of liability*

Limit of liability section is typically a major issue during Agreement negotiation. The total amount is frequently capped at the Agreement amount (or a multiple thereof). However, the Party owning less IP and shipping more products often want to carve out intellectual property infringement portion from the total limit of liability amount, and make the patent owning Party responsible for any damages in an award or settlement of a third party claim of patent infringement.

8.8. Technology Transfer Agreement/Software License Agreement

Technology transfer agreement, besides having similar common issues discussed above, also deals with deliverables and acceptance procedure, as well as subsequent technical support at various levels. We'll use a software source code license agreement as an example to illustrate main issues that need special attention.

For a software license agreement, the typical issues relate to delivery and acceptance, rights and restrictions, warranty and representation, and limit of liability. It also includes detailed exhibits describing licensed program, support terms, and escrow agreement if source code needs to be kept by a neutral third party for specific purposes. These exhibits should be reviewed carefully by technical teams. However, in the following, we'll mainly discuss the main issues related to the main body of the Agreement.

8.8.1. *Delivery and acceptance*

Delivery is often controversial because licensee wants licensor to deliver not just the original program, but subsequent enhancements. Licensor and licensee need to agree whether each minor revision, major revision, internal and external bug fixes are all part of such enhancements.

Acceptance is problematic because parties often can't agree upon the criteria for evaluating the software program. Licensee wants to use what it deems appropriate, while licensor doesn't want unlimited rework, especially if two parties are newly partnering with each other and haven't built enough trust. Typically a process should be agreed upon where if a bug is found by licensee, licensee will return the program for rework, licensor agrees to resubmit after fixing the bug. Licensee will want to be able to reject the program, stop any remaining payment, and terminate the agreement. Licensor will want to obtain some nonrefundable upfront payment to discourage such termination.

8.8.2. *Rights and restrictions*

Besides of obtaining licenses to modifying the source code, and distributing the object code, licensee may also need a license to the documentation and photograph.

Licensor may restrict licensee from removing its own copyright notices, or reverse engineer the software program for purposes not covered by the agreement.

In addition, if parties are collaborating with each other on source code modification, there will be an issue regarding ownership of derivative products.

8.8.3. *Patent ownership — avoid jointly owned patents*

During a collaboration relationship, derivative product or modifications to the original technology may contain patentable inventions. Usually the easiest approach in dealing with patent ownership is each party owns its own invention during the collaboration.

However, if an invention involves both parties and the contributions are not divisible into separate inventions by each party, then you face an issue of how to deal with such co-invented patent filing process and who owns the patent.

For jointly owned patents, each party has equal right to the patent, unless specified expressly otherwise. Such joint ownership may devalue a valuable patent significantly. Considering the scenario in which you plan to use a patent to assert or sue another party. You spend lots of time, effort, and money to develop claim charts, ensuring no relevant prior arts. Thereafter, you approach the target company with your patent number or claim charts. The target company can easily undermine your efforts by striking a deal with the joint owner of the patent and obtain a license. Then, all your efforts are flushed down the drain.

According to US IP law, all true inventors need to be put down as the co-inventors for the patent. However, parties should agree in the Agreement that one of parties own the patent, while the other party obtains a license. Each party may have signed certain cross-license agreement with several other companies ("encumbrances"). As soon as the patent is filed by a party, the encumbrance usually attach to that patent if such a new patent falls within the capture period of the cross-license agreement. One optimum approach is to let the party with the least encumbrances own the patent in order to optimize the value of this patent.

After parties agree that one party will own the patent, it is important to write in the Agreement that the other party will assist with inventor declaration, assignment, etc. Inventors of the other party will have to sign an assignment agreement agreeing to assign all his/her rights to the patent owning party. You may also want to include a section dealing with the situation when the other party doesn't cooperate with such assignment and declaration.

8.8.4. *Warranty and representation*

Other than general warranty and program specific warranty, there is often a "No Patent Infringement" warranty required by Licensee. Licensee usually wants Licensor to warrant that the program and documentation doesn't infringement patent, copyright, trademark, trade secrete or other proprietary right of a third party. Licensor typically will change this to a narrower representation "to Licensor's knowledge". Some attorneys would attempt to change the knowledge qualifier "to Licensor's actual knowledge". The advantage of actual knowledge is that it is limited to what the Licensor was in fact aware of.

This section will also include a section regarding IP Indemnification, requiring Licensor to defend, at Licensee's option, and hold harmless Licensee from IP related claims, suits, or proceedings. Licensee will demand Licensor to pay all damages associated with such claim or settlement of the claim. Licensor will want to exclude any infringement caused by combinations of Licensee product with Licensor product. Licensee will insist on to only exclude combinations not authorized by Licensor. Licensor will also exclude unauthorized modifications.

In case of such infringement, there needs to be a cure process for the benefit of the Licensee. This could include Licensor procuring for Licensee the right for continued use, or replace with a non-infringing alternative. If none of solutions is viable, Licensee will demand certain refund, perhaps a portion of the original payment.

8.8.5. *Limit of liability*

Similar to limit of liability issues discussed above, both parties will want to limit the liability to expressly exclude any special or consequential damages (including loss of profits) arriving out of any performance of the Agreement, regardless whether it is based on tort, warranty, contract. However, Licensee will want to expressly state that Licensor is responsible for paying any damages such as award or settlement due to IP infringement. Licensor will insist on capping it with a multiple of contract value. The outcome will depend on the power of negotiation of each party.

To cap off this Agreement negotiation section, transaction lawyers and negotiators often have a tendency of trying to negotiate and obtain a near-perfect legal document, with no or minimal risks. However, you must keep in mind that just like a perfectly written (scoring 100%) patent that doesn't read onto a current or future product is of no real value, a perfectly written contract with 100% risks contained that doesn't enable an eventual partnership has zero value as well. Therefore, the ultimate goal of Agreement negotiation is to:

(a) Enable a successful business partnership optimized for your company; and
(b) Minimize legal risks while enabling such a partnership.

Index

Printed in the United States
By Bookmasters